Praise for Cocaine Cowboys

'*Cocaine Cowboys* is a rollercoaster ride that takes the reader right to the heart of how and why cocaine became Europe's favourite drug and the tapestry of characters that makes sure it is available in every pub in every rural town. Nicola's wealth of experience as Irelands top investigative journalist shines through in the incredible detail and the fascinating tapestry of characters and stories she has woven through the chapters. If you read nothing else this year, read this!'

Donal MacIntyre

'An insightful and explosive exposé of Ireland›s cocaine epidemic and the drug lords who fuelled it. Nicola Tallant is one of Europe›s most respected crime journalists who has been at the very top of her game for years. *Cocaine Cowboys* is the definitive account of a boomtime which turned street dealers into billionaires'

Stephen Breen, author of *The Cartel* and *The Hitmen*

'Another absolute page turner from Ireland's finest journalist'

Mick McCaffrey, journalist, and author of *Cocaine Wars*

'Nicola Tallant joins the dots and follows the trail of white lines from the jungle labs of south America to the dinner tables of middle Ireland. *Cocaine Cowboys* tells the global success story of Ireland's own narcos. How they hit the big time, and how they unravelled the fabric of our communities and society as they created a wild west drug frontier right here at home'

Neil Leslie, Group Editor, Reach PLC

Nicola Tallant is a three-time winner of Crime Journalist of the Year in Ireland. She is Investigations Editor of the Sunday World newspaper and the host of the Crime World podcast. She lives in Dublin.

COCAINE COWBOYS

The Deadly Rise of Ireland's Drug Lords

Nicola Tallant

eriu

First published by Eriu
An imprint of Black & White Publishing Group
A Bonnier Books UK company

4th Floor, Victoria House,
Bloomsbury Square,
London, WC1B 4DA

Owned by Bonnier Books
Sveavägen 56, Stockholm, Sweden

X @eriu_books

@eriubooks

Trade Paperback – 978-1-80418-4-028
Paperback 978-1-80418-5-995
Ebook – 978-1-80418-4-110

A CIP catalogue of this book is available from the British Library.

Typeset by IDSUK (Data Connection) Ltd
Printed and bound by Clays Ltd, Elcograf S.p.A

1 3 5 7 9 10 8 6 4 2

Every reasonable effort has been made to trace copyright holders of material reproduced in this book, but if any have been inadvertently overlooked the publishers would be glad to hear from them.

Eriu is an imprint of Bonnier Books UK
www.bonnierbooks.co.uk

'There is no calamity greater than lavish desires.
There is no greater guilt than discontentment.
And there is no greater disaster than greed.'

– Lao Tzu

CONTENTS

PROLOGUE

The football came over the wall first as if casing the derelict yard. It was followed with a thud as its teenage owner landed on the broken concrete ground. It was 5.02 p.m. and the September evening sun was shining at the picturesque Dunlo Harbour of Ballinasloe, a large town outside Galway city. The harbour area was once just a small outpost consisting of a harbour master's house and two stores. In the years following the turn of the century, expansion had seen it become more populated with modern duplexes, terraced homes and apartments, often marketed as perfect residences for first-time buyers.

But there were still some disused yards that had fallen between the cracks of progress, remaining empty and abandoned, like the one the teenager had followed his ball into. To the casual observer, it would be an everyday scene of bored after-school mischief. But the only ones there to witness it were far from casual. The drug squad detectives watched as the boy took some latex gloves from his pocket and headed towards a school lunch box. As he unpacked its contents of six sandwich bags containing white powder, the detectives sprang from the shadows.

Almost two years later, members of the public would be asked to leave the courtroom due to the young age of the offender whose case was about to be heard in front of Judge Brian O'Callaghan at Galway Circuit Court. The accused, now aged 17, sat flanked by both his parents. The teenager had no previous convictions. He wanted to become a teacher, the court heard. He loved soccer and was an avid player too. The average kid next door. He told the court he was pleading guilty to the charge of possession with intent to supply cocaine valued at more than €44,000 at the disused harbour yard on that Sunday evening in September 2021. The cocaine had been packed into the lunchbox in six sandwich bags and was ready for sale. Lab tests following the youngster's arrest would show he had 620.7 grams to offer his local community. At the in-camera hearing, counsel for the teenager parroted a line that has now become familiar in provincial, rural and city courtrooms around the country: the boy took full responsibility for the drugs, he had mixed with a bad crowd and had since turned his life around. He had wound up in the yard with a large quantity of cocaine, the court was told, because he had taken responsibility for a debt that friends had accrued. The boy's age was on his side. A custodial sentence for the Section 15 offence carried a mandatory minimum 10-year prison sentence, but because the defendant was under the age of 18, he was in luck. He was handed down 120 hours' community service.

❦

Twenty years ago, when drugs like cocaine were only available in Dublin and a handful of large urban centres in Ireland, the idea of a schoolboy peddling coke around a provincial Irish town would have caused a sensation. The remarkable thing now is how unremarkable it has become for an Irish teen to be a small link in a globalised chain of money, misery and murder. Since it first started tumbling in on the shores of West Cork in the 1990s, and in the stomachs of drug mules travelling from Miami, cocaine has become the drug of the nation. It has swept in like a blizzard to dust every corner of every small town, from Donegal to Wexford and Kerry to Louth. While a line of cocaine may have once been the stuff of movies to rural Ireland dwellers, it is now a central part of every night out, every occasion: communions, christenings, weddings and local sporting celebrations . . . It is available to order just like a pizza, through social media sites like WhatsApp, Snapchat and TikTok. So swift and total has been the spread and availability that Ireland is now one of Europe's most prolific users of the drug. One in every 40 of us admits to having snorted it in the past year, according to the United Nations. Unlike other drugs, cocaine respects no social boundaries. Farmers, GAA players, first-time users in their 50s, and even pensioners are presenting more and more for treatment. Former Limerick hurler turned counsellor Ciarán Carey has said 'many young GAA players are destroying themselves with drugs, particularly cocaine' and believes 'we need to start educating kids when they are in sixth class, because this is around the time that drugs are first introduced in many of their lives'. Professor Colin O'Gara, consultant psychiatrist and the clinical lead of addiction services at Saint John of God Hospital, says it is now a 'public health emergency' the scale of which needs to be recognised by the government.

But to unravel how a small island on the edge of Europe ended up such a big player in the major cocaine leagues, we must follow the white supply lines back to the beginning. And we must also follow the money. Each bag that passes from dealer to user in clubs and pubs is completing an incredible journey from farm to nose, a journey that relies on grinding poverty, greed and corruption in order to reach its final destination on the table-tops and toilet cisterns of every county in Ireland. Every step of the way, cocaine multiplies in value at a rate that puts every other commercial trading activity in the shade. It is the ultimate capitalist product, siphoning money at every link back up the chain to a mega-wealthy few who sit at the top of a ferocious and violent underworld economy. They use fear to rule over a global business, which has grown to threaten the very stability of states, and even the planet itself, such is the impact of the cocaine trade on biospheres like the Amazon rainforest, which are vital to combating climate change.

The bloodied trail starts high in the Colombian hills, where impoverished farmers and casual labourers pick millions of leaves of the coca plant and haul their product to dangerous jungle labs. In neighbouring Peru and in Bolivia, similar production lines are also in place. The product's route to markets like Ireland will be long and treacherous, but also extremely valuable. By the time cocaine hits our streets, its value will have multiplied almost 500 times. The profit margins of narco-economics are what makes people kill for it. A workforce in the Andes mountain range, which extends along the western edge of South America, will be paid just over a dollar for each of the 125 kilos needed to produce one kilo of cocaine. By the time it reaches our shores, that single kilo can fetch €70,000. In the labs, poor workers earning a few dollars a day crush the leaves and douse them with chemicals, including diesel oil, caustic soda and cement. Through a series of processes, they turn it into a white paste, a kilo of which, when refined further into powder, will be worth between $1,500 and $7,000. By other calculations, the price of production is much higher. At one point at the height of the Colombia drug wars, it was estimated that each kilo processed, shipped and distributed cost six human lives.

The next step in the supply line – the transport of Colombia's most famous export – is by far the most important after production. Routes go back to the notorious cartels that began in the late

1970s with Pablo Escobar's Medellín operation and the Rodríguez Orejuela brothers' Cali cartel. Mexico soon followed as it became an important transshipment point into the US. In recent years, the Sinaloa and Gulf cartels took over trafficking of Colombian cocaine to worldwide markets. Today other groupings are major players in the market too – in the narco economy, as in every other trade, stable supply lines are crucial.

From the jungle labs of South America, the cocaine moves north through Central America and, traditionally, onwards to Caribbean outposts. A majority of Europe's product then heads east for the unprotected shorelines of West Africa. It crosses into lawless territories where terrorist organisations like Hezbollah hold sway, across war-torn states that are rife with corruption and where many use their military to protect their share of the global drug supply line. The 2017 World Drug Report estimated that two-thirds of all cocaine bound for Europe now makes its way through West Africa. The UN Office on Drugs and Crime described three main hubs: the northern, made up of Guinea-Bissau, Guinea, The Gambia and Senegal; the southern hub of Benin, Togo, Ghana and Nigeria; and the eastern hub of Mali and Mauritania. As the chain grows, so does the value of the product, and the violence that is a central component of the narco economy. Along the way, guerillas, traffickers, drivers, shippers, mules, gang members, cartel bosses, hitmen, wholesalers and dealers will all take their cut.

From West Africa, the cocaine goes on the move again, restless to reach its final destination in the clubs and on the dinner tables of affluent European towns and cities. It will now have to traverse the thin blue line of law enforcement desperately trying to stop it in its tracks. European crime fighters have banded together in a bid to cut off the container shipments. The Maritime Analysis and Operations Centre (MAOC) is the agency that co-ordinates anti-drug trafficking for member police forces, including Portugal, Spain, the UK, Ireland, France, the Netherlands and Italy. They try to track smuggling operations by air or sea and deploy military forces to intercept shipments before they are landed. But the trade is relentless, and waves of boats and flights flood towards Europe where more than €10.5 billion worth of cocaine makes its way through the vast ports in Belgium and the Netherlands. Galicia in Spain, an area synonymous with smuggling, is another popular landing point for Colombian cocaine into Europe. Boats meet at sea and divide the shipments, landing some into Galicia, taking some north to Madrid and Barcelona, and more towards Antwerp in Belgium – the biggest entry point – and Rotterdam in the Netherlands.

When it finally comes ashore, drug gangs begin the next phase of the business: to cut the product. They bulk up what they have to sell, using agents like laundry detergent, caffeine and laxatives. The narcos are now following a well-worn corporate template as they diversify for the retail market, adding more illegal money to the bottom line – and usually more violence and murder too, every entry to the ledger inked in blood. The wheels of the global enterprise are driven on remorselessly by huge profit margins, where a kilo will be worth €70,000 on arrival in Ireland, a mark-up that has seen one-time street dealing punks become millionaires in a cocaine gold rush. And driven also, of course, by the seemingly insatiable demand.

∽

The 2023 Global Report from the UN's Office on Drugs and Crime shows that Irish people are among the top cocaine users in Europe, with just the Netherlands and Spain outstripping our love for the white powder. The same report warns of the link

NICOLA TALLANT

between that usage and violence on our streets. The lucrative Irish market has caught the attention of gangs as far away as Albania, increasing the likelihood of more bloodshed. It also warns of some of the 'business trends' – increasing intimidation focused on drug users unable to pay debts, and the growing use of children as young as 10–14 years old for intimidation of those who owe money by attacking homes and cars and even people, and as underage couriers.

But our love affair with cocaine has placed us firmly on the drug map in more ways than one. Not only are we among its biggest customers, we also have our very own multinational corporation mixing with the big boys. The Kinahan organisation emerged from a young and hungry generation of criminals perfectly placed to benefit from the country's economic boom. It has become Ireland's first truly trans-global crime group. It has grown so influential that it is now the target of US sanctions, with its leaders running from the law deep into the Arabian Gulf and territories such as Iran where they have washed their dirty money and helped fund terrorism.

The story of the rise of the Kinahan mob from street dealers to a cocaine conglomerate is an extraordinary tale of our times. Less than a decade after they first appeared on the Costa del Sol, jostling for position with Russian and Italian mobs, they had become the number one target of Europol, the law enforcement agency of the European Union. And less than ten years after that they had caught the attention of the powerful US Drug Enforcement Administration (DEA) after creating a European super cartel with the Dutch Moroccan mafia – who control the ports of entry into Europe – the Italian Camorra group and an Eastern European mob. The Dublin street gang had swapped shell suits for shell companies and joined the narco A-list moving cocaine across Africa in air ambulances, buying off officials for use of landing strips, and taking control of the key route into Europe. Together with their peers in the drug trade, they set the price and the tonnage of product flooding into the massive drugs market, which saw 200 tonnes seized in 2020 alone.

US authorities who sanctioned Christy Kinahan Snr and his sons Daniel and Christopher in April 2022, along with a number of associates, first uncovered the extent of their power in 2017. In scenes reminiscent of *The Godfather*, they observed meetings between the Kinahans and Europe's other mafia 'families' at Daniel Kinahan's wedding at Dubai's Burj Al Arab, the world's most luxurious hotel. At that point, concerns about price-fixing and a flood of cocaine through the ports of Rotterdam and Antwerp had raised alarm bells among US law enforcement officials. Undercover operatives in Africa also discovered the Kinahans' role as the controllers of the African drug pathway to Europe, which involved isolated landing strips for motherloads from Colombia, Peru and Chile, and the use of air ambulances to move smaller cargos onwards to the north of the continent, from where the cocaine then made its journey to Europe. The planes even kept flying during Covid lockdowns in the guise of emergency medical transporters. Malawi and other African countries have the perfect ingredients of poverty, unemployment and corruption that make them ideal places for the cartels to operate. Ireland's 'Dapper Don' Christy Kinahan Snr had re-invented himself as an aviation boss from his headquarters in Dubai, while his son Daniel became CEO of the lucrative logistics wing dealing directly with South American suppliers and European buyers. They had perfected the business model.

When the cocaine arrives into Europe's cities and towns, another tier of dealers is waiting to take it to the retail market. Below the narco CEOs, these are the 'Instagram Gangsters' who keep the wheels of the cocaine epidemic grinding every day. Young and armed, they rule the streets of their own communities with fear. They brazenly show off their wealth on social media sites, directing armies of young men to do their bidding while customers queue to make them rich. These big-shot cocaine cowboys seem like a different breed to some of the early entrepreneurs, who saw the drug as something clean and sophisticated, taken by the rich and famous, and which held none of the negative images associated with heroin. While murder and violence were always part of the drugs landscape, the triumph of cocaine has changed the rules. The fast money on offer has dangerously upped the stakes and forged a harder and more ruthless gangland ruled by the gun. But for those at the end of the incredible transcontinental production line, that is an ugly world they prefer to turn a blind eye to. They refuse to join the dots from their weekend party fuel to the feuds, the daylight murders and the bodies slumped in cars in suburban driveways. As activist Fr Peter McVerry has correctly pointed out, 'The vast majority of drug dealers' money comes from middle-class people who are using cocaine.'

Despite the warnings and headlines, the reports and the cost of policing, the demand for cocaine keeps growing. Maybe, as addiction expert Prof. Colin O'Gara describes, it is simply in our DNA: 'Are we genetically predisposed? I think most of the literature would suggest we are. You can look at population genetic studies, but culturally there is no question that we have a very unhealthy relationship with alcohol and have done for a very long time. The type of people we are? We like to have fun, we love the craic and that is very important, and then you have this very important link between alcohol and cocaine.

They combine to form a third product, cocaethylene, which was marketed back in the 1800s as a wine and it was endorsed by the Pope. At the time it was a very popular tonic, so that combination was world famous for strengthening you up. If you feel lethargic, listless and depressed, they said you needed some of it and this really reflects what is happening today. Life is stressful, people are under huge pressure and turn to stimulants to cope. The availability of cocaine in every small town, in every place across the country, means that people are turning to it for those very reasons.'

Whether or not it's part of our DNA, the story of how Ireland took its place at the top table of both global demand and supply of the cocaine trade is a fascinating journey into the dark heart of a nation. It's a tale of Ireland's place in a world where organised crime has become bigger than many nation's economies. It's a tale of journeymen traffickers who honed their craft to compete with the world's leading players, and one of the tragic victims who have lost their lives on the way. It's ultimately the unlikely story of our doomed love affair with a product from the jungles of South America, a deadly infatuation branded onto the very soul of Irish society by our own cocaine cowboys.

CHAPTER ONE

THE FIRST ARRIVALS

The politician got to his feet in the Dáil. Jim O'Keeffe represented Fine Gael in Cork South West. He knew his area well and he was worried. It was June 1993, Europe's internal borders were down, and the Gardaí had just seized £5 million worth of cannabis that had washed up in bales along the Cork coast near Rosscarbery, a picture-perfect tourist village on a shallow estuary surrounded with blue flag sandy beaches. 'Unfortunately, it is now very clear that the hundreds of miles of rugged coastline in West Cork have become a honeypot for drug smugglers,' Deputy O'Keefe said.

Just 12 months earlier, the then State Solicitor for Cork, Barry Galvin, had caused consternation when he went on the popular Friday night chat show, *The Late Late Show*, and told the country that the West Cork coast was 'leaking like a sieve'. Cannabis, he had said, was being brought ashore by the tonne load and nothing was being done about it, suggesting that crackdowns in Britain and the Netherlands had meant that Ireland was the easiest entry point for drugs into Europe. What was more, Galvin had insisted, wealthy drug barons were living in splendour in the area and the Gardaí didn't have the resources to deal with them. Not long after his appearance, one of those residents, a Dutch man called Jan Hendrik Ijpelaar, who owned stunning Glashnacree House overlooking Kenmare Bay, was arrested in the Netherlands. He was later convicted of leading an organised crime gang and distributing drugs, including heroin, ecstasy and hash. Ijpelaar had been a regular visitor to County Kerry from the late 1980s, maintaining a low profile while there.

West Cork and parts of the County Kerry coastline, where the focus of much attention was being placed, had a long history of smuggling and, hundreds of years ago, locals would take their fishing boats out to meet larger boats carrying drink and tobacco from France or Spain. While the area had gone from a poor backwater to a desirable bohemian and multi-cultural mecca, one thing that hadn't changed over the centuries was that when darkness fell, it was almost impossible to track an approaching yacht. While Galvin's comments had been dismissed by politicians and Gardaí, Customs were listening, and they had announced a new Drugs Task Force with special powers, made up of 74 members, half of whom had been allocated to Cork. They had also been given another inflatable dinghy to patrol the vast area, doubling the fleet from one to two.

Cannabis smugglers, mostly coming from Europe and North Africa, had been using the coastline since the late 1980s when authorities started to find large supplies of the drug on boats, in camper vans, and even chucked overboard in waterproof wrappings. In the early 1990s, officials believed that cannabis made up almost 75 per cent of the illegal drugs market. At that time the mathematical equation measuring what was being nabbed versus what was getting in suggested that Ireland was simply high as a kite but, of course, much of the drugs were destined for the UK. While smugglers and Gardaí were pitted against one another in a game of cat and mouse on the high seas, it was largely accepted by both sides of the divide that once a load was landed, it had a pretty good chance of making it to its onward destination.

What probably should have been more concerning, yet was missed in the hype of the cannabis hauls, was an incident in 1989 when a ship in a deep-water berth at Ringaskiddy was discovered with a cargo of £1 million of cocaine on board. The South Americans had been eying up the European market for years and had established a strong network of buyers and distributors in the UK and the Netherlands. To get their product to them, the South Americans had simply drawn a straight line northeast from the Caribbean coasts of Colombia and Venezuela to the shores of Spain and Ireland. But despite the early warning signs of the blizzard of cocaine that would follow, it was the larger cannabis hauls that continued to hold the attention of many and made the headlines. Bulky and easy to find, hauls were regularly discovered bobbing in the high seas, washed up on shorelines or found in specially modified boats. At Courtmacsherry in 1991, over £7 million worth of cannabis created shockwaves when it came fast on the heels of a £1 million seizure the month before.

'The question that needs to be addressed is how many of these shipments have got through,' Jim O'Keeffe TD told the Dáil in 1993, citing one example he said he knew of relating to a landing on Schull that was never traced. Cleverly, he recognised the threat from the other side of the Atlantic and the possibility of the European Union needing to put its might behind resources in West Cork. 'There is also some evidence that because the United States is more successful in disrupting South American drug supply routes that drug producers are turning their attention to the European market. West Cork is, of course, right on the shipping line between Europe and the Americas and is particularly vulnerable as a possible access for drug traffickers to the UK and mainland Europe.'

Adequate manpower would be needed, he stated, to police such an enormous stretch of coastline, in particular as the lighthouses, including the Old Head of Kinsale, Galley Head, Fastnet Rock and Mizen Head, had become automated, meaning the eyes and ears of humans, once the keepers of the shorelines, were no longer at sea. 'We need to make available to the Garda modern gear which is as good as, if not better, than anything available to the drug smugglers. I am talking about high-powered binoculars, night-sight equipment, infrared cameras and scrambler radios,' O Keeffe said, while urging that the Navy and the Air Corps with their ships, helicopters and planes needed to be on hand for surveillance. He finally asked the public to come together in an army against the drug smugglers who could watch and report any suspicious activity on the coastlines and 'combat this growing evil'.

While it may seem quaint now to consider fighting what would become a tsunami of cocaine from South America with binoculars and four lighthouse keepers, the people of West Cork were acutely aware that they were in the eye of the storm. O'Keeffe's party colleague PJ Sheehan called for European Commission funding for a coast-watch service that would serve all of Europe. But the then Minister for Justice Máire Geoghegan-Quinn was quick to dismiss the drama, saying that Cork was well served by the 17 officers that made up the drug squad based at Anglesea Street, and that she had been assured that Ireland was not a major importation route for drugs, but that most of what was discovered was for home consumption instead.

The minister had just weeks earlier attended a meeting in Copenhagen and, together with the 11 other European Commission ministers, signed an agreement to enable the first phase of the establishment of Europol. With the border controls gone, the member states were on their way to creating the Europol Drugs Unit to combat the international trafficking of drugs. In Ireland, drug enforcement was the remit of the Garda National Drug Administration Office, up and running for three years, and the recently established Customs National Drugs Team with a focus on intelligence gathering and maritime-based activity at entry points including Cork.

Months later O'Keeffe was back on his feet with news that another seizure in Kinsale was valued at £3 million, and that with over £30 million worth of drugs seized in Ireland in less than a year, records were set to be broken. 'An emergency drugs plan has to be formulated by the government to stem the tide, so to speak, in this area,' he said. With 1,970 miles of coastline covered with coves and inlets to police, garda numbers were critically low and a halt on recruitment in the Defence Forces and the Navy meant that they, too, were restricted with resources. While the Garda Síochána had vast experience dealing with terrorism, it had limited experience with drugs and only a small group of officers had gone undercover in Dublin to buy heroin off dealers. Like a slow spread, hustlers of all varieties had seen the potential of drugs, the growing market for them, and the easy money that awaited anyone who got in on the game. It wasn't only the West Cork coastline that was being targeted by entrepreneurs of the New Frontier. Homegrown criminals, who had come of age in an era of armed robberies and kidnappings, could see the potential to turn drugs profits into millions, and many were already eyeing up cocaine as the fastest way of all to get rich. Some were already trying to establish their own routes directly from Miami in Florida, which lay at the heart of the action and where almost three-quarters of Colombia's finest started out.

Eamon Kelly had emerged as a criminal from Dublin's north inner city in the 1960s when he began his career with burglary. On the Garda radar since he was a teenage tearaway, he had joined the IRA and stayed with the Official, old-school faction when it split with the Provos in 1970. His links to the paramilitaries gave him an extra edge in Dublin, along with access to firearms, and he quickly became a ruthless criminal with a fearsome reputation for violence. He was clever, too, and from an early stage in his career he used a company as a front for his activities. Kelly was a formidable force and someone not to be crossed. Outside the old Workers' Party Club on Gardiner Street in 1984, it was said that a simple political debate had got heated but angered Kelly enough to knife his 21-year-old rival almost to death. He was convicted and got a 10-year sentence for the attack, the first lengthy term behind bars he would receive.

Kelly was a complex character and held all the anger and rage of the old-school IRA against the rule of law and social injustice. He challenged the justice system that had taken him away from his family, and he managed to have a retrial ordered, this time being found guilty for assault and landing a far lesser three-year sentence. Although only in his mid-30s, Kelly had a head for business, planning and how to wash dirty money through the legitimate system. He found himself advising other criminals, including the likes of Gerry 'The Monk' Hutch, who looked up to the older criminal and followed his migration from the north inner city to the suburbs, where each would rear their families. Out of prison, Kelly was adamant of one thing, that he wasn't going to mess up again and find himself back behind bars. While armed robberies were risky, he'd a few contemporaries who were making a pretty penny on cocaine and he, too, believed that the white powder, with a far better reputation than heroin, was going to set him on a path to riches.

For most of the 1980s, heroin had been seeping into underprivileged neighbourhoods across the city like a cancer, infecting a generation of willing users and turning them into the walking dead. Communities had turned on the dealers and joined forces under the umbrella of the Concerned Parents Against Drugs, a grassroots movement that had begun as a working-class response to the drugs problem, to the spread of HIV, and to the deaths of teenagers and young adults in huge numbers. It had begun in the Hardwicke Street flats complex – an area which would later become a stronghold of the Kinahan Organised Crime Group – and quickly spread across the city into other social housing complexes. Marches were organised on the homes of the big drug dealers such as Tony 'King Scum' Felloni and Thomas 'The Boxer' Mullen. The ensuing mob rule that came when the Republicans muscled in meant a huge amount of focus and Garda attention was on heroin. Jailing characters like Larry Dunne, nicknamed 'Flash Larry', and his brother Mickey 'Dazzler' Dunne, who had got rich and wore a swagger as they lived it up on the proceeds of their crimes, became the top priority for cops. Then there was the colourful Martin 'The General' Cahill who had robbed gold and diamonds, priceless art and placed a bomb under the car of the chief forensic scientist James O'Donovan. His activities and his attitude had embarrassed the State so much that a special task force nicknamed the 'Tango Squad' had been placed on him and his gang on a permanent basis.

Eamon Kelly liked the look of cocaine, it didn't carry with it the same negative connotations around health and misery as heroin did; instead it was the epitome of cool and was being used by the beautiful, the famous and the rich. The classic film *Scarface* only served to increase its popularity, despite the plot and the violence. Starring Al Pacino as the ruthless gangster Tony Montana, who launders millions in cocaine money and, ultimately, loses his mind as he hoovers up his own supply, the movie would become a cult classic. As Kelly was tempted to dip a toe in the market, Ireland was slowly shaking off the chains of poverty of its past, and nightclubs, restaurants and wine bars were now populated by the movers and shakers of Irish society. The Berkeley Court Hotel in leafy Ballsbridge, White's on the

Green, and the Mirabeau restaurant in Dún Laoghaire were all popular with a rich and powerful set who drank expensive wines and partied into the night. Kelly reasoned he'd have a solid customer base and a network of contacts, including an Irishman living on Miami Beach called John Francis Conlon. Conlon appeared to know all the right people and introduced Kelly to dealers selling high-quality cocaine for a steal at $20,000 per kilo, enough to make around £500,000 when cut and bulked up and sold back in Ireland. While Miami might have been a playground for the rich, it was also a place of grinding poverty for immigrants struggling to get a starring part in the American dream, so there was no shortage of those willing to mule the drugs to destinations for a few thousand dollars.

Kelly was an unlucky cocaine cowboy in many ways. Rumours would later abound that Conlon was double-jobbing for the DEA in a bid to penetrate the network of Pablo Escobar, having made contacts in American politics from an earlier career as an arms dealer. Kelly also didn't know that the Gardaí had been tipped off that the 'Provo' was attempting to develop a new cocaine route into Ireland through direct contact with the cartels.

On September 3rd, 1992, Conlon arrived at Dublin Airport on a flight from Miami along with an overweight Cuban woman. They parted company and he made his way out to the arrivals hall alone while she took a taxi to the city centre. In a classic Quentin Tarantino-style cluster, undercover gardaí had been tailing Kelly for hours, unaware he was meeting a man with serious connections in secretive US law enforcement, but knowing a deal was about to go down. The Serious Crime Squad had watched Kelly park and make his way to the arrivals lounge where he made eye contact with Conlon before they walked out separately and got into a Renault. Kelly drove the car with Conlon in the passenger seat, and first they went to Kelly's home in Furry Park in Killester before they hit the road again, driving around various parts of Dublin until Conlon got out and went into a bank near Pembroke Road. Subsequent enquiries would reveal that he withdrew £2,000 in cash while Kelly waited outside. Back in the car, the pair drove immediately to Jury's Hotel in Ballsbridge where Kelly parked and Conlon again got out. He went inside the hotel and returned with a bag which both men examined before they placed it in the boot. They were eventually stopped at the East Link Toll Bridge and both were arrested and taken into custody. The bag, containing a white powder, was sent for technical examination, but officers knew it was cocaine. Other evidence collected included a piece of paper under the driver's seat with details of flights from Miami to Dublin on it. A second piece of paper that fell out of Conlon's shirt contained the name of the Cuban woman, Elisabeth Yamanoha, who'd accompanied him on the flight and who had just been picked up by officers at the hotel. A search of her room would unearth more evidence linking the three to a plot to import cocaine, including a bank-note band with £2,000 written on the adhesive tape and a jumper she wore on the flight, which covered the cocaine she hid in folds of skin to avoid detection. The sting was a huge success for the then Inspector Martin Callinan, who would later become the Commissioner of An Garda Síochána, and his team, who had a fleet specially modified as secret surveillance vans. While the operation had been expensive, it was a success, and Kelly was a big prize given his background in the IRA and his advisory role to younger ambitious criminals. From the moment he was caught, Kelly denied point blank that he had anything to do with the drugs and told officers that he had simply been asked to pick up Conlon by a friend called James Beirne. He said Conlon had told him the bag contained money 'for a friend of Jim Beirne'.

While Kelly was more comfortable mixing with paramilitaries, armed robbers and street-wise criminals, James 'Danger'

Beirne, a former Roscommon football star, preferred to associate with celebrities and high-rolling Londoners living a champagne lifestyle of limos, cocaine and fast women. Larger than life, loud, gregarious, and popular, Beirne enjoyed a flutter and had a habit of going through money like water. A privileged start to life had changed course when he dropped out of dentistry college and headed to London to earn his fortune instead. There he made friends with rich and fun-loving socialites and rubbed shoulders with some dangerous criminals who liked his personality and his head for their kind of business. His reputation as a popular sports star back home had suffered a hammer blow when he was arrested and sentenced for defrauding a Jersey bank out of 353 gold Krugerrand coins worth the equivalent of more than €100,000. He'd gone to jail but, when he got out, he came straight back to Ireland and set up a series of companies before embarking on a major fraud against the Norwegian government involving dried fish. Beirne's scam had gone so far that, by the time he was found out, Norway was down millions, but he simply went bankrupt and retreated to the shadows. As far as the Gardaí were concerned, Beirne was off their radar – out of sight, out of mind. Whether Kelly was naming him and breaking the criminal code of *omertà* as part of a grudge against him or in a desperate bid to convince his overlords in the IRA that he had nothing to do with drugs was irrelevant. They had their evidence and they were going to trial without any complications.

Kelly and Yamanoha were remanded in custody without bail but Conlon, on a second attempt, won his freedom pending trial after a £140,000 bail bond was paid. Although he'd had to surrender his passport, he'd managed to get his hands on a British one and flew back to Miami, later ringing the Gardaí to apologise for having absconded. It later emerged that Conlon was a suspected DEA tout who'd been monitoring Escobar's ambitions to push his product into Europe, while playing the role of a fixer for new customers from across the Atlantic. Kelly remained in custody vehemently pleading not guilty and feeling foolish and furious that he was left to face the music with his Cuban mule. During his trial, the court heard that detailed forensic tests had been carried out on adhesive tapes and the jumper worn by Yamanoha, who worked in the service industry in Miami. Dr Sheila Willis, a forensic scientist, told the trial that samples of the tape found in the bin in the hotel room matched fibres on the green jumper. At one point the judge, jury and legal counsel all visited the hotel and saw for themselves where the Garda surveillance van had been placed in the car park, and heard how undercover officers had watched Kelly and Conlon as they handled the plastic bag containing the cocaine. A car similar to the one which Kelly had been driving was even placed where the court heard he had parked. Despite his protestations of innocence, Kelly was found guilty and given a 14-year sentence with his co-accused Yamanoha receiving eight, although she would be later freed on appeal.

Between his conviction and sentence hearing, the *Irish Times* had published several articles which not only covered the evidence given at the trial, but also Kelly's background and his deep links with Republicanism and organised crime. In the newspaper, journalist Paul O'Neill, who would go on to become the *Irish Times* editor, had focused on one of the unanswered questions of the trial, namely why the Gardaí were watching Kelly in the first place. O'Neill, through a series of sources, had been able to put together a profile of Kelly as a violent criminal involved in fraud and drug smuggling, who was closely associated with leading criminal figures in Dublin. Kelly, ever the agitator, described the article as 'malicious and pernicious lies' and he complained to the Court of Criminal Appeal where he argued that two articles published had been prejudicial and that the trial judge should have acceded to applications to discharge the jury as a result. *The Late Late Show*, where the trial had also been discussed, was also cited for straying into illegal commentary. The ruling went somewhat in Kelly's favour, but instead of throwing out the case as requested, the Court of Criminal Appeal simply ordered a new one. Kelly went back to the High Court asking it to stop the second trial, claiming he could not get a fair hearing because of the publicity surrounding the case, but that didn't work and he found himself back in the dock.

After the second trial, Kelly was again found guilty and later sentenced to the same 14 years, but his legal agitation would govern trial reporting by the media for years to come. During the trial, Detective Sergeant John Fitzpatrick of the Garda Drugs Squad had told Mr Peter Charleton, prosecuting, that cocaine was widely used in Ireland by more affluent sections of society. It was generally sold, he said, with a purity of between 25 and 30 per cent, but the cocaine in the possession of Kelly and others had an 85 per cent purity and would, therefore, be bulked and mixed once it arrived safely. Going on that ratio, gardaí had estimated the drugs found in Kelly's possession were worth about £500,000, an indication of the profits that could be made and the quality that customers were prepared to buy.

Kelly settled down to life behind bars in Portlaoise Prison, where he befriended the terrorist Dessie O'Hare, but he continued to argue to have the cocaine rap lifted, repeatedly asking judges to overturn his conviction. In 1996, three years after he was first sentenced, the Court of Criminal Appeal dismissed his second legal challenge centred on allegations that the former head of the City of London CID and Fraud Squad, then Commissioner Thomas Dickinson, had given information to the Gardaí after Kelly's arrest which would have been essential to his defence. His claims that he'd been the victim of a miscarriage of justice due to

John Conlon's role in the conspiracy fell on deaf ears, and he had to accept that he was going to have to do his porridge after all.

Around the same time Eamon Kelly was dabbling in the cocaine market, another Irish man had even higher ambitions for himself as a cocaine cowboy and a direct route between the South American cartels and the coastlines of the UK and Ireland.

Businessman Brian Wright was convinced that it was literally going to be plain sailing to get his product from the Caribbean to the UK once he could get an introduction to the suppliers. His chance came when he met with a Brazilian called Ronnie Soares, who had a direct line into the cartels in Bogotá and Medellín, and just like that, his massive cocaine operation got underway. A professional gambler who'd grown up in Cork, Wright had moved to the Kilburn area of England along with his 11 siblings, who were all reared in grinding poverty, instilling in him an insatiable appetite for money and a fearless demeanour. He'd started out as a small-time gambler but he'd become so flash that by the time he was transporting cocaine, he already had a box at Ascot where he was bribing jockeys and running rings around the authorities. Just like his heroes the Kray Twins, Wright courted celebrity and one of his closest friends was the comedian Jim Davidson, who would give evidence at his trial. Authorities in the UK had no idea how big Wright had got until bad luck and a freak storm would combine to begin the unravelling of his carefully constructed empire, which was based on a delivery round so guaranteed that he earned himself the nickname 'The Milkman'. Likewise, Gardaí in Ireland had no idea of the enormity of what they would uncover when a yacht called the *Sea Mist* was forced to dock at Cobh on a stormy night in October 1996.

The boat had been caught in the bad weather and needed shelter, but when it arrived, the skipper and another crewman on board behaved so suspiciously that fishermen and locals were alarmed enough to call the Gardaí. They boarded the vessel and discovered that it had been specially modified to hide almost £6 million of cocaine. Brian Wright was immediately suspected of being the bigwig behind it. He was already on the radar of the US and UK authorities, who were jointly monitoring his involvement and friendly relations with Colombian cartels, and together they were sitting back waiting for the right moment to pounce. In August 1996, just one month before *Sea Mist* veered off her course for England, his son, Brian Wright Jnr, had been spotted and documented in intelligence files as having been in the Caribbean. While officers were monitoring his activities, they had no idea just how big a player Wright Snr had become.

The *Sea Mist* didn't have its flag raised as it realised it wasn't going to make it past the southeast coast of Ireland towards Dover, and the fisherman who had guided her became suspicious when the two crewmen appeared more panicked than grateful as they were directed to safety. Initially there was confusion over the amount of cocaine on board the yacht and its purity, but as officers started to dismantle the interior of the boat, they uncovered more and more cocaine. The Gardaí began with estimates of about £40 million, but one tabloid hit the highest end of the scale when it coupled a 'dusky Venezuelan beauty' as being one of five arrested with a 'record £500 million worth of cocaine'. The 'dusky beauty' was a 19-year-old who would later be acquitted of any involvement in the importation of illegal drugs. Four men were also brought to court. Graham Howard Miller, then 47, from Cumbria in England, the skipper Gordon Richards from Brighton, James Noel, 51, and Roman Smollen, who was 50 and from the honeymoon island of St Lucia.

Within days of the chance discovery, the group appeared at a special sitting of Cork District Court following what was described as 'Europe's biggest ever cocaine seizure' on board the Norwegian-registered converted cruiser. Superintendent Kieran McGann opposed bail for all five due to the seriousness of the charges, the amount of drugs said to be involved, and because he believed the defendants would not stand trial if released. All were remanded in custody and a two-year-old child was placed with foster parents under the care of the South Eastern Health Board as the Irish authorities faced a decision on whether to keep him in Ireland or return him to relatives in South America. While the seizure had been a coup in terms of size, scale and headlines, many of those nabbed were pawns and totally dispensable to the ambitious Wright, who had funded the voyage. However, among the bits of intelligence found through documents, phone records and from statements was information that a yacht called the *Selina* was due to rendezvous with the *Sea Mist* off the UK's Dorset coast near Poole. The information would provide a breakthrough that would allow UK police to dig deep into the Wright network and set up a proper plan to take down the cocaine giant and jail him and his lieutenants for a long time.

Back home Irish police weren't in a celebratory mood, despite the massive seizure and the international kudos that had come with it. Just months before the storm forced the *Sea Mist* to dock in Cork, the murder of journalist Veronica Guerin had brought politicians and police chiefs out in force with promises to crack down on organised crime. Guerin had been driving her car back to Dublin from a court appearance when she was shot dead by a gang led by the cannabis kingpin John Gilligan. The crackdown that followed had scattered Gilligan's gang and had seen new legislation brought in to allow Gardaí hold suspected drug traffickers for up to seven days. More importantly, the outcry had seen draconian Proceeds of Crime legislation speed through the houses of parliament at an unprecedented rate, which facilitated the set-up of the Criminal Assets Bureau (CAB) with the remit to go after the money.

While some senior criminals had fled Ireland, any who had invested their ill-gotten gains openly in property were vulnerable, with the onus of proof on the target of CAB investigations to prove their innocence as opposed to the other way around. The Bureau had a long list of those it intended to look at, but first up were a slew of serious organised crime figures from both the UK and the Netherlands who had moved to Ireland during the early 1990s to run their illicit operations. They were the ones that Barry Galvin was referring to when he complained on the *Late Late Show* about crime lords living it up in rural Ireland. Now at the helm of the new Bureau as its Chief Legal Officer, Galvin was intent that the blow-ins were about to start to feel rather unwelcome.

First on the list was Johnny Morrissey, a violent Manchester criminal suspected of gangland murder, money laundering and cocaine smuggling. He'd left England and set up shop in Kinsale in County Cork, where he splashed around cash, diamonds and jewellery, earning him the nickname 'Johnny Cash'. Balding Morrissey had arrived in like a hurricane and snapped up a building just yards from the waterfront in the pretty fishing village and told locals he planned to open a restaurant there. Massive renovations followed, which were carried out by mainly UK workers. He poured buckets of money into his new venture; it was rumoured he spent at least £600,000 paying everyone, from the painters to the plumbers to the serving staff, in notes pulled from his bulging wallet. Known as a boisterous individual, he became a familiar figure around the town, giving generously to local charities and fundraisers and picking up bar tabs, which he'd often pay in sterling.

He eventually opened the doors of his business venture, a high-end restaurant which he called the Annalise. At night he worked the tables or drank in local bars, but by day he took to the seas in what Gardaí suspected was his real business. When the fledgling CAB made enquiries with Interpol about Morrissey, they set up a series of raids that found a handgun, half a kilo of cocaine, cash and Cartier jewellery. Officers believed that Morrissey had been using the jewellery to pay Russian criminals, who were transporting cocaine into Europe and delivering it to the fishing enthusiast on the way, but Gardaí couldn't get enough evidence for a case against him. An ocean-going rigid dinghy was, however, discovered along with commercial diving equipment, which could reach greater depths than normal sub-aqua gear, but they proved nothing alone.

Morrissey was at the time closely associated with George 'The Penguin' Mitchell, an entrepreneurial criminal based in Amsterdam who had attempted to set up Ireland's first ecstasy-making factory before his plans were foiled. Mitchell had an entire wing of his operation based in Cork, where his sidekick, Alan Buckley, lived. Mitchell had also managed to make contacts directly with the Colombians and was fast adding cocaine to his list of products for wholesale in Ireland, the UK and Europe.

Morrissey was incensed that CAB was out to ruin his fun and destroy what he had built up in Kinsale. In a plan to hit back, he put together a plot to murder Barry Galvin. With a reputation as a hitman for the gangsters in England, CAB took no chances with their man and Galvin was the first ever civilian to be issued with a firearm for his own protection. The Bureau foiled the murder plan and demanded £100,000 from Johnny 'Cash' and froze another £500,000 of his assets. Morrissey eventually gave up the fight and walked away from the money and from Kinsale for good, and the CAB turned their attentions on another of his contemporaries.

The international criminal mastermind David Huck had been one of the first of the smugglers to see Ireland as a safe haven and moved from Ibiza to County Clare in 1988, buying a luxury home and moving part of his fortune to an Irish bank account. Just like Morrissey, he posed as a suave businessman and flashed his cash about. His big interest was in cannabis and as a criminal he had enjoyed quite a share of luck. He'd started with cigarettes but moved to hash after he realised how easy it was to buy it from the Moroccans and land the drugs from sea. In 1993 he just managed to escape when his yacht, the *Brime*, was stopped off the Kerry coast laden with hash, and although he'd been arrested and questioned about the consignment, he had been released without charge. Huck had bought and refurbished the ketch, which was due to meet another yacht off the Kerry coast travelling from Wales. The second boat had run into difficulty at Ballinskelligs Bay and had to pull into shore for repair, where eagle-eyed locals reported that the two men aboard were acting suspiciously. The duo had phoned Huck, who'd made his way down to the port just as Gardaí boarded the Welsh vessel, on which they found a small quantity of drugs.

While they were suspicious that there was a bigger plan afoot, they didn't realise that the boat was due to meet the *Brime* and divide its load. They had to let Huck go and he immediately left Ireland on a flight from Dublin to London. Later that day, the *Brime* crew phoned a mobile that had been seized by Gardaí. The officer who answered the call kept his cool and the voice on the other end gave details of their location and made plans to meet up off Loop Head, where they would switch the loads. They were met instead by the naval vessel the LÉ *Orla*, and the operation was deemed a huge success despite the fact that Huck had got away. In his absence, the Bureau moved in to pick through his abandoned belongings, which included two houses and land. Not long after, Huck's legendary luck finally ran out off the coast of Cornwall when

British Customs nabbed him on board the *Fata Morgana* with £10 million worth of the drug.

Mickey Green was another criminal superstar who'd decided to seek refuge in Ireland, and while he'd fled by the time the Criminal Assets Bureau was set up, they immediately went about mopping up the substantial assets he'd left behind. Green had only been based in Ireland for a couple of years, but during that time he was suspected of identifying and funding routes for cocaine to be landed in the country. Thanks to his talent for disappearing just as he was about to be captured, Green was dubbed the 'Pimpernel' and would inspire movies and TV crime dramas for decades. One of the notorious 'Wembley Mob', he'd built his reputation in armed and violent robberies and pulled off some of the most daring heists in British criminal history. But when the mob leader, Bertie Smalls, was given full immunity in return for giving damning evidence against his men, Green had found himself with an 18-year sentence.

Green didn't even serve half that stretch in jail, and by the early 1980s he'd been released, reuniting with one of his Wembley Mob pals, Ronnie Dark, the duo getting involved in an ingenious and highly lucrative VAT scam. It was one of the first ever rackets involving gold Krugerrand, South African coins that weigh exactly one ounce. Green and Dark flew vast amounts of Krugerrand, which were exempt from VAT, into Britain using a private jet. They then melted them down into gold ingots or bars, and sold them to bullion houses, making sure to charge them VAT. In just six months, they made the equivalent of about €6 million today. It was a beautifully simple shakedown.

Once rumbled, Green fled to the Costa del Sol in Spain, which still had no extradition treaty with the UK, and there he discovered the world of drug smuggling and, in particular, cocaine. Always quick to reinvent himself in the underworld of crime, he quickly became one of the leading figures in the burgeoning European narcotics trade. On the Costa he lived it up with all the trappings of a cocaine kingpin: a luxury penthouse apartment, a white Rolls Royce, a red Porsche, and the obligatory yacht. By the mid-1980s, he was worth tens of millions of pounds and had a collection of expensive cars and 11 yachts. Describing himself as a car dealer, he bought a huge villa on the outskirts of Marbella and became a part-owner in a club on the harbour in Puerto Banús, enjoying his status as a major player in full view of the authorities.

But in 1987 his life of pleasure on the Spanish coast was seriously disrupted when he was arrested by Spanish police after they seized two tonnes of hash. Green got bail and fled to Morocco, leaving behind all his properties, cars and yachts. Within a few months, he popped up again, this time in Paris, where French police, after being alerted by Interpol, swooped on his apartment on the Left Bank. They found vast amounts of cocaine and gold bullion, but the 'Pimpernel' had once again made his escape. A French court later sentenced him in his absence to 17 years for drug smuggling and possession.

In 1993 another court, this time in the Netherlands, handed him down a 20-year prison term for smuggling cannabis, but Green was happily based in California by then, where he was living in a rented Bel Air mansion. The DEA, trying to get a handle on the Colombian cartels, kept an eye on Green and watched as he met with key figures and negotiated big shipments. In 1994 he was linked to a one-tonne shipment of cocaine worth £200 million, which was seized by customs at Birkenhead in Merseyside after being shipped from South America through Poland. The Americans eventually made their move and burst into Green's California mansion, and an arrangement was brokered to send him to France where he was set to start his 17-year prison sentence. But in an extraordinary sequence of events, Green was bundled on a plane for transport to Paris with his Irish passport tucked into his pocket and a master plan in his mind. When the plane stopped off at Shannon to refuel, he simply walked off and used his passport to waltz through customs and make his way to Dublin.

In Ireland, pre-Google, he managed to settle into an anonymous, albeit high-society life, posing as a wealthy retired English businessman with an interest in horse racing. In reality, he was successfully running cocaine across the Atlantic while using Ireland as his headquarters. He bought a house to match his persona; Maple Falls in Co. Meath was set on four acres of land and surrounded by high walls and trees. It was a huge stately manor measuring 5,500 square feet, complete with five bedrooms, three reception rooms, a sauna room, a snooker room, and a heated indoor swimming pool. Outside there were stables and an all-weather tennis court. For nights out in Dublin, he bought a two-bedroom luxury penthouse and became a regular in the Berkeley Court and Westbury hotels, along with the celebrity-favourite club Lillie's Bordello.

In his early 50s, he hooked up with a younger Irish woman, Anita, who would become his long-time partner. Green liked Ireland and reckoned it was a good location to run his empire, and an easy place for his friends and family in the UK to come and visit him. Setting standards for the many big-league cocaine dealers who would come up behind him, he tried to rub shoulders with politicians and business people by attending fundraisers and giving generously to charities. He loved nothing more than a big night out, and it was after one of those soirées in April 1995 that life in Ireland changed for good.

He'd been drinking and was driving his Bentley in the city centre when he smashed into a taxi. Instead of calling an ambulance, Green immediately fled the scene, but when he was caught by two gardaí on patrol, he refused to give a urine sample to test if he was drunk. In the meantime, the fire brigade had responded to calls about the crash and it took 45 minutes to cut the taxi man and father of nine Joe White from his car. He died later in hospital from shock and severe blood loss.

Green was charged with dangerous driving but got two witnesses to lie about details of the crash. It emerged years later that Michael Michael, a drug baron and one-time head of a London-based criminal gang known as the Organisation, had linked him up with the 'witnesses' and even travelled to Dublin to bail him out. In a case of crime pays, Green got a rap on the knuckles from the court and a £950 fine, and Joe White's widow was left with nothing but a pension to raise her large family, never receiving a penny from his insurance company or from the gangster himself. Green, who was believed to have been worth more than £100 million at many points in his long career, never said sorry or offered to help them out.

The outcome might have been a win, but it wasn't all good news for Green, and with his cover blown he found he was no longer welcome among the horsey set. Any political ties to anyone of any influence were also quickly snipped, and then came the news that the IRA were sniffing around him and rumours that the terrorists were possibly planning to kidnap him, to either demand a ransom from his girlfriend, Anita, or to persuade him to cut them in on his drug-dealing action. Green didn't hang around to find out and, just like David Huck, he fled Ireland, leaving his properties behind for the CAB to move in on.

As the Bureau got busy with the criminals' proceeds of crime, Eamon Kelly's old foe James 'Danger' Beirne was finally caught in the UK trying to smuggle cocaine worth £6.5 million sterling into Britain. At 51, 'Danger' was older than the average cocaine dealer, as was his co-accused, who was in his late 50s.

Together with a Peruvian, they had done a deal with a gang based in the Andes and ordered 50 kilos of cocaine and devised what they believed was a foolproof plan to get it into Britain, which involved hiding it in timber bound for Estonia. At the time Estonia was the biggest exporter of wood into Europe, so they wagered that if it came from there and not Peru, it would easily get through customs. However, they forgot to check the ship's log and didn't realise that its first stop was Felixstowe in England and not Estonia. When the boat docked at the port, the timber did arouse suspicion, but only because of the zig-zag route the boat was due to take. Customs officers examined the cargo and found the cocaine, but to discover who owned it they had to be clever and let it continue on its journey as planned. It was only when it arrived back to the UK some weeks later, and when the trio showed up at the port for their timber, that officers moved in on their targets. In the years that followed, Beirne and his cohorts would face three trials before they were eventually found guilty and sentenced to huge jail terms.

A year after 'Danger' Beirne was nabbed trying to pick up his cocaine, John Conlon was finally back in Dublin to face the music for his role in the Eamon Kelly conspiracy to use human mules from Miami to carry drugs to Ireland. Conlon's address was given as Allison Road, Miami Beach, and his sentence was backdated to 1994 when he had been taken into custody in England and held for extradition. During his trial, then Detective Superintendent Martin Callanan told the court that Conlon, a native of Westport in County Mayo and a father of three, had left Ireland in 1959 and owned properties in Miami, where he had lived for some years, and in Norfolk in England. He had no previous convictions. While in custody he had contracted hepatitis C after picking up bloodstained clothes belonging to an infected fellow inmate who had cut his hand.

Across the water, UK police were working hard to break up the 20-strong Wright mob, which they had discovered were the most powerful cocaine gang at the time, thanks to the shocking find on the *Sea Mist*. The Wright Group was so big that the £50 million value of the cocaine they had lost in Cork had hardly affected them at all, not even causing a ripple in the operations. The human losses hadn't appeared to bother them either.

A year after they were arrested on the boat, skipper Gordon Richards, three crew and his girlfriend had gone on trial in Cork. Richards pleaded guilty but gave the court a window into the tentacles of the Wright organisation that stretched from the UK into Venezuela. Richards told the judge that he and his Venezuelan girlfriend, Teresa da Silva Roy, and her two-year-old son had made the journey which ended in Ireland because they were under threat from gun-toting South Americans working for Wright. He said that three months before the doomed trip, he had been approached by people who offered him money to take the *SeaMist* to France. He said he'd agreed after they told him that he wouldn't live if he didn't captain the ship, and he said he'd left Puerto La Cruz in Venezuela and first stopped at Trinidad, where the boat was repaired. 'An aeroplane dropped the shit off while we were at sea. I knew it was contraband and was pretty sure it was cocaine,' he admitted.

In his statement, he said he'd received $6,000 for supplies and $1,000 for himself, initially telling Gardaí that his girl-friend stowed away on board with the child, but in a letter to the judge claimed that he took them with him because he believed they were in danger. Richards told Justice AG Murphy that he had fallen on hard times and was to be paid $400,000 for the voyage. Crew members Roman Smollen, James Noel and Graham Howard Miller were found not guilty by a jury, along with Ms da Silva Roy.

During his appeal, further details about Richard's distressing story were heard, including the fact that he had no criminal history and had worked hard all his life as a boat builder. Brought up in the West Indies by relatives, Richards, whose real name turned out to be John Ewart, had earned enough money to live a nice lifestyle, but when a hurricane struck, he said, he'd lost everything. In prison in Ireland, he was working building model boats and selling them to prison officers but his health was failing, the court was told, and he hadn't seen his girlfriend as she'd returned to South America. Richards, or Ewart, had named Wright as the mastermind behind the plan and detailed the extent of his operation.

Between 1996 and 1998 alone it was estimated that the Wright Group had smuggled a staggering £300 million of cocaine across the Atlantic. Surveillance had identified Wright's most trusted allies, who were his son Brian, his pal Kevin Hanley and the middleman, Brazilian Ronnie Soares. Just like the *Sea Mist*, officers believed that boats had picked up the drugs at sea and then sailed them over to the UK, docking at night and transferring their cargo to waiting vans. Boats like the *Moonstreak*, the *Cyan*, the *Flex* and the *Lucky Irish* were all identified by officers as having carried drugs worth about £50 million each.

In 1998, a year after the *Sea Mist* crew were tried, undercover officers in the UK eventually got the break they needed when Hanley was arrested with cocaine in the boot of his car. Unaware his every move was being watched, Wright called a meeting and booked into an expensive hotel, but Customs got there first and bugged the suite and photographed him on the balcony. Conversations about drug movements and money transfers were recorded, while undercover officers followed his key lieutenants to a farm where they were stashing almost 500 kilos of cocaine. When they attempted to move the drugs, Customs swooped in, fearing the gang would break up and they'd miss their one opportunity to catch them red-handed. Typically, that meant letting Brian Wright, who was out of the country, slip through the net for the time being, but his son was arrested along with Soares and seven others. In the years that followed, 15 members of the organisation would be tried, convicted and sentenced to more than 200 years in jail.

⁓

If 1996 was a significant year for criminals in Ireland with the establishment of the CAB and the seizure of the cocaine on the *Sea Mist*, 1998 would prove to be quite the match – even down to another cocaine haul discovered on a boat that had to limp into harbour in Cork after engine difficulty.

When Customs officers started to search the 50-foot catamaran in Kinsale Harbour, they couldn't believe the amount of drugs on board. Wrapped in packaging and concealed beneath the bunks as well as under diesel tanks, they found a total of 320 kilos over the course of three different searches. Dubliner John O'Toole, in his early 50s and with an address in Panama City, was the registered owner of the boat and he was on board with an Englishman called Michael Tune, who lived in Tenerife. Both were arrested while stories began to emerge about what had led Customs to the catamaran. Some said that, just like *Sea Mist*, *Gemeos* had failed to lift her flag; others said that she had moored illegally. It was far more likely that it was an intelligence-led operation with the information coming from UK Customs, who were dug right into the cocaine gangs at the time. But whatever the truth, the haul from the *Gemeos* was enormous, and police at one point valued it at £120 million, dropping to a more conservative estimated street value of £40 million with 75 per cent purity by the time the two were brought to court.

O'Toole first told cops that they had sailed into Kinsale from Tenerife in the Canary Islands, but that they had come via the Azores to get better winds and it had taken them around 20 days. Charts told a different story and markings used by navigators to plot their course showed the ship had been 400 miles east of the Bahamas in the Caribbean just weeks before it reached Cork. Confronted with the evidence, O'Toole changed his story and told officers that he had taken the boat from his wife and had decided to sail it across the Atlantic to sell it in Europe. A court would later hear that Customs officers had been alerted to the 50-foot catamaran by Harbour Master Captain Phil Devitt, who noticed the boat had anchored at a mooring belonging to another boat and had failed to pay harbour dues. A local man had towed it to the mooring with his speed boat after three crew on the *Gemeos* signalled to him for help. Both men pleaded not guilty at Cork Circuit Criminal Court to five charges, and the trial got underway in May 1999.

O'Toole proved to be typical of the colourful characters that seemed to populate the cocaine trade during the 1980s and 1990s. During his trial he got into the witness box – usually an ill-advised move by anyone who is caught red-handed – and said he didn't approve of drug dealing and he didn't like people who dealt in narcotics. Born in Enniskerry in County Wicklow, he'd moved to Canada with his late wife Gabriela, who had cancer, he said, and who needed money for her treatment. But he'd fallen on hard times and someone had damaged another boat he'd used, leaving him with nothing except for the *Gemeos* and rising bills. It was a familiar tale, albeit Gabriela had actually passed away four days before the trial began. O'Toole said that he'd been introduced to a man in Panama, described as 'Mr X', who asked him to take drugs to Europe. 'I don't like drug dealers because of what they do. It's all mafiosa, gangs, killings, and that sort of thing. I don't agree with it. It's just not in me. Drugs are totally wrong,' he said. 'I was sort of shocked. I had never been approached like that before . . . I refused point blank.' Despite taking $5,000 to help with his wife's medical costs, he denied that he knew he'd be expected to do anything for the money. 'I made it plain that I did not want to get involved. I never thought it would come to what it did – it was a nightmare. I thought at the time that he was genuinely sorry for me and my wife, and he had money and he wanted to help,' he said, adding that he was beaten up in a car park in Panama City and forced to agree to the indecent proposal.

The court, however, heard details of monthly payments of $5,000 amounting to more than $70,000 over the course of a year. He was also to be given $300,000 for the trip on the *Gemeos*, less the $70,000 advance. The payday to ship a load of cocaine was tax free and clearly tempting. O'Toole had once had a successful career in yacht chartering and, in Tenerife, his wife worked in diplomatic circles and regularly brought in business. Their companies were very successful with a million-pound turnover, but a series of tragedies, including the death of his brother Robert on board one of the yachts, his father's death and Gabriella's breast cancer, followed in quick succession.

Giving evidence, Detective Sergeant John Healy said he also believed that O'Toole came up against red tape and ran into difficulties with the Tenerife authorities. These problems revolved around regulations about the employment of locals, as well as increased competition in the yacht charter business. O'Toole's most prized yacht, the *Shogun*, was also destroyed by unknown persons, the officer told the court, and the family moved to Gabriella's native country of Panama where the hospital treatment bills for her cancer cost thousands of dollars every month.

O'Toole got to know the shadowy drug boss 'Mr X' in a night-club through contacts.

Michael Tune was to receive £100,000 for his role in the enterprise and was hoping to use it to move to England with his girlfriend and their 18-month-old daughter.

In a last-ditch effort to convince the judge to be lenient with O'Toole, counsel Blaise O'Carroll asked the court to listen to Gabriella from the grave through a letter she wrote to her husband while he was in prison. He also produced a letter from O'Toole's 13-year-old son, but the judge said that he had to put emotion aside. 'I have a function to send out a message to people involved in the drug world on behalf of society,' he stated. Tune changed his plea to guilty towards the end of the trial, a smart move which got him a lesser sentence of 14 years for his role compared to the 20 years handed down to O'Toole.

While a large seizure was always welcomed by police, there were gaps everywhere for ambitious dealers to move cocaine, and at the very heart of the trade lay poverty, ambition and a never-ending stream of drug mules willing to fill their stomachs or luggage with the drug. As the threat of cocaine escalated, Ireland and the UK decided to get together in a deal to clamp down on the couriers transporting the drugs, and they agreed to swap names of suspected mules and work together to track boats and planes used to transport drugs. Irish Customs director, Frank Daly, and chair of HM Customs and Excise, Dame Valerie Strachan, signed an agreement at Dromoland Castle in County Clare in 1998, and by 1999 new legislation was brought in so those caught transporting drugs could face up to 11 years in prison. No doubt the objective was to convince the mules to think twice before taking a job and put the squeeze on the drug barons, but what resulted was a major headache for the Irish prison system.

Mountjoy jail had housed female criminals convicted of offences since it opened in 1858, but by the mid-1950s, the women's wing was given over to younger offenders and became St Patrick's Institution. Since then, there had been only a small number of women incarcerated, but their numbers had been growing with the arrival of cocaine, and in 1999 a new female-only prison, called the Dóchas Centre, was opened. It was a campus-style prison designed for twice the number of prisoners as the old basement, complete with an ethos for them to live as close to an ordinary life as possible. Each had a cell with their own bathroom and inmates could clean, cook and launder their own clothes in seven separate houses that accommodated 10 to 12 in each, with a larger house called Cedar where 18 inmates would live together. With their ensuite rooms and keys, the women could move about relatively easier, and mothers were allowed keep newborns with them until the children reached 12 months old, at which point they had to leave the prison. The centre offered training and educational programmes to inmates, including hairdressing and beauty therapy, photography and FETAC training programmes to equip them for life on the outside.

The opening of the new facility was lauded as a bright, new era in rehabilitation and compassion, and it became a home from home for a large group of foreign prisoners who were there because of cocaine. They had been promised an escape from poverty, but instead many had been caught working as pack mules to ferry drugs from their home countries, many of which were places of no opportunity. Behind the walls of the Dóchas, the women from Africa, South America and the Caribbean had few friends and virtually no visitors, but the then Governor John Lonergan felt a lot of sympathy for them and so devised a way for them to feed their children back home. By carrying out prison work, many earned a small weekly wage, which they faithfully sent back to their families. Many never even told their loved ones they were in prison, instead spinning a yarn that they were leading free and respectable lives in Ireland and earning good wages. Enclosed with the money was a note to their families telling them how good life was in Ireland, how their job in the hospital or the restaurant was paying well, and how happy they were. In reality they were on a work initiative in the jails, which allowed them to earn £33 for every 100 pairs of shoes they hand sewed. For many the work was the only thing that kept their double lives a secret from their loved ones. In an interview at the time, Governor Lonergan said, 'It's tragic, really. Most of them just saw drug smuggling as a quick way of making money. I suppose you could call them naive, but they are here now and for a lot of them their families don't have a clue. Some of them send home every penny they earn. They ring home and say they are working in a hospital. They make the best of their lot.'

Growing numbers of the convicted drug mules meant they made up almost one in five of the female prison population in the year it opened. Brazilian Maria Emilia Bilibo, a 32-year-old artist, was the first to plead guilty to importing drugs under the new Act. She had been caught trying to smuggle £2.5 million worth of cocaine through Dublin airport. She had no previous convictions and was a good mother to her two children, and the court heard it was out of the need to support her children that she agreed to carry the drugs. A dealer had offered her $35,000 along with $1,500 expenses to take the flight to Ireland with the cocaine. She agreed, planning to return to Brazil to open a souvenir shop with the money. Instead, she was sentenced to seven years.

As more and more of the couriers were processed through the court system, it was clear they were terrified of the repercussions in their home countries and most refused to name the dealers who promised them the fortune they had dreamed of. Governor Lonergan said that, despite their crimes, the women deserved praise for their positive attitude and determination to make amends. They coped, he said, with isolation from their families, lack of friends and often a language barrier, yet worked into the evenings sewing shoes.

As the world prepared for a new millennium, cocaine worth £4.5 million was found in a warehouse in Dublin hidden amid a cargo of bananas, accidentally sent onwards from Antwerp. Fifty-two kilos of drugs were found in three boxes in the fruit, which had originated in Colombia. Gardaí who were called to the warehouse believed that the drugs had been distributed in error. In a Europe of no borders, the free movement of goods was making it ever easier for the cartels to move their product. The CAB may have run some of the key players out of Ireland and scattered them to the wind – successful crackdowns and intelligence-led operations on major drug barons had seen many of them locked up, with their skippers serving long sentences behind bars – but cocaine production was heating up in Colombia, Venezuela and Peru, where political corruption was fuelling a dangerous and growing trade, and where poverty and desperation would facilitate a never-ending supply of workers.

Undoubtedly Cork and its coastline had featured heavily in the first decade of Ireland's love affair with cocaine, but there were bigger players eyeing up the huge ports of Europe like Rotterdam and Antwerp as an easier route for the drug, believing it could be hidden in the massive shipments of bananas and coffee and other commodities making their way from South America.

George 'The Penguin' Mitchell was one of the first to have made serious contacts with suppliers from Colombia. He had a tight-knit inner circle in Dublin headed by his brother Paddy, partners in London and Liverpool, and a close association with a grouping known as the 'Cork Mafia' run by Edward 'Judd' Scanlon and Alan Buckley. Scanlon, from Bishopstown, was a middle-class, privately educated and privileged type with a nose for trouble. He'd been first caught with drugs in the 1970s in New York, and later in the UK in 1980 driving a lorry load of heroin from Turkey to England. He was eventually nabbed at Heathrow Airport with a woman carrying four ounces of heroin in her knickers and was landed back in jail. But Scanlon had been an early convert to the potential of cocaine and was on the radar of British Customs throughout the 1980s. In Ireland he was the focus of the Cork City Divisional Drugs Unit, not least for the flash way he lived his life, with a taste for designer clothes, fast cars and splashing his cash. Just like his pal Johnny Morrissey, Scanlon had tried to hide in the cosmopolitan foodie port of Kinsale, where he owned a restaurant and where his friends called him 'Giorgio' because of his never-ending supply of Armani threads.

In his arrogance, Scanlon had believed he was untouchable, despite a history of going to jail, and he had a tendency to be hands-on with his supply. Under surveillance in March 1997, he'd been seen handing a holdall bag to a known Dublin drugs courier and, when he was stopped, he was found with ecstasy and cocaine. In court the courier refused to identify Scanlon because, he said, he was threatened and feared for his family, but eyewitness evidence of their meeting and statements from senior drug detectives was enough to convince a jury of his guilt.

In court, officers said that Scanlon was in the 'upper eche-lons' of the drug trade and had been on their radar for 10 years. He'd presented himself to communities as a respectable busi-nessman, all the while pushing cocaine and ecstasy into a willing southern market and dealing directly with Mitchell for his supply. Scanlon, renowned for his love of fine dining, was floored when he got 22 years, the heaviest drug sentence ever handed down to a criminal, and was refused leave to appeal. The crackdown on Scanlon, which was a joint effort by the Gardaí and the CAB, was ultimately focused on his boss and Cork Mafia godfather Tommy O'Callaghan, a far rougher type who had introduced Mitchell to many of his associates, including the ex-Irish National Liberation Army gunman Tommy Savage. Feeling the heat, O'Callaghan had moved out to Europe and settled between Spain and the Netherlands after he'd been hit with a tax demand of £700,000 by the Bureau.

His line manager Alan Buckley also sensed the impending doom and managed to leave Ireland just as Scanlon felt the full force of the law. Just like Mickey Green, Buckley had earned himself the nickname of 'The Pimpernel' due to his incredible ability to get away with things. Another fast-car-driving Romeo, he had based himself in the posh Cork town of Douglas for years, where he used an antique shop as cover. When Gardaí had targeted Mitchell's ecstasy factory, it was Buckley who was one of the key dealers under surveillance, but he'd cleverly slipped the net and couldn't be arrested at the time. After the crackdown the mob regrouped, expanded and settled in as wholesalers in the two key European locations of the Netherlands and southern Spain. Buckley moved to Marbella while Mitchell and O'Callaghan based themselves in Amsterdam. One of their enforcers, Michael 'Danser' Ahern, moved to Portugal while Scanlon did time in jail in Ireland.

In their new HQ, the group also began to do business with a newcomer on the international scene. Fresh out of jail from Ireland, Christy Kinahan Snr was making his presence and his ambition known in Amsterdam, where he was determined to take his place at the top table of organised crime. They would be perfectly placed in the years to come to take advantage of Europe's growing love affair with cocaine.

CHAPTER TWO

A NEW ORDER

While a coterie of swashbuckling, old-school armed robbers had been the first to see the potential of cocaine and the riches that came with it, beneath the surface lay a young and hungry generation desperate to get in on the action. And if the 1980s and 1990s belonged to blaggers and gamblers who lived it up and courted celebrities, the new millennium marked a distinct change in the attitudes of those who wanted to make a name for themselves as a fresh breed of cocaine cowboys whose ambition was equalled only by their propensity for violence.

While there had been a scattering of gangland murders in the 1990s, many of the assassinations had been put down to personal disputes or hard business decisions among the criminal fraternity, who seized opportunities to take out rivals after much consideration. Paddy Shanahan, known as 'the Builder', had helped many gangsters launder their money through property developments, but when he was shot dead outside a gym in October 1994, his murder had been put down to his own associates. A year later, gangland enforcer Michael Crinnion from Cork was killed outside a bar in the city in a hit suspected of being organised by the rival Cork Mafia who had grown to hate him. A year after that, PJ Judge, known as 'Psycho', was shot dead in a bar in Finglas, making way for his understudy Martin 'Marlo' Hyland to take over his drug patch.

The arrival, however, of the new order of ruthless young criminals prepared to take on and take out the older crews was cemented when drug dealer Pascal Boland was shot dead outside his home in Mulhuddart in January 1999. Boland was a tough-talking dealer who had stood down the notorious Judge and thought nothing of pushing in on territory in west Dublin, which was fast becoming the turf of a teenage gang known as 'the Westies'. They were nicknamed after the notorious Irish mobsters who terrorised New York's Hell's Kitchen over two decades through murders, kidnappings, extortion, gambling, dealing, loan sharking, fraud and counterfeiting. The original Westies had eventually been taken on by the tough-talking Rudy Giuliani, who led the federal prosecution of New York mafia bosses as US Attorney for the Southern District. Over the course of the high-profile trials, the group had been described as one of the most savage in the long and violent history of New York gangs; their Irish counterparts would earn a similar reputation, albeit on smaller turf.

Led by Shane Coates, only 18 when he shot Pascal Boland, and his sidekick Stephen Sugg, the gang had come onto the drug scene like a hurricane. They hailed from Blanchardstown, a Dublin suburb that had exploded outwards from what was once a small rural village into the largest urban area of north Dublin. Coates and Sugg, along with their friends Andrew and Mark Glennon, literally epitomised what flash Larry Dunne had prophesied as he was led off to jail in the 1980s: a new generation of drug dealers who were far more ruthless and ambitious than those who had gone before them. Of the gangs of violent young criminals who had popped up across the city, staking their claims on geographical areas and their customers, none would define this new breed more terrifyingly.

Coates and Sugg were already top targets for the Gardaí while still teenagers and had started their criminal careers stealing and joyriding cars. They quickly honed their driving skills to good use in smash-and-grab raids across the country, making the inevitable transition to armed robbery and drugs. Both racked up a string of convictions along the way and spent short stints in prison. For Gardaí policing the area, they became public enemy number one and eventually, in April 1995, were caught red-handed as they attempted the armed robbery of a butchers in a shopping centre. They were convicted and sentenced to five years each for the attempted robbery and possession of sawn-off shotguns but, given their young ages, a judge decided to give them a chance and suspended the end of the sentences on the basis they didn't associate with one another. They ignored the conditions and were sent back to jail for another year. On their second release they were careful to keep their association under the radar until the ban on their friendship was lifted.

It was their reputation for violence that ensured they stood out from the growing number of dangerous gangs populating the Blanchardstown area. They'd begun selling heroin but quickly added cocaine to their supply. With the Glennon brothers, Mark and Andrew, at their side they elbowed their way past other young pretenders to take over some of the vast estates that made up Blanchardstown and out towards Ballymun. Several dealers either moved out or began working directly for them. Their operation was well organised and, in their first year in business, it was estimated they pocketed £1million in clear profit. Theirs was a simple business plan: there was absolutely no credit and stories abounded of people getting cut up and shot by them, of the addict who owed them a few quid being hung by his ankles from the top of one of the Ballymun towers, and of the beatings they were reputed to dole out at will.

In reality, the Westies were far worse than the rumours going around about them, and by their use of extreme violence, they assumed, in a very short space of time, absolute control over the neighbourhoods. Over the next five years they dominated the drug scene and multiplied their profits times over. They told dealers to buy their drugs from them or they wouldn't be alive to sell their lines of coke, wraps of smack and quarters of weed. Defiance led, inevitably, to a visit to intensive care. Even debts as small as £50 would be collected with violence and hundreds of incidents were reported. One dealer was tortured by having jump leads attached to his nipples; a chronic heroin addict with nine children was burned with cigarettes over a £500 bill; other users were thrown from balconies, breaking bones and smashing skulls in the process. Andrew Glennon notoriously used a pliers to pull a tooth from the mouth of one young addict who could not pay, while another accomplice held the victim down. The terrified victim refused to complain. They used guns, baseball bats, vice grips and broken bottles to intimidate those who bought their supply, and together with the Glennon brothers and 12 key lieutenants, they operated with relative impunity because of the fear they struck in anyone whose evidence could be used against them.

At times, Gardaí constructed seemingly watertight cases against them that, for various reasons, fell apart. Boland, who'd been working the area for years, came into their sights when he tried to take back some control, moving in on their pushers and trying to undercut them on the supply price. His greatest mistake was likely when he told them 'you're nobodies'. With Boland riddled with bullets, the Gardaí upped the Westies on their list of targets, began gathering intelligence around the group and set up a special task force to deal with them.

Months after they shot Boland, the Westies burst into the home of a teenager and shot him in his bed. The youngster had been a friend of Sugg, but had angered him when he began dating a female friend without asking his permission. The victim's brother was beaten with an iron bar on that same occasion when he tried to intervene, and the Gardaí were called. Statements were taken but neither was prepared to give evidence by the time the case was ready for court, terrified that a far harsher punishment awaited them if they co-operated with the authorities. Confident they had got away with it, they shot three more dealers over bad debts, including Paul Ryan from Raheny, whose body was found in a County Offaly field in 2003. A crime-scene examination would find he'd been assassinated with one bullet in his head, while his hands were tied behind his back. A muzzle was discarded on the ground beside the body.

The violence the group doled out inevitably turned inwards and the Glennon brothers moved to take over from Coates and Sugg at a time when they were beginning to make huge profits from cocaine and using a huge amount of the drug themselves. Sugg fled to Alicante after an attempt on his life in 2003, which he believed was made by his old pal Mark Glennon, and he was soon joined by Coates, while the younger Bernard Sugg stayed behind to look after their interests and manage their army of dealers. In Spain the duo used the same tactics to muscle in on territory in the Costa Blanca, believing that their terrifying reputation would work there. But, while they were away, Andrew Glennon walked into a pub and shot Bernard Sugg twice as he enjoyed pints with a group of lieutenants.

The CAB identified €500,000 in assets but the money, like the Westies, had gone to Spain where Coates and Sugg intended on building a second empire. Months after the shooting of Bernard, Shane Coates, then 31, and Stephen Sugg, 26, went missing with reports that they had been abducted over a drug debt owed to an associate of John Gilligan. It seemed the tide had finally turned and their own heavy-handed tactics had now been used on them, and their bodies, intelligence suggested, were buried in an isolated mountain area.

Their time in Spain had been brief, but they had made the most of it. Coates had been living in a luxury villa overlooking the village of San José while Sugg had bought an apartment in nearby Alicante. They'd thrown themselves into the holiday life-style of women, champagne and cocaine, and pictures showed them dancing in clubs wild-eyed and soaked in sweat. It had seemed like the ideal location with a large population of expat residents from the UK and Ireland offering them anonymity.

As the hunt for their bodies continued, the Glennon brothers got their comeuppance and were both shot dead within six months of each other, Andrew in the middle of the night in County Meath in a scene straight from *The Godfather* when his car was surrounded and he was riddled with bullets, and Mark six months later in September 2005, when he was gunned down outside the family home in Hartstown. When two bodies were found buried six feet under concrete in an industrial estate in Spain the following year, the mystery of the disappearance of Sugg and Coates was solved, bringing to an end the notorious reign of the Westies. Those who had killed them had gone to great lengths to make sure their bodies would never be found in the warehouse in Catral, 30 miles from Alicante, where a section of concrete had been dug into a six-foot grave where their remains were dumped, before a layer of fresh concrete was poured over them.

∽

The Westies' greed and ambition to be cocaine cowboys would be mirrored by many other gangs that came after them, but they weren't exactly pushing their product to an unwilling public.

Quite the contrary, in fact, as would be proved again and again over the decades to come. It was the increasing demand for Colombia's finest powder that lay at the very heart of the supply problem and the type of violent youth it was attracting.

The warning signs were there from the beginning, with academic research showing that cocaine was transitioning into mainstream society and becoming normalised in clubs and bars where it was readily available. In one study conducted by the Health Research Board (Maycock, 2001), strong indicators of both the increased availability and use of cocaine were found. The study had used interviews with a small sample of recreational users to measure the problem, and not just statistics from Gardaí and addiction and probation services as indicators of the levels of the drug's availability. It conducted in-depth interviews with ten social users, all of whom reported an increased visibility of cocaine on the club and pub scene, a development viewed in 2001 as new. While cocaine had largely been the drug of the wealthy, the study also noted signs of increased cocaine use in disadvantaged urban areas, particularly within Dublin city.

The National Advisory Committee on Drugs (NACD) 2003 report, *An Overview of Cocaine Use in Ireland*, noted anecdotal information that there was an increase in cocaine use across the general population outside existing problem drug users. Reports of an increased level of cocaine use in the pub and club scenes was again noted and put down to greater availability of the drug, cheaper prices and the fact that ecstasy appeared to be losing its attraction due to reports of poor and fluctuating quality. The report said that cocaine was being sold for between €30 and €40 per half gram, with each gram giving cocaine users 5 to 10 lines for snorting, which could last between a few hours and a whole night, depending on tolerance.

In 2002, the Citywide Drug Crisis Campaign organised a meeting of community, voluntary and statutory representatives to discuss cocaine use, and attendees reported that new cocaine users, who were not problem drug users, perceived the drug as 'clean and acceptable with minimal health implications'. The meeting also reported that the drug was readily available and acceptable, especially in pubs, in a way that heroin had never been. The NACD report later noted users were 'attracted by the perceived effects such as the absence of hangover and an increase in sex drive'.

The *European Journal of Anaesthesiology* was also warning of the potential for health complications given cocaine's transition from 'higher socio-economic groups' to the general population. In conclusion, the report gave a long list of medical complications that could be caused by short- or long-term use of the drug, including acute and chronic diseases of the central nervous, cardiovascular, respiratory and renal systems, as well as foetal abnormalities. 'Cocaine is capable of causing this morbidity or mortality on single or repeated use. It remains a very dangerous recreational drug, particularly in the light of its increasing availability and decreasing street price,' it concluded.

The European Monitoring Centre for Drugs and Drug Addiction in 2003 warned of problems that would be faced with the enlargement of the European Union to 25 member states and also pointed to recreational use, saying, 'A clear consensus on appropriate intervention strategies in this area doesn't exist.' Two years later, the Lisbon-based centre cited an estimated 4.5 million young cocaine users in member countries, a jump from the estimated 1 million from the previous year. The report suggested that around 13 per cent of 16- to 29-year-olds in the UK who visited pubs and wine bars used cocaine, with the figures dropping to under 4 per cent for those who didn't.

The figures were likely far too conservative compared with the real situation on the ground. The fact that wealthy countries in Europe had been experiencing an economic boom, Ireland's so notable that it had been nicknamed the 'Celtic Tiger', meant that a whole generation had enough money to splurge on cocaine at the weekends. Labourers, previously unemployable, were pocketing eye-watering wages as the construction industry embarked on a decade of unprecedented growth, while foreign computer and IT companies swamped the country, attracted by tax incentives and offering huge salaries to a well-educated workforce. For the first time, Ireland felt rich and prosperous. A new middle class shook off the shackles of its grim and miserable past, as cocktail menus became the norm in every pub, wine bars opened their doors, coffee shops lined every main street, and clubs were packed at night. The nation embraced a never-ending party fuelled by champagne and cocaine.

Under the surface, in working-class areas untouched by the economic boom and forgotten by shiny new development, groups of socially disadvantaged teenagers, many of whom grew up under the shadow of the first crime bosses like Martin Cahill and John Gilligan, were desperate to get in on the action – and more and more seemed to be willing to kill to get rich. By 2005 the gangland murder rate in Ireland had hit an all-time high, with 21 assassinations, many linked to cocaine wars that had broken out in areas of Dublin, Limerick and Sligo. Just eight years after the then Taoiseach Bertie Ahern declared war on Ireland's emerging gangland culture, it was clear that the government was failing to stem the bloodshed, and the underworld was becoming more violent than ever before.

To add to the problem, the killings were notoriously difficult to solve, with less than a 10 per cent chance that the gunmen, or those on whose orders they were working, would be convicted.

By and large the public and politicians remained apathetic about the killings, which had begun to suck up a huge amount of Garda resources with most murder investigations centred on victims who were involved in the drugs trade and who were young. Drug dealer Simon Doyle, 22, was gunned down days before Christmas in 2001 outside his home in Clondalkin. His murder, along with five others, would be linked to a feud between two warring gangs. Patrick Lawlor was only 18 when he went missing during another feud centred in Ballyfermot. His body showed up three years later near the Grand Canal in Dublin. The body of 19-year-old Niall O'Hanlon was found in a shallow grave in Crumlin after he'd been abducted and stabbed over 30 times in a killing linked to a feud. Twenty-five-year-old Michael Scott was shot dead in his home in Ballymun. Some older criminals, too, found their careers cut short as they were taken on and taken out by a younger breed of gun-toting gangster. There was career criminal Maurice 'Bo Bo' Ward, who died aged 56 when a gunman, working for a young Clondalkin outfit, entered his home, and Seamus 'Shavo' Hogan, a 47-year-old former member of Martin Cahill's crew, who was shot dead as he sat in a car in Crumlin.

In 2006, however, one shooting would cause a public outcry and pile the pressure on politicians. Anthony Campbell was fixing a radiator in a house in Finglas where Martin 'Marlo' Hyland was sleeping. The young apprentice had no idea when he arrived at the house in Scribblestown Park that there was even anybody upstairs, nor had he heard of the notorious 'Marlo' Hyland. The plumber, who was just 20 years of age, was intent on learning his skills so he could one day go out on his own fully qualified and enjoy a steady income. He didn't have time to run when a gunman burst into the house, ran upstairs and riddled Hyland with bullets as he slept, then turning the gun on the youngster on his way out so he could never give evidence in court. His plumbing boss only escaped because he had left the house half an hour earlier to get supplies and returned to find his apprentice slumped in a pool of blood. Days from Christmas, the gun murder was a deeply shocking loss of another innocent life caught up in a brutal takeover bid by Hyland's own crew, a mirror image of how he himself had taken the throne years before from his own boss PJ Judge.

At 39 Hyland had become the country's biggest drug baron and was believed to have been involved in at least six murders himself. He had taken control of Finglas when Judge was shot dead and had made millions flooding his turf with cocaine, funding his operation with armed robberies. Before his murder, Hyland had been the subject of Operation Oak, a Garda crack-down on the Hyland gang, which had resulted in the seizure of more than a dozen shipments and created huge paranoia within the ranks. Hyland was undoubtedly the biggest player of the time and he had been working with the Bradley brothers, Wayne and Alan 'Fatpuss', and had a mob under him supplying Finglas and Ballymun with cocaine and heroin. A group of young men known as the 'Filthy Fifty', in their late teens and early 20s, had helped make him rich. They had a reputation for being coked up and willing to take on any job as getaway drivers in robberies and drug deals. The best known were John Daly, a trigger man, Anto Spratt, an expert on big armed robberies, and Deccie Curran, an enforcer. Collie Owens and Eamon Dunne were among Hyland's most trusted. Many said the group was cursed by a gypsy, as Spratt had died from hanging in Mountjoy prison, while Curran also died in a cell from drug complications while awaiting trial. In the aftermath of Hyland's murder, many others would follow him to an early grave in the years to come.

Under the direction of Hyland, the group had been ripping off ATM machines, banks, post offices and even grabbing cash from pubs and bookies. Hyland never got his hands dirty with any of the robberies, but he divided the profits, taking the largest chunk for himself and pumping it back into his drug business, allowing him to control the wholesale supply of heroin, cannabis and cocaine across his turf. Hyland was a Finglas lad himself and had been involved in serious crime for years. Legend had it that he had turned bad when his sister Julia was raped and murdered years before by her husband Michael Brady. When Brady got out of prison, Hyland tracked him down and assassinated him as payback, and the murder became his calling card.

When the Gardaí established Operation Anvil in 2005 to target organised crime, Hyland found himself at the top of the list of targets, but it wasn't until the special operation was up and running for a few months that the extent of his business was understood. He'd become so big from the profits of cocaine in the previous few years that the separate Operation Oak had been established to focus on just him, and the State put all its resources into him and his cronies, including CAB, the surveillance units, and drugs and organised crime divisions, along with the specialist National Bureau of Criminal Investigation. His solicitor's offices had been raided, properties identified, firearms seized, and €23 million of mainly cocaine seized by officers in a series of targeted operations. In August 2006, when €400,000 worth of cocaine and nine firearms were seized in County Meath, the drugs were traced to Hyland's gang. One of those arrested was Paul Reay, 26, and such was the paranoia of the gang at the time that Hyland had him shot in case he spoke to the Gardaí.

Hyland had been mentored in his life of crime by Eamon Kelly, who'd taken on the role of an advisor after serving his time for his own ill-fated attempt to use Miami mules to bring cocaine into Ireland. Kelly hated the pillars of the State and, in particular, the media, having had his own lengthy battles with the *Irish Times* and *Late Late Show*. Despite his lengthy career and his status as a Godfather of gangland, Hyland had no major convictions save for a lengthy list of motoring offences, so when he was named by the *Sunday World* newspaper as a major-league criminal, he sued, under the guidance of Kelly, and the company was forced to pay him compensation. Hyland had gloated in his success and put it around that the €100,000 had come directly from the crime journalist Paul Williams' own pocket, and that he was going to enjoy every penny of it. He appealed the termination of his dole money when the CAB began investigating him, and he claimed he'd bought a winning Lotto ticket from a man known to him and used the €250,000 winnings to explain his wealth.

Unknown to Hyland, Kelly was also mentoring an ambitious and dangerous criminal working under him who was eyeing up the crown and who was ready to step into his shoes once the boss was taken out. Before Eamon 'The Don' Dunne got his hands on the prize, the underworld that he and others inhabited became the focus of the national agenda by a public shocked that its crude ways could spill into ordered society and claim the innocent life of the apprentice Anthony Campbell. Under pressure in the Dáil, Minister for Justice Michael McDowell hit out at the gunmen who'd carried out the brutal attack and said the murders of Hyland and Campbell were a direct result of Garda success against the Finglas group. Amidst lots of remarks about 'the wrong place at the wrong time', McDowell saved his sympathies for Campbell. 'It was a barbaric killing and the perpetrators are ruthless, savage people, and my heart just goes out to the family of the young man caught up in this. In relation to the particular individual who was the target of today's operation, the Gardaí had scored massive successes in recent times and that may have provided the reason why this operation was mounted against him.' Labour leader Pat Rabbitte was incensed and said somebody needed to take charge of the growing murder rate in gangland: 'Somebody needs to get a grip on this situation. There have been 120 gun attacks since 1998. The Minister for Justice doesn't seem to have any grasp of the reality of life.' Former Taoiseach Bertie Ahern agreed: 'There isn't a town or village in Ireland that isn't affected by the drugs menace. I utterly condemn these barbaric and senseless killings.' Fine Gael's justice spokesman, Charlie Flanagan, had, only a year earlier, echoed the sentiments and criticised the government's record on gang crime. Following three assassinations within 72 hours, he had sought the non-stop surveillance of gangland bosses.

Those murders were part of the gang feud in the Crumlin and Drimnagh areas of Dublin, which had been dubbed the 'Cocaine Wars' and which started after the Garda seizure of a huge consignment of cocaine in a hotel in the city in 2000. The teenage gang had come up under John Gilligan and were once his dealers, but when his mob murdered Veronica Guerin and his gang were dismantled, they saw an early opportunity to fill the vacuum. Brian Rattigan and Declan Gavin were the leaders, and they had been trusted and admired by Gilligan – he'd even brought them to meet his suppliers in the Netherlands when they were just 16 years old, teaching them valuable lessons in the supply chain. They had gone out on their own with a crew of school friends, but they had a difficult business relationship, with both wanting to be boss. They'd started buying larger amounts of cocaine and when they ordered two kilos of the drug and 49,000 ecstasy tablets from the Dutch suppliers, they planned to divide the money and reinvest it in another load. But the Gardaí had got wind of the plans and when two of their underlings, Graham 'The Wig' Whelan and Philip Griffiths, booked hotel rooms with Gavin, where they would cut up the consignment, everything went badly wrong. The three had intended to work through the night to break up, grind and bulk the large block of cocaine into individual one-gram deals, which they could sell for €80 a bag. Once mixed, they had estimated a profit of €750,000, which was to be divided between 10 of them, including Rattigan. When the cops burst into the room, Whelan and Griffiths were literally caught red-handed with the drugs, but Gavin was having a lie down and wasn't physically touching any of the gear, meaning he had to be released after questioning.

While many may see that as a stroke of luck, in the paranoid drugs underworld there are no coincidences. Rattigan and Gavin had immediately gone to battle, each accusing the other of informing, and their pals had chosen sides, creating two clear factions. At Gavin's side were Freddie Thompson, his friend Paddy Doyle, and money man Darren Geoghegan. Doyle was a natural born killer, a hitman for hire who honed his skills to be a cold and calculated assassin; Geoghegan was bright and able to manage the business; Thompson was violent and ruthless. Tensions grew between the two sides and a year after the hotel bust, Rattigan was celebrating his little brother Joey's 18th birthday, full of cocaine, when he heard Gavin was in the area ordering a takeaway. He made his way to the Abrakebabra and set upon Gavin, stabbing him repeatedly in front of horrified onlookers – the first murder of 16 in Ireland's most vicious cocaine feud.

Thompson took over from his boss and gained a notorious reputation as a terrifying gangland star known as 'Fat' Freddie in the tabloid media. The next person killed was Rattigan's beloved younger brother Joey. Retribution was swift when the man suspected of pulling the trigger, hitman Paul Warren, was shot dead. His murder was suspected of being organised by Rattigan, despite the fact that he was behind bars for shooting at a patrol car. John Roche, suspected of the Warren hit, was next to die. Then, in November 2005, the murders peaked when there were three killings in two days: first Darren Geoghegan and Gavin Byrne were shot dead as they sat in a car; two days later Noel Roche, a brother of John Roche, was shot dead as he sat in traffic in leafy Clontarf. His was the 20th gangland murder of the year.

The following morning on his radio show, popular DJ Gerry Ryan lamented how drug crime had come to his own neighbourhood, saying his family had been forced to walk past a crime scene on their way to school. Ryan was a proud resident of Clontarf, one of the best addresses north of the river Liffey, but he was also rumoured to be a heavy cocaine user and, when he died some years later, a coroner recorded a verdict of death by misadventure with cocaine as a significant risk factor. A doctor who gave evidence at his inquest said he had a chronically damaged heart with the presence of myocarditis, which suggested previous use of cocaine. The DJ's reaction was typical of the disconnect at the time and one which would continue as the years went by.

Comfortable in their belief that it was OK to snort cocaine, a growing number of middle-class users would not see themselves as connected to the wider issue and to the gang wars that were raging around the country, because they only took the drug at the weekend. The feuds seemed a world far removed from lengthy lunches in Ballsbridge and late nights at Lillie's Bordello, yet both were often fuelled by cocaine. Noel Roche's mother knew the reality of it all and she took to the airwaves and told RTÉ that her son's murder had all started with an argument about a motorbike, an incident that happened well before the hotel seizure. 'People don't realise, it's so simple. Two young fellas took to arguing over a stupid motorbike five years ago. . . . It escalated to houses being shot, my own house was shot up twice in two weeks, just because Noel and John knew one of the fellas that had been arguing. . . . It's just madness.

Total madness,' the mother who had lost two of her sons to gun murders said. In response to the publicity and criticism, Minister for Justice Michael McDowell announced an extra 15,000 Garda hours to combat gun crime in Dublin and to assure the public that he had control of the situation.

It wasn't just in Dublin that the profits from drugs had set communities and childhood friends against one another. Gangs west, south and north had turned to guns as a wave of cocaine-charged feuds erupted. In Sligo a mob known as the 'Irwins' had been causing chaos in their hometown and using it as a base to pump the northwest with cocaine. Initially run by the oldest brother Hughie Irwin, he had gone to war with another gang in the town and survived a number of attempts on his life. Following the murder of his rival Hughie McGinley in April 2005, Sligo's first gangland murder, Hughie Irwin was arrested and ate his own excrement in an effort to make officers sick.

He later moved to Lanzarote and continued to help run the operation from there, but the day-to-day running of the business was taken over by his younger brother Patrick Irwin, a Lothario who took his lead from movies like *Goodfellas*. Patrick was dubbed the new King Scum as he lorded it over the town and behaved like a Hollywood gangster, with a weakness for women and a luxury lifestyle. A young hairdresser, whom he was dating, managed to apply for planning permission in 2005 to build a beautiful home in scenic Dromahair in Leitrim when she was just 23 years of age. Construction on the house started a year later, but the CAB weren't fooled and knew where the money was coming from.

Patrick Irwin was eventually caught in October 2006 with €67,000 worth of cocaine in Roscommon after a surveillance operation was set up on him. He was about to do a drugs transaction in an area called Doon when officers swooped and caught him sitting in the passenger seat of a Mercedes with €55,000 in cash and 962 grams of cocaine. He was charged with a drug offence which he denied, but in November 2007, under the tutelage of Eamon Kelly, he requested a forensic examination of the Mercedes, which had by then been returned to its owner. He then took judicial review proceedings arguing that he couldn't get a fair trial because the car wasn't available to him, but Mr Justice Nicholas Kearns, then President of the High Court, criticised Irwin's delay in seeking the review and said any supposed 'failure' by Gardaí to retain the car could not have produced any information of the slightest use to him. The judge said that the bringing of 'missing evidence' cases was almost a matter of routine to prevent a trial taking place, and he said he could only imagine the sense of 'bewilderment' in the justice system in the minds of victims by such delays. Irwin eventually conceded defeat and pleaded guilty to the charges at the Dublin Circuit Criminal Court.

Two years later, the CAB swooped on Irwin and members of his gang and seized his house, an ice cream van, a boat and a 4x4. Irwin had close relations with 'Marlo' Hyland and his successor Eamon 'The Don' Dunne, as well as strong links with the notorious McCarthy–Dundon gang in Limerick. As she had a child with Irwin, hairdresser Avril Boland was top of the pecking order and had been living with him, despite having no connections with criminality and coming from a very respectable family. At the same time, he also managed to lure another woman into his world from a very different background.

When she stood in the dock of Court 7 in the Central Criminal Court for sentencing on gun-running charges, Deirdre Moran couldn't have fallen farther from the hopes and dreams of her parents. Just 26 years of age, she was handed a five-year sentence by Judge Patricia Ryan after the court heard her relationship with Irwin brought her straight into the heart of organised crime. The daughter of a cancer specialist, life as she knew it changed for good on September 1st, 2009, when she was arrested transporting a Smith & Wesson .22 LR revolver on the Lucan Bypass on the M4. The gun had been deactivated in England in 2006, but was later reconditioned so that it could fire live ammunition. Gardaí had set up a surveillance operation near the Liffey Valley Shopping Centre and pulled her car over following a tip-off. She told officers she had only gone shopping to buy a jumper for her son, who had started school that day, but inside the car, detectives from the Organised Crime Unit found a revolver supplied by 'The Don's' drug gang. During her court case, it was suggested that she was involved with an organised crime gang through her association with her son's father, who was described as someone of 'significant interest' to Gardaí. But Deirdre emphasised that she was simply a single mother living on the €180 a week she received from working in a clothes shop plus €160 a month in lone parents' benefit. Her barrister told the court she had 'an unblemished character' and had been planning to move to Manchester 'to start a new life', but she had fallen for Irwin when she was just a young teenager after her hospital consultant father moved to the town, and had a child with Irwin when she was 18. A third woman, living in a council home in Sligo, was also in a relationship with him until he was jailed.

While Dublin's cocaine wars were spread out in areas of the suburbs and the sprawling housing estates that surround the city, Limerick had a completely different feel and the disconnect between the users of recreational drugs and the gangs that supplied them felt much more cheek by jowl. Like other cities in Ireland, Limerick had benefited from the economic boom of the beginning of the century, with new bridges arching over the

Shannon, new luxury apartment blocks, and a cosmopolitan feel to the shopping and restaurant areas of the city centre. But within minutes from the centre, one battleground made way to another as housing estates like St Mary's Park, Southill, Moyross and Ballinacurra Weston became the strongholds of Limerick's four families of organised crime.

Despite the intimacy of the city and its small population of less than 100,000, the names of the criminals were known across the country. They struck fear wherever they were mentioned, such was the ferocity of the Keanes, the Ryans, the Collopys and the conjoined McCarthy–Dundons, who took ownership of their territories house by house in an extraordinary decade of senseless drug wars that were more violent than anything seen before. With armies topping an estimated 500 foot soldiers, the gangs shored up their social housing fortresses, just a stone's throw from the bustling O'Connell Street. Such was the compact nature of the city that Gardaí often had to organise for dole payments to be made estate by estate so rival criminals didn't collide in the social welfare office, which was located off the city's main street where professionals sipped oat milk lattes on their breaks. With unemployment rates in some estates topping 70 per cent, it was fertile recruitment ground for the gangs.

Eddie Ryan was the first man down when he was shot in The Moose bar. Kieran Keane was rumoured to be his killer, and he was paid back when he was abducted during an extraordinary double-cross focused on a fake plot to kidnap Ryan's two sons. Keane was executed on the side of a road and his nephew Owen Treacy miraculously survived after he was stabbed a dozen times and left for dead. Eddie Ryan's elder brother, John, was next, shot by a youth on a scooter with a balaclava over his face. Retaliation followed with the murder of Michael Campbell-McNamara, who was found in a field, eventually shot dead after being tortured, bound and gagged. His death led to the killing of teen Aidan Kelly, whose body was dumped in an isolated country lane on the city outskirts. The murders just kept coming and, like in Dublin, most were passed off as criminals living by the gun and dying by the gun in an inevitable fashion – until two children were badly injured.

Mum Sheila Murray had declined to give two men a lift, it was as simple as that. Later when she tried to start her car, it exploded in flames trapping her two young children in the blaze. Gavin, four, and Millie, six, were rushed in 'critical' condition to the hospital and the nation reeled in shock and horror. Politicians called for at least 100 extra gardaí to regain control of the estates; others looked for the army to be brought in, describing the attack on the Murray children as the final straw, but nothing changed. Three teenagers, two aged 17 and one aged 16, were sentenced for their roles in the attack; the younger would later be shot dead at a family wedding.

For those who cared to comment, the gangland murder rate was put down to the dark side of the Irish economic boom, an era of more dangerous and better-tooled criminal gangs. But most preferred not to join the dots with the likes of reports from the UN that listed Ireland among the richest in the world with the third-highest cocaine use in Europe.

Of course, most of those left at home to fight it out for turf, respect and power were the underlings of the higher echelons in the Netherlands and Spain where George 'The Penguin' Mitchell and Christy Kinahan Snr had blazed a trail to become the biggest wholesalers to the country. While they sanctioned many murders back home, both liked to keep their heads down and their noses clean in their adopted homes of Amsterdam, Antwerp and Malaga. Murder was bad for business and sure to attract the attention of the police. Sometimes the bloodshed did spill over to the European drugs supermarkets of the Dutch capital and along the Costa del Sol, but efforts were made to hide the dirty work or at least blame it on the Russians.

In June 2000, 'The Penguin' Mitchell got a wakeup call to just how high the stakes had become when murder came to his door and his son-in-law Derek 'Maradona' Dunne was killed at the Amsterdam apartment he shared with Mitchell's daughter Rachel. One-time professional footballer, Dunne, known as 'Maradona', from Dublin's north inner city, had escaped a life of poverty with his footballing talents, and as a young teen he was seen as a local hero for his clean-living ways and interest in sport. He was a fitness fanatic and never took drugs himself, but his reputation soured after it became clear he was selling heroin to his local community. He was charged in relation to drug offences but got off on a technicality and remained in Ireland for a period, despite being publicly exposed as one of the main movers on the Irish drugs scene. Gardaí suspected him of being one of those involved in Mitchell's plans for a huge ecstasy factory uncovered in the Irish midlands in 1995. A year later he was one of three major drug dealers, along with Mitchell and his sidekick Thomas 'The Boxer' Mullen, named in the Dáil as being responsible for flooding Ireland with heroin. Detectives tried hard to pin something on him, but under the guidance of his father-in-law he proved difficult to trap. Ironically, it was his dealings with other crime bosses that had eventually driven him out of Ireland, and he was forced to flee after he fell out with paramilitaries and his life was threatened. He initially moved to the UK but wound up in Amsterdam with Rachel, who witnessed his violent death after unwittingly opening her front door to a gunman.

The publicity surrounding the murder had drawn media attention on the notoriously private Mitchell, who was not long out of prison after serving two years for hijacking a lorry containing £4 million worth of computer parts. To add to the interest in the story and Mitchell's activities in Amsterdam, the shooting had come just weeks after three young Irishmen were brutally murdered in the city as the first-timers attempted to muscle in on the drugs trade. Brothers Morgan and Vincent Costello and their friend Damien Monaghan were tortured to death in their Amsterdam apartment after a bust-up with drug bosses as they tried to buy a consignment of cocaine.

Four years later drug dealer Sean Dunne went missing from Alicante, and as was often the case of those who disappeared in Spain his body was never found. Dunne had been running a cocaine smuggling operation and VAT fraud scam in association with paramilitary criminals and had become extremely rich and powerful. After a massive trawl through the Dunne finances following his disappearance, the CAB seized 13 properties from his estate and an expensive site near Fairyhouse Racecourse in County Meath. While they also identified large tracts of development land bought by him and criminal associates in Alicante, they never would get their hands on them. Dunne was known to Gardaí since the 1980s, but it was in the 1990s that he became involved in armed robberies and quickly moved on to drug dealing. After the collapse of John Gilligan's gang, he'd muscled in to fill the vacuum. He based himself on the Costa Blanca in Spain, where he organised huge drug shipments to Ireland and Britain and where, at one stage, he was believed to have had more than 30 tonnes of cocaine warehoused somewhere in Alicante, which he supplied to Republican and Loyalist gangs along with major gangsters in the UK. He was also coining it from an IRA VAT fraud involving the construction industry. He fronted a money-making scam which saw innocent sub-contractors forced into using their C2 tax-compliant certificates for bogus work that made millions for Dunne and his associates, but he got greedy and fell foul of the paramilitaries when they realised he was taking a bigger cut. In 2000, he was arrested and questioned in connection with the murder of Joseph Foran – a former associate of the notorious criminal PJ Judge. Foran had been assassinated by a suspected IRA hitman in 1996 in a row over drugs turf. In the years running up to his disappearance, Garda intelligence suggested that he was one of the biggest players in the cocaine trade in Ireland and was laundering his criminal proceeds in Spain. A major covert surveillance operation had been launched and he had been identified at meetings with major drug dealers in both Ireland and the UK.

By the time of his disappearance, Dunne and his wife, Deirdre, were sitting on a portfolio that rivalled those of the Celtic Tiger millionaires. Along with a long list of homes across Dublin, he had also purchased extensive property interests in Donegal and Westmeath. While he'd fallen out with the IRA and had previously survived a murder bid by them, his disappearance was put down to a feud involving rivals in Spain, but without a body, the story and interest soon died away.

When local police in Portugal stumbled upon a body in a freezer in 2004 and identified the remains of Cork drug trafficker and gangland heavy Michael 'Danser' Ahern, it was suspected that the job wasn't quite finished. The gruesome find was made when officers in Albufeira on the Algarve responded to a call of suspicious activity at an apartment complex and found him stuffed into a freezer. The 37-year-old had been beaten and shot in the head. Ahern was part of the exiled Cork Mafia and a central player in their international cocaine-smuggling ring. The murder brought to a dramatic end a three-month-long joint investigation between the Portuguese police and the Garda National Drugs Unit into 'Danser' Ahern and his role between

Portugal, which was less policed than Spain, and Ireland. Soon after his body was discovered, Gardaí moved in on 15 properties and discovered a cocaine processing factory in Balbriggan in north County Dublin, seizing 25 kilos of cocaine along with 60 kilos of mix used to bulk out the drug, which gave a good indication of the profit margin and the quality of cocaine going up customers' noses. Had his killers completed the job, it is expected Ahern would have never been found and, just like Sean Dunne, remained on the missing list.

John McKeown, known as 'The Mexican', was another dealer who vanished without trace from the Torrevieja area of Alicante in late December 2006. He had been supplying Martin 'Marlo' Hyland's outfit with cocaine and went missing around the same time his boss was murdered. While police in Spain have continued to pursue a missing persons case, underworld legend is that McKeown is 'swimming with the fishes'.

Disappearing bodies meant no murder inquiry and no major calls for crackdowns on the criminal gangs who would operate with impunity from their foreign headquarters. It was good for business, good for politics and, in particular, good for tourism, which was arguably the second most important economy on Spain's south coast next to organised crime. In a way, leaving no trace of the dirty work was also a measure of respect that criminals had for their adopted soils and, in particular, the Costa del Sol and Costa Blanca, which were finishing schools of sorts for the young and ambitious drug dealers of Europe. But just like the tide of change back in Ireland, cocaine was transforming everything, and those who still believed in the old rules of gangland, where rivals brokered a peace deal and where no trouble was brought too close to home, were dwindling in number. The new breed of rich, ruthless and impulsive drug lords fuelled by cocaine and steroids would ultimately force a change in more ways than one, and the decade to follow would see the carefully laid structures of the old guard ripped apart.

∽

It was during the 1960s that the Costa del Sol was first transformed into a tourist hotspot for Europe and where planeloads of early package trippers landed in three-piece suits, with suitcases stuffed with sausages and pork chops, to experience their first taste of the Mediterranean. The tourists carved it up to their own social etiquette, with working-class holidaymakers beating a path to the beaches of Benalmádena and Fuengirola, and the middle classes feeling more at home in Marbella and Puerto Banús. But the criminals came too and, according to legend, signed up to the unwritten rules that they could live and work there as long as they didn't bring trouble.

As drug dealing became the stock in trade of the old-school robbers, the location of the Costa couldn't have been better, with just 10 miles of water separating it from Morocco, the world's largest producer of hashish. Boats sped under cover of darkness to coastal beaches with packed cannabis, which was picked up and driven through the country for distribution onwards. The proximity of the large port of Algeciras, the tax haven of Gibraltar, and the coming together of mobs from all over the world meant that it remained relevant when cocaine started to make waves. The Costa became home to gangs from the Netherlands, Italy, France and Belgium, and the Europeans were joined by representatives from Colombia, Venezuela, Peru and the African regions where cocaine was routed. Serbians, Estonians, Russians and Turks gathered in what became a melting pot of the underworld. Weapons, drugs and even humans were all commodities dealt in whispered conversations, while at night gangsters partied hard with the rich and famous who came to holiday. For decades there had been an agreement to the unwritten rules and only the most serious and urgent of business was handled in the open so as not to scare the tourists. Corruption seeped into police departments, where poorly paid officers were tempted by the easy money that came with turning a blind eye. Criminals even boasted about having the judiciary in their pockets but, like all good things, the party on the Costa would come to an end. In the meantime, many just couldn't stay away.

CHAPTER THREE

GENTLEMEN OF THE
TRACK

Since his son, his right-hand man and his fixer, along with other members of his £340 million cocaine conspiracy, had been locked up, Brian Wright Snr had been kicking back in northern Cyprus enjoying the fruits of what the *Sunday Times* rich list had estimated to be his £600 million fortune. At arm's length from the law and confident that he couldn't be brought back to the UK, he revelled in his own cunning. He'd been out of the country just as police and Customs realised they had to move in on his mob or risk losing them, but after the biggest and most expensive surveillance and undercover operation ever, they had recordings of Wright talking about cocaine shipments and had caught the gang with their hands on 500 kilos of cocaine as they shifted it to a farm building. Wright, like other top-tier criminals, had always managed to stay one step ahead of the law. He had moved fast when he heard that Customs had busted his son Brian Jnr along with his fixer Soares – he'd locked up his villa and fled the Costa Del Sol, making his way by private jet to Turkish Cyprus, a territory which had become popular with criminals on the run. Northern Cyprus suited his lifestyle with casinos and bars, a warm climate and cheap booze. At 55 Wright was already a veteran of the cocaine trade and was feared and revered in equal measure, and he watched from a distance as his gang were jailed one by one and details of the six-year Operation Extend were described as 'without parallel'.

Over the course of five trials, he'd been kept up to date as his 34-year-old son was sentenced to 16 years, his lieutenant Kevin Hanley to 15 years, and Ronald Soares, his direct link to the Colombian cocaine barons of Medellín, to a lengthy 26 years. A skipper on one of the boats got the longest sentence of 30 years in Miami, and in total 15 gang members had been sentenced to jail terms that added up to more than 200 years. It had been an irritating success for the authorities, and Wright Snr had been named as Britain's most wanted by the end of the 2002 court cases.

A series of contempt orders along with a news blackout had been imposed, so the cases hadn't been reported on as they proceeded, but as soon as Judge John Foley at Bristol Crown Court gave them the go-ahead, the media had a field day linking Wright to Pablo Escobar and a horseracing scandal. During the trials, ex-jockeys Barrie Wright, who was no relation, and Graham Bradley had admitted under oath to being paid for passing on insider information on horses. The Jockey Club had also vowed to reopen an inquiry into Wright's involvement in laundering millions of pounds of dirty money through racing.

The court heard that Wright had met the Brazilian, Soares, in Sotogrande in Spain, and that he had a direct line to the barons of Medellín who were prepared to airdrop the cocaine directly onto ships as they headed across the seas, cutting out middlemen and excessive logistics costs. For Wright, it was like winning the lottery ten times over. The DEA had identified the coasts of Ireland and the UK the terminus, where smaller boats would meet the yachts and bring the loads onto land. Skippers and crewmen had been identified over the course of the probe, as well as Hanley, who held the vital role as the main onward transport director who got the product to the dealers.

Hanley was the first to be nabbed in November 1998 as he drove through London with cocaine in his boot, and it was at that point that Wright panicked and called off any further shipments. However, after meetings with Soares, he was convinced it was just bad luck and got his flotilla going again. In February 1999 Customs were watching a farm in Middlesex when the gang moved a large consignment of freshly arrived cocaine. They moved in, their years of patient surveillance work coming good.

As the back-slapping of Customs officers died down, Wright bedded in to Cyprus and vowed he wasn't going home to face the music – but everyone knew where he was. The country was even named during post-trial press conferences focusing on his whereabouts. Despite the absence of an extradition treaty with the UK, Wright knew he was a liability because of his high profile and, in particular, as the country made efforts to join the European Union.

In March 2005, Wright's time in hiding came to an end when he was arrested back on the Costa del Sol. At 58 he put up no fight against extradition, and he was back in the UK within a month and charged before the courts. Announcing his arrest, an HM Customs spokesman said he had been involved in horseracing fixing and cocaine smuggling, and John Maxse of the Jockey Club said: 'Brian Wright is banned from going racing and from liaising with jockeys and trainers.' Wright did an interview with the *News of the World* in which he denied he was ever involved in anything dodgy on the racetrack and claimed he had made his fortune from gambling. On April 15th, 2005, Wright appeared briefly at London's Bow Street Magistrates Court where he was placed in custody awaiting trial and, two years later, aged 60, he took to the witness stand in Woolwich Crown Court to defend himself. Again, it was horse-doping and race-fixing allegations that irked him far more than the accusations of global drug trafficking.

The court had heard that over the course of recordings by officers during Operation Extend, Wright had been taped giving out after a number of jockeys had been arrested by police investigating a doping scandal. Wright had been arrested at the time but released without charge. He told the court he was never investigated over the alleged scandal, telling a jury: 'To begin with, the press insinuated certain things that were completely ludicrous. It was never followed up . . . I knew the allegations and insinuations coming out that I was involved in the corruption, the doping of the horses. If you read the papers and press there were certainly insinuations that you could read between the lines . . . I was very angry about it. The first person to suffer if the horses aren't running is me, because I'm a big punter.' He told jurors that he was someone who had just got lucky and portrayed himself as a gentleman of the turf, saying that by the 1990s his knowledge of the track and contacts in the industry were bringing him in at least £400,000 a year, and that his biggest win came in the 1000 Guineas Stakes in 1989, when a series of bets on Musical Bliss racked up a profit of close to a million pounds.

Wright also denied he was involved in drug trafficking, but despite his efforts to defend himself, he was found guilty by a 10–2 majority verdict. His QC Jerome Lynch pleaded for some leniency: 'The reality will be that he knows, as does his family, that he will probably die in jail.' As Wright was led away, a huge financial entanglement of his millions got underway and a spotlight was firmly placed back on the horseracing industry – the sport of kings which had been trying to clean up its image for years.

Back in 2002, the BBC's flagship show *Panorama* had delved deep into the huge profits of cocaine it was alleged were washing around the tracks, and the corruption in the industry that had made it all too easy for the likes of Wright to wash his dirty money. The Jockey Club, which regulated the industry, had come under the spotlight and had recently appointed a new Director of Security, the former head of the SAS, Major-General Jeremy Phipps. He had just taken over the role from Major Roger Buffham MBE, who had served in the Special Military Intelligence Unit in Northern Ireland during the Troubles. In secret recordings, the pair had been filmed meeting and talking about the Wright Organisation trials, which had just completed and which had heard evidence from a number of figures in the industry, including the former jockey Bradley. During the conversation, Phipps said the transcripts were dynamite and Buffham claimed nobody in racing wanted to do anything about the situation. Buffham, it turned out, was working with *Panorama* and had furnished them with Jockey Club files which laid out the extent of Wright's corruption of horseracing.

The programme went on to detail how betting had been left largely unregulated and it focused on Wright's long career at the track, during which he entertained both law-abiding people and major criminals in private boxes at Ascot. Wright apparently placed bets for jockeys who weren't allowed wager, and he offered others money to throw races and make sure their horses didn't come in first across the finishing line. The investigation linked Wright to a major doping scandal in the 1990s, where a number of horses had tested positive, and accused the Jockey Club of lax security protocols which could have nipped it in the bud when instead it turned a blind eye.

When Buffham came to work at the regulating authority in 1993, he knew that Wright was a suspect and even claimed there was an intelligence file on him associating him with named jockeys. The major bumped up security, installed CCTV cameras at racecourses and used his background to build intelligence on Wright. By 1996, Buffham said that there was solid information that Wright was fixing races. But the information wasn't enough for the Jockey Club to act, and so Buffham tried to bring in rules that would mean jockeys associating with known criminals could lose their licence. But the same year that he lost the *Sea Mist* cargo, Wright had doubled down his activities on the racecourse and had a bumper year, despite the suspicions around his activities. *Panorama* detailed how he brazenly mixed with jockeys and entertained them in fancy London nightclubs, gifted them expensive jewellery and often flew them to Spain to meet with him.

During the trial of his son, Brian Wright Jnr, it had emerged that the Wright Organisation were in permanent communication with their racing contacts looking for inside information on the form of horses. A former jockey had admitted that he'd been offered a bribe, Buffham said, and in 2000 he'd compiled the full 'Wright' file and named 24 jockeys, whom he believed were associated with the cocaine baron. He concluded that the involvement of organised crime was so great that racing had no integrity, and that horseracing was particularly vulnerable as jockeys could influence the outcome by making sure their horses lost.

Phipps came out fighting in the aftermath of the scandal, and in an interview with the *Racing Post* in August 2002 he said disciplinary enquiries were underway and admitted that robust action was necessary to ensure the future of racing: 'You used to be able to sort things out by taking a jockey to one side, or whispering in a trainer's ear, but you can't do that anymore, which in some ways is a great pity. But I am keen on some form of a warning system, which would have to be recorded but which would enable us to make a point to, say, a young jockey who was in danger of going off the rails, or a trainer who has a horse for a dodgy owner.' He told the journalist Howard Wright that the trial evidence had re-opened old wounds: 'It reminded us that in the 1990s there was a particularly nasty gang in operation, doing a lot of damage, bringing drugs into this country, laundering money, blackmailing jockeys and putting pressure on owners.' And he concluded: 'We now have to ask, where is Brian Wright Mark 2? He's not in racing, but he's out there, and all of us in the industry have got to make sure our defences are up.' Ironically, Phipps and others in the racing industry wouldn't have to look too far for Brian Wright Mark 2. Over the years that Brian 'the Milkman' Wright had been in exile, other cocaine barons were circling the racecourses looking for a way to get in on the action and wash their millions. Just as Wright had done, his criminal associate and fellow Irishman Christy Kinahan Snr sent his son in to have a look at the opportunities that remained on the tracks.

∽

Kinahan Snr had a very different upbringing to the impoverished childhood of Brian Wright. He had grown up in a wealthy family in Dublin in the 1960s, in a redbrick period property in Cabra where his mother ran a successful guesthouse. He'd shown sporting prowess in his early years and was academically intelligent, but in his 20s he'd dabbled in heroin and got mixed up with working-class career criminals in the city. His posh accent and middle-class background made him useful as a fraudster and a fence who could shift stolen goods into the legitimate economy. He amassed a handful of convictions for burglary and using forged cheques before seeing an opportunity in the heroin business after the demise of Larry Dunne in 1984.

Kinahan proved a fast mover, and within a year he had become one of the most significant dealers of the drug in Dublin. He was placed on the Garda radar and in 1987 an apartment he had rented was raided and officers found heroin valued at £117,000 and evidence of his links with a significant Algerian drug supplier. It should have been a swift end for the gangland outsider, but instead, aged 30, he used his six-year prison sentence to his advantage by doing a degree behind bars, studying languages, and hooking up with his future partner in crime, the Jennifer Guinness kidnapper John Cunningham. Nicknamed 'The Colonel', Cunningham came with a serious criminal calibre and had been part of the Cahill mob who had run rings around the Gardaí in a decade-long orgy of robberies, including those of expensive jewellery and fine art. Known for his military precision, he had connections with major movers in Amsterdam, the supermarket of Europe's drug trade. Together Kinahan and Cunningham shared a career ambition to become the biggest drug and weapons wholesalers in Ireland and, indeed, parts of the UK.

Kinahan's sentence ended in 1991, at which point his sons Daniel and Christopher Jnr were teenagers and had surrounded themselves with a group of friends from the north and south inner city who were ambitious and ready for success in the fast-emerging drug trade. Many were a new generation of the Hutch family, headed by Gerry 'The Monk' Hutch, who'd built his career and reputation as being anti-drugs. Two years after his release, Kinahan was nabbed again in possession of stolen travellers' cheques, but out on bail he moved to the Netherlands where he hooked up with Curtis 'Cocky' Warren, a Liverpudlian drug baron with direct links to Colombian cartels and just about everyone else Kinahan needed an introduction to. By 1996 he was joined by Cunningham, who'd escaped from an open prison after serving just 10 years of his 17-year sentence.

In an extraordinary stroke of luck, the two found themselves in prime position when John Gilligan was put out of business following the murder of journalist Veronica Guerin. It wasn't long before Kinahan was arrested with cocaine and firearms and was jailed for another four years. Again, he used his time to his advantage, building up extensive contacts in the drugs world. Released from jail again, he'd returned to Ireland for his father's funeral but was lifted on an outstanding warrant, landing him another four years in Portlaoise Prison. True to form, he used his time to direct operations while Cunningham built up the business on the ground in Amsterdam. As large weapons and drug seizures in Ireland led straight back to the operation, Dutch police were alerted and nabbed Cunningham with the illicit goods in a successful undercover sting.

Out of jail by 2000, his business partner back behind bars, Kinahan moved straight to the UK where he started building up the business again, and where he began to eye up the racetracks as a way to launder his funds. He moved to north Surrey, where he opened a number of companies, and soon his sons were registered as living in a house in Chertsey. All three remained on the move, travelling in and out of Spain, the Netherlands, Belgium, the UK and Ireland. But by 2007 Daniel Kinahan took a starring role in a court case of the high-profile jockey Kieren Fallon, accused and later acquitted of race fixing.

While Kinahan was never charged, surveillance pictures of him taken in 2004 were shown over the course of the evidence, which centred on an alleged bet-to-lose scam that the prosecution said was masterminded by the high-stakes gambler Miles Rodgers. Police, believing he had fixed races over a two-year period, had put Rodgers under surveillance and placed a bug in his car. In May 2004, after Kieren Fallon had won on Russian Rhythm, the trial heard that Rodgers had tried to confront the jockey after losing heavily but failed and, days after the race, Daniel Kinahan had flown into Leeds Airport where he was met by Rodgers. Rodgers drove Kinahan to a hotel where they were joined by another man and Philip Sherkle, described as a barman with an address in Tamworth in Birmingham. The police watched as the young Kinahan and Sherkle travelled to another hotel and checked in under false names, using cash to pay. At 1 a.m. Kinahan and two others drove out to visit Fallon at his family home, only to turn back when they realised they were under surveillance. They checked out of the hotel at 2 a.m.

While Fallon and others would later be acquitted after a major trial at the Old Bailey, a series of intercepted phone conversations heard Daniel Kinahan being described as a 'formidable' and 'menacing' character. 'He is only a little fella but you know when you've been spoken to,' the court heard in taped chats. Rodgers was recorded saying he had met many intimidating characters over the course of his business but they 'paled into insignificance beside D'. It was 'D' who, the court heard, was losing his patience because Fallon kept winning races instead of losing them. Kinahan, who was not named, was described as a former Dublin furniture shop owner who had once employed Sherkle. The significance of Kinahan's presence could not be overestimated, with his father's drugs outfit on its way to becoming bigger than Brian Wright's ever was.

Investigators had initially become suspicious of Rodgers in 2002 when he bet heavily on a horse owned by his own company, Platinum Racing. His Betfair account was closed down and information was shared with the Jockey Club. In other races horses were also wagered heavily to lose, and 27 in total were investigated as part of the alleged conspiracy. But he was acquitted after the trial on direction of the judge, who said there was no case to answer following two months of prosecution evidence.

Kieren Fallon, who had always denied his involvement, was soon back in the saddle. Rodgers was also acquitted of hiding the proceeds of crime. While Daniel Kinahan was terrifying Rodgers, two other dodgy dealers on the racecourse were far more robust characters when it came to dealing with associates of his father's enormous organised crime network, and while the Wright and Rodgers cases may have damaged the reputation of the sport, their unproven bet-to-lose scams were nothing compared to what was to happen next.

It was around the same time as Rodgers' trial came to an end that another two characters, with lots of money to spend and a whiff of danger about them, started raising eyebrows among the racing fraternity. The pair, Maurice Sines and James Crickmore, owned a company called Leisure Parks Real Estate Limited, which had been buying up caravan parks across the UK, many marketed as retirement homes for downsizers. Sines introduced himself as a Romany Gypsy to anyone who would listen, and the pair had already gained a reputation of being difficult landlords. In one of their retirement villages, residents had begun to move out in their droves, many claiming intimidation, and other residents had got a court order preventing Sines from threatening them and blocking sales of their homes.

Sines, a round-figured and noisy man, would later go head to head with the singer Elton John when he set in place plans to turn a site close to John's Windsor Castle neighbourhood into a caravan park. Sir Elton and 300 neighbours met to protest the plans for the site, which backed onto the singer's immense property. In court Sines would later be described as a 'self-made man' who bought up 16 caravan sites over his career. But it was his activities on the racecourse that were becoming more concerning and, along with Crickmore, his reputation as a big spender was drawing attention.

In 2009 Crickmore took part in a charity auction, paying more than £500 for jockey Kirsty Milczarek to be at his beck and call for a day, and while the day out with Racing Welfare in Newmarket was for fun and the auction garnered plenty of laughs, things would turn far more sinister. This time the British Horseracing Authority (BHA) took on an investigation after suspicions arose that Sines and Crickmore had jockeys in their pockets and, just like Wright, had convinced them to lose on odds-on favourites. A number of races became key to the inquiry, including a March 2009 race at Lingfield where jockey Paul Doe seemed to stop the horse Edith's Boy as it came out of the stalls. The jockey had been observed doing the same thing at another racetrack on another horse. Jockey Greg Fairley also appeared to have slowed a 15–2 favourite at Wolverhampton as it set off on perfect ground. Ten races on five different tracks came in for scrutiny, and the female jockey Milczarek, who Crickmore had won at auction, and who was in a relationship with Kieren Fallon, was placed under investigation.

The results of the findings were sensational, with Sines and Crickmore described as the 'instigators' and banned from racing for 14 years. Doe and Fairley were banned for 12 years while Milczarek and Jimmy Quinn were put off the track for two years. The inquiry showed how Sines and Crickmore had run their bet-fixing by hiding their involvement and only using the names of associates to place their bets. Sines' telephone records showed frequent calls to a number of well-known jockeys, including Frankie Dettori and Fallon, while he bet through accounts owned by Peter Gold and his son Nick. Gold was a wealthy businessman with a colourful past and his son was a dark-haired Romeo who courted models and liked to drive fast cars. He was also a part-owner of The Box, a celebrity hangout in Soho renowned for its debauched nightlife. The British Horseracing Authority found that they were engaged from the outset in providing Sines and Crickmore with their largest and most convenient route to the lay-betting markets. And they did this in the knowledge that inside information inspired the selections, even if they did not know that the information sometimes extended to agreements with jockeys to lose if necessary.

Nick Gold described himself on his company website, Nick Gold Investments, as chairman of a business with interests in more than 30 companies and with a turnover of £300 million yearly. Gold had met Sines in 2008 while playing poker in London and, according to the BHA, he went 50/50 with Sines and Crickmore, allowing them to use his Betfair accounts, but they'd fallen out when the young entrepreneur claimed he was owed money.

On appeal, Milczarek had her findings of corrupt and fraudulent practice and breaching the rules by passing on inside information overturned when her former boyfriend, Fallon, gave evidence in relation to text messages which cast doubt over her guilt. Sines and Crickmore had their appeals dismissed but their bans reduced to 13 years. While the entire investigation was hugely embarrassing for the billion-pound racing industry, the integrity of which was vital to lure punters and their money, the BHA took solace from the fact that at least there were no drugs involved. This time those caught up in the net had been dodgy businessmen and people working in the industry, not big cocaine networks like the Wrights or Kinahans. It would take just a few years for that hope to die.

⌒

In February 2016 a group of people gathered at a house in Raleigh Square in Crumlin where the Byrne family were waking their son David. It was just days after the now infamous Regency

Hotel shooting. The attempted murder of Daniel Kinahan by rivals at a boxing weigh-in had been planned with military precision and would mark the beginning of the brutal Kinahan and Hutch feud, claiming 18 lives – including Byrne, who was shot in the hotel lobby. The Kinahan Cartel had closed ranks as they prepared for a mafia-style funeral to cement their fearsome reputation, and only a tight inner circle of friends and comrades were welcome to offer their condolences to veteran criminal James 'Jaws' Byrne and his wife Sadie. Most of those who went through the doors of the house where David's body was laid out were easily recognisable: mob boss Daniel Kinahan, his sidekick Christopher Kinahan Jnr, cocaine kingpin Liam Byrne, enforcer 'Fat' Freddie Thompson and senior cartel lieutenants Liam Roe and Sean McGovern. Then came the big man from England, Thomas 'Bomber' Kavanagh, a brother-in-law of the murdered David Byrne.

Bomber was big league and one of the most prolific cocaine smugglers operating in the UK. His organisation was based in Birmingham, where he had moved after he had become the focus of Garda attention and the first Irish target of the Criminal Assets Bureau when it was set up in 1996. There he had teamed up with his drug-dealing cousin James Mulvey, and together they would develop a drugs route through the ports of Belgium and onward to the UK and Ireland using specially modified industrial machines and cars. To hide the source of his incredible wealth, Bomber had established a car sales firm, TK Motors, which purported to deal in luxury second-hand cars.

Outside the Byrne house, undercover cameras snapped those being welcomed to Raleigh Square, gathering intelligence to identify the dark heart of the cartel as fears grew of a ruthless retaliation and escalation of the Kinahan–Hutch feud. Not so instantly recognisable to the Gardaí were the faces of Maurice

Sines and James Crickmore, who had arrived with Bomber and who would stay by his side over the course of the ceremony. While Sines had been spotted in the company of members of the Byrne family, the closeness of their friendships hadn't previously been identified. At the funeral service, Sines stood front and centre with the 'godfather' Bomber Kavanagh, greeting mourners while surrounded by an army of young men in matching uniforms.

Information later provided by UK police showed that in the years since the race-fixing scandal, Sines and Crickmore had continued to display their thuggish qualities on their caravan sites and had been forced to pay £400,000 in fines and compensation for bullying elderly homeowners on one of them. Leisure Park Real Estate admitted 11 charges of using bullying tactics and Portsmouth Crown Court heard that one homeowner had had their water and sewage pipes disconnected, while others were forced to move and sell their homes for low prices. Both Sines and Crickmore had earlier been given personal fines in relation to the allegations. Residents who were too frightened to be identified later told how elderly women in particular were targeted by the thugs who terrified them. Sines' wealth had grown to an eye-watering degree; he had a chauffeur-driven Rolls-Royce Phantom and was living in a mansion in the plush Wentworth Estate. The millionaires' playground nestled in the heart of leafy Surrey boasted a who's who of neighbours and had been home to Sir Bruce Forsyth, Sir Elton John, Sir Cliff Richard and even the Sultan of Brunei. Sines had been regularly photographed posing outside one of the UK's most exclusive addresses with a collection of cars while entertaining members of the wider Byrne and Kavanagh group.

While the origins of the friendship between Kavanagh's cocaine mob and the race-fixing mates remained unknown, officers were able to see that they were so close they had holidayed together and gathered for significant family occasions, including weddings and children's birthdays, while they also swapped and borrowed high-end motors. The previous summer, Sines had even been made godfather at the christening of Liam Byrne's new baby with partner Simoan McEnroe. Sines' son Fred Jnr and his wife Amy were also in attendance, along with his daughter Vienna and her husband Billy Britton. He had travelled to Dublin for the christening at the Radisson Hotel in Dublin 9 where the Kinahan brothers, Daniel and Christopher Jr, attended along with other associates from the UK and Spain. At that point it was David Byrne who was acting as driver for the mob and he chauffeured pals to the occasion in a Mercedes-Benz G-Wagen owned by Sines. Liam and his pal Sean McGovern had recently registered their company, LS Active Car Sales Limited, to an address at Raleigh Square, and used the occasion to show off other top-of-the-range motors.

Just weeks after the funeral of David Byrne, the CAB used an angle grinder to get through the bullet-resistant door at the front of his brother Liam's home. Number 2 Raleigh Square had been subject to major home improvements, made without planning permission, and had been doubled in size, dwarfing all the neighbouring properties. A few doors away, a similar renovation job was under construction on an unoccupied property. As the Bureau officers began to pull apart the house, they found a bar, a jacuzzi room and a roof-top playground. Estimates would suggest up to €750,000 had been spent on the €250,000 property to bring it up to spec. Inside, drawers were stuffed with Rolex watches and designer shoes, wardrobes were full to the brim with Moncler coats and other fashion labels, and they found evidence of travel and heavy wagers, including a betting slip that showed a €38,500 punt that Liverpool would beat Newcastle. At nearby LS Active Car Sales, 23 cars and six motorbikes were seized, including luxury Mercedes, BMWs, Lexus, Land Rovers and turbo diesel Volkswagen Golfs. Byrne was furious, but he also knew he was by now the country's number one organised crime target. He left Ireland and soon registered a new company with an address of one of Sines' mobile home parks in Essex.

As the CAB case continued, officers started to unravel a car's currency method of payment for drugs and found an interesting link with the home a few doors away from the Byrnes' where construction had ground to a halt. The house had been sold in 2015, but the new owner had yet to place their name on the Land Registry file. The buyer, it emerged, was Maurice Sines, and the house was being renovated for Liam Byrne's teenage son Lee – who'd once been collected to attend his school graduation ball in Sines' Rolls-Royce Phantom. They also discovered that James Crickmore's company transferred funds electronically to LS Active Car Sales' bank account, providing seed capital for the business to start trading.

On early compliance visits, Liam Byrne had stated that Crickmore was providing vehicles to him on a 'sale or return' basis, a scheme used by criminals in the motor industry. The links between Sines and the mob became even deeper when Liam Byrne moved his family to the UK full time and into a house on Dosthill Road at Two Gates in Tamworth. The house had been purchased for £460,000 by Leisure Parks Real Estate, and was located in the same neighbourhood where his brother-in-law Thomas 'Bomber' Kavanagh and sister Joanne Byrne lived in gated splendour on the Sutton Road.

∽

While Brian Wright was the first of the Irish cocaine cowboys to see the opportunities in the lax controls over betting on the racetracks and through mobile betting agents, he was really just following a well-worn path laid decades before by Howie Winter, the one-time leader of the Winter Hill Gang in Boston and a crime partner of James 'Whitey' Bolger. Winter had been indicted along with 20 others in 1970 by federal prosecutors on a race-fixing scam. Jockeys in France had also been investigated years before Brian Wright ever dipped his toe into a race-to-lose syndicate.

Racing wasn't the only sport that would be corrupted by organised crime over the golden era of cocaine; boxing and football, too, would be infiltrated by mobs overwhelmed by the money they could make from dealing powder and desperate for a way to spend and launder it. In the years to come, Daniel Kinahan would make extraordinary inroads in boxing, becoming a fixer for one of the biggest purse fights in the world. Other attempts by the group to spread its tentacles into football were also identified.

The Europol Serious and Organised Crime Threat Assessment of 2017 identified corruption in sport as one of the 12 main activities of organised crime within the European Union. A UN Office on Drugs and Crime report of 2020 warned that regulators needed to tighten their grip on sports within their own jurisdictions to strengthen them against the threat: 'The failure to effectively tackle the involvement of organised crime in sport is a serious threat not only to the integrity of sport but also to the social role and ethos and values that underpin it. Organised crime groups . . . exploit sport through illegal betting, competition manipulation and human trafficking to generate illicit profit. However, they also use sport as a vehicle to project power and influence in local communities.'

While it was obvious to everyone that mobs and boxing had long links, an insight into the less explicit reasons was given by the notorious Salvatore 'Sammy the Bull' Gravano back in 1993 when he addressed US politicians to tell them how the Gambino family had been laundering funds through the sport for decades. Apart from the clear opportunities to wash dirty money, he told those listening how his 'Family' had hoped they could make useful connections with wealthy businesspeople through their role in boxing, like hotel owners Donald Trump and Steve Wynn. The mafia turncoat had admitted his role in 19 murders and his testimony resulted in a life without parole sentence for John Gotti. When asked why it was important that organised crime had no role in sport, he answered: 'We do have that habit of cheating a little bit.'

CHAPTER FOUR

AN HEIRESS AND
A TRAGIC MODEL

Anne Bullitt was a difficult woman. When her US lawyer, Robert Pennoyer, phoned Palmerstown House in Dublin looking for her, he could hear her whispering in the background to her house-keeper: 'Tell him I'm not in.' Pennoyer was Anne's lawyer, a stalwart of New York and a man with an office in the famous Rockefeller Center. He was in a bit of a bind, having responsi-bility for her vast estate but unsure that he was the only one in charge of her final wishes. Pennoyer was anxious to speak with Anne for a number of reasons: as executor of her will, he needed to keep in touch and wanted to know if she had found someone to replace him in his role. As the years went on, he also wanted to know when the wealthy heiress would return to New York, anxious that she sign up someone to have power of attorney for her should her faculties wane.

Their first meeting had been in 1988 when Anne, aged 64, had come into his office like a hurricane, dripping in couture clothing and fine jewels. She was an incredibly wealthy heiress who was the sole descendant of her father, the late William C. Bullitt Jnr, America's first ambassador to the Soviet Union, who had left his vast fortune to his only child. She had travelled the world, married four times, and collected paintings, designer clothing, jewellery and furniture on her way. She'd had an odd upbringing that had taken her from Moscow to Paris and right into the heart of the American establishment. William had reared her alone after splitting with her mother, and the father and daughter had enjoyed an incredibly close relationship. When he died in 1967, she'd locked up their summer house in Massachusetts – a New England stately home called Ashfield with grounds of almost 400 acres of woodlands, streams and fauna – and vowed to retire there one day. But her first meeting with Pennoyer was for a different matter.

A biography had been written about her father and his adventures on the American diplomatic stage, tracing his relationship with President Woodrow Wilson and his secret missions into Russia where he had met with Lenin. It had gone on to describe him as an eccentric character who'd been President Franklin Roosevelt's ambassador to the Soviet Union and to France. Anne was furious about a number of things in the book, particularly the suggestion that he was of Jewish origin and that he was gay. She was adamant that she would defend his honour and wanted Pennoyer to go through the manuscript of the book page by page and note her objections.

Later that year, the heiress came back to the offices for a second time and asked Pennoyer to write her will. 'She wasn't talking to any of her family at that point and seemed to have no friends. She asked me to write the will and to be the executor. I explained to her that it was normal to name a member of the family but she was insistent that she wanted me to take on the role. She was living in Ireland and she would come back to New York every few years. Every so often I would call Ireland to see if she'd another lawyer or if there were any changes she wished to make but she wouldn't talk to me,' he said. Anne never did come to the phone but in 1995, aged 71, she called into the office unannounced on a visit to the city and Pennoyer took the opportunity to talk with her about her power of attorney. Again, she asked the lawyer to sign up for the role. 'You usually wouldn't do that,' he said. 'But she didn't want anybody else.' Anne returned again to Ireland where her health started to deteriorate, and she became more reclusive in the huge expanse that was Palmerstown House.

The house and vast estate on the edge of Dublin and the borders of Kildare had a long history of British aristocracy and had been burned to the ground in 1923 by anti-Treaty forces. Rebuilt, it had changed hands again until it was bought by WJ Kelly, a businessman with a love of horseracing who had developed it as one of the leading stud farms in the country. Anne and her father, William, shared an interest in all things equestrian, among other things, and she was interested in a career in horse breeding, which had brought them to Ireland in the first place. With her second divorce, from American diplomat Nicholas Duke Biddle, under her belt, she soon found her third husband in Ireland: Roderic More O'Ferrall, a horse breeder and a descendant of a landed family who owned Kildangan Stud. The marriage was brief but Anne emerged from it with a 100-carat diamond necklace, specially made for her by Cartier, and Palmerstown House, which her father bought her so she could pursue her career as a trainer and breeder. According to Pennoyer, Anne loved Ireland and wanted to stay, so William had offered WJ Kelly £50,000 for his home and stud and he accepted.

Derby winners followed and she soon became one of the top owners in Ireland, racing horses, in navy and white colours, and clocking up more than 100 champions. In 1966 she made Irish racing history when she became the first woman to saddle a winner. But a year later her father died and she married once more, this time to US Congressman Daniel Brewster; this marriage only lasted two years.

Over the next three decades, Anne stayed on at Palmerstown House, training and breeding her beloved racehorses while becoming ever more reclusive and eccentric in her ways. By the mid-1990s she relinquished her licence and locked herself away in the house with few visitors except her staff, legal executives and financial advisors. Together they managed her affairs and made sure she was up to date with her bills. The family's old summer home in Massachusetts lay crumbling, but she'd kept up payments for the land and any taxes owed on it. She still insisted that she would retire there, but anyone who had seen it knew it was unfit for human habitation; the house was completely overgrown with vegetation. In Palmerstown House her maids looked after her needs as she retreated to the darkness of a three-bed apartment within the property. Few suited Anne's temperament or her insistence that she live with the curtains always closed; she had no friends, only staff, with many of them forced to use the servants' entrance, not being allowed through the front door.

As her sight began to fail and her health to deteriorate, it became apparent that the huge house and stud were no longer suitable. Her lawyers agreed a deal for the sale of the property to a buyer prepared to hand over €8 million, but Anne was not happy and, fiercely independent, decided to step in herself. In an extraordinary move, and behind the backs of her advisors, she sold the property to the millionaire businessman Jim Mansfield Snr in 1998. Bizarrely, Mansfield and his son Jimmy Jnr had befriended Anne and were two of the very few visitors she invited into her home. The story of how it all happened is told a number of ways, but the simplest is that Mansfield Snr saw an opportunity, trumped the original offer by €2 million and promised Anne she could live out her days in Palmers-town House no matter what her health. They did the deal and Mansfield Snr moved into the house, to the concern of Anne's advisors, who didn't believe she was capable of such a decision, given her state of mind. They hired psychiatrists to assess her while Mansfield had practitioners look at her too, until it was eventually ruled that she was incapable of managing her affairs and she was made a ward of court in February 2000. The sale of the property and its contents was put on ice.

James Mansfield Snr was on the crest of a wave at that point, and his companies were behind huge developments in West Dublin. A shrewd businessman, he told a story of hard toil in gravel pits before starting a plant hire and machinery business which he expanded into England. Myth has it that he had seen an oppor-tunity after the Falklands War that had made him very rich. The story was slightly different each time it was told, but the general gist was that Mansfield had made millions buying up all the ancil-lary equipment used by the British forces to retake the islands and sold it on at a huge profit. The bit that was often left out was that he was charged with VAT fraud in the UK and had become involved with the gangland criminal Paddy Shanahan, who specialised in robbing antiques and worked as a money launderer for criminal gangs until he was assassinated in 1994. Mansfield Snr had paid a hefty fine after being found guilty of recklessness in completing VAT returns, but he was acquitted on fraud charges.

When he moved back to Ireland, he focused on property development and bought and sold houses with Shanahan, before his murder, and with associates of Eamon Kelly and Gerry 'The Monk' Hutch. His first big purchase had been the Clondalkin paper mill site, which he turned into a shopping centre and sold at a big profit. He then bought the huge Tassagart House and land in West Dublin in 1990, and for the next 10 years he blazed a trail as one of Ireland's biggest and brashest developers who flouted planning laws, cosied up with politicians, and secretly mixed with senior figures in paramilitary and organised crime groups. He built Citywest Hotel, which became a favourite venue for the annual Ard Fheis of the Fianna Fáil and Fine Gael parties, without a commencement notice and expanded it enormously and often without planning permission. He built a golf course, houses, apartments and private estates. Most of the money for his ventures was borrowed from banks, but rumours abounded that his friends in low places were also investors.

While Anne's advisors had managed to have her placed in nursing home care, the biggest headache for them was the contents of the house, which Mansfield Snr, and later his son Jimmy Jnr, was now living in. Pennoyer had repeatedly asked Anne to have an inventory of the contents drawn up at the cost of $25,000, but she'd refused, and as the Mansfield father and son bedded down in the house, the patriarch insisted that his purchase included everything that was in it.

In the meantime, in New York Pennoyer had tidied up her affairs and used a $250,000 yearly alimony payment from one of her ex-husbands to fix up the property in New England, which had gone to rack and ruin. He restored it and set up the William C. Bullitt Foundation to establish it as a reservation to be enjoyed by the public. But the proceeds from Ireland needed to be consolidated to the trustees for the upkeep of the estate and Pennoyer knew that the contents of Palmerstown House were likely worth at least the sale price again. A committee was appointed to represent Anne and legal proceedings were issued against Mansfield, while the High Court impounded the €10 million and negotiations started behind the scenes. While nobody knew exactly what was kept there, Palmerstown House was a treasure trove of Anne and her father's travels overseas and their incredible lifestyle, which had brought them into the orbit of famous artists, historical figures and collectors. Boxes of William Bullitt's papers from his time in Moscow and during the war lay in the basement, collections of couture clothes filled the wardrobes, expensive jewellery lay on dressing tables, and among the paintings that hung from every wall were two Pablo Picassos, hand-gifted by the artist to William. Fine French period furniture bedecked the rooms, Persian rugs lay on the floors, Chinese pottery balanced on bookshelves, Japanese screens divided vast rooms, and drawers were stuffed with silver cutlery while porcelain dinner sets were stacked alongside each other in carved cabinets. Of more historical interest, apart from the boxes of papers and documents, was a pair of 18th-century pocket pistols, given by George Washington to the Marquis de Lafayette for his services after the Battle of Yorktown in 1781. In an interview before his death, William Bullitt had said that the guns were on display on a mantelpiece in his daughter's bedroom at Palmerstown House.

Business was booming for the Mansfields and, initially, Mansfield Snr moved to Palmerstown alone in a bid to start handing over some control to his son, but passing the torch to the younger generation wasn't going to prove that easy. While Mansfield Snr was proud of his rags to riches story, his incredible wealth had meant that his sons had grown up in privilege and extravagance, which gave them access to private helicopters, chauffeur-driven cars, and the hotels, restaurants and other developments in the family portfolio. An endless stream of hangers-on who were at the epicentre of a hedonistic Celtic Tiger culture of champagne, cocaine and money to burn were forever in their company. Tony Mansfield was the sensible one and had settled down with his wife, Anita, but Jimmy Jnr and PJ were hot property for a queue of models and socialites who wanted nothing more than a seat at the VIP table. PJ was more outgoing and a regular on Dublin's party scene, including clubs in the city like Lillie's Bordello and Renards, but Jimmy Jnr preferred the crowds to come to him and, within weeks of his father moving less than 20 kilometres down the road, he'd turned Citywest into his own party palace.

Along with the high society circles he moved in, Jimmy Jnr, just like his father, had a darker side, and a collection of less desirable pals, too. One of them was a car dealer, Lee Cullen, whose company, Exclusive Cars, was based in Saggart and who was laundering dirty money for a network of drug dealers and paramilitaries. Another was Troy Jordan, a horse dealer who had been closely linked to John Gilligan and members of his criminal gang. From his base in Palmerstown House, Mansfield Snr called one of his most trusted members of staff and asked him what was happening in Citywest. The news was not what he wanted to hear, Junior had opened the doors of the hotel to a collection of the criminal underworld who were drinking and staying there for free, staff were frightened and many were threatening to leave. Included among Jimmy Jnr's guests one evening was the drug dealer Derek 'Dee Dee' O'Driscoll from Ballyfermot. A furious Mansfield Snr asked for a meeting with his son and warned him against such open relations with known criminals, and the pair had a blazing row, during which Junior smashed a bottle of whiskey and told his father he could keep Citywest. Mansfield Snr weighed up the situation: his son had recently split from his wife and needed his own space to rebuild his life and, while the row with Anne's committee was ongoing, he wanted to make sure that Palmerstown House was occupied and lived in. He told Junior that he could live at the mansion until such time as development plans for it were underway, on condition that he keep his private parties there.

In the public eye, the Mansfields continued to make waves on the business pages, with plans for a conference centre, another golf course, a retail village, and a never-ending stream of luxury houses and apartments. In the nursing home, Anne lost her sight and became very passive as the teams of solicitors and financial advisors worked in the background to return to her estate the unknown contents of Palmerstown House. Solicitors negotiated behind the scenes, but the case was by now caught up in the courts and time was on Mansfield Snr's side as the antiques expert picked his way through the contents and remaining horses that were still at the stables. And as Pennoyer remarked of the contents: 'There was no way of knowing what was there and what might have been taken or sold as all that was going on.'

Around the same time that he snapped up Palmerstown House, Mansfield Snr bought Weston Airport for £10 million, adding the private airstrip to his vast assets. Without seeking authorisation, he made the hangars bigger, added a huge new car park and turned a small bungalow on the site into a new control tower and viewing gallery. Locals feared he was trying to turn it into a commercial airport, but he shrugged off any negative publicity by saying he had simply carried out some refurbishments. He had plans for Palmerstown House too, and he set about turning it into a second Citywest, building a golf course there in 2004, which was designed by his friend, golfer Christy O'Connor Jnr, who had also been the architect of the two at Citywest. The *Irish Times* newspaper and its Environment Editor Frank McDonald pursued him vigorously through the planning process, reporting on each setback to his designs to build a major hotel and business park in the grounds of the house. At one point, Kildare County Council granted permission for a 290-room hotel and a massive conference centre, but An Bord Pleanála reversed it to protect the listed property.

The Mansfield family, in particular the sons, were by then regular figures in the gossip pages, with showbiz journalists following the trail of every rumoured romance or flirtatious gaze. They travelled around town in their father's Rolls-Royce and collected their own Ferraris and Maseratis. While they mixed with models and socialites, they kept their distance from the media and stories that were emerging about their pals who were under investigation by the Criminal Assets Bureau.

The Celtic Tiger financial boom that had started in Ireland in the mid-1990s hadn't only made money for developers; criminals had also prospered. At the heart of the underworld boom was the growing use of cocaine, which had settled right into a heady social scene never seen before in Ireland, and it was firmly the drug of choice for cash-rich recreational users who frequented the coolest pubs and hottest clubs. Cocaine had enjoyed a tenfold increase in just five years, and by the mid-2000s the market was estimated to be worth €120 million a year, with addiction experts reporting that it had exploded in use at the same time the economy had taken off. While figures from An Garda Síochána were often a reflection of the resources that were being put into a particular crime, the seizure figures, too, were notable. In 2002, just 23 kilos of the Class A drug had been found during search operations carried out by the National Drug Unit, but within three years a record 300 kilos had been discovered, indicating that at least another 3,000 kilos had hit the streets. At the same time, addiction services were reporting one in six patients seeking treatment for cocaine addiction, mostly young professionals in their 20s and 30s. The trend would continue for many years to come, and with it the feuds between the gangs vying for turf and control over the market.

With the boom stretching well into the 2000s, Mansfield Snr was adamant that he was going to get his money back on Palmerstown House and saw potential for development everywhere. To keep the Bullitt advisors happy, he had relinquished some of the disputed contents of the house, in particular the papers stored in the basement, which were letters and documents that had belonged to Anne's parents. The papers were gifted to Yale University and negotiations continued about the furniture, the paintings and other items in the house. In 2005 the golf course became the home of the Professional Golfers' Association, a nod to its construction and quality.

The house, in all its splendour, was a cash cow in itself, and despite the fact that it was the home of Jimmy Jnr, it was regularly rented out for functions. The then Minister for Finance Charlie McCreevy hosted a lunch for EU finance ministers there. But despite his efforts, Mansfield Snr kept coming up against opposition when he looked for planning permission for bigger developments on the vast lands. A green light given by Kildare County Council for a 290-room hotel and a 1,200-person conference centre along with a business park, tourist apartments and detached houses was again overturned when An Bord Pleanála decided it was not suitable for the green belt area. It did grant approval, however, for the 18-hole golf course and driving range already constructed, as well as the go-ahead for a clubhouse. Another application for a major golf tourism development was again rejected and described as 'obtrusive'.

In the absence of planning for Palmerstown House, Jimmy Jnr continued to live there and his parties became the stuff of legend, with a jacuzzi installed on the roof and a never-ending flow of guests. He purchased a herd of llamas for the lawns and a flock of ostriches, and he moved one of his regular girlfriends in. Surrounded by Anne Bullitt's personal effects, he often hosted dinners and family parties there. At Kylemore House nursing home, Anne's health continued to deteriorate while her financial team doggedly negotiated with Mansfield Snr for the return of the contents.

In 2006, the Mansfields hit peak Celtic Tiger extravagance when PJ tied the knot with his partner, model Andrea Roche, and the pair hosted 270 guests at Palmerstown House. Reports noted that Roche's new father-in-law was then worth €1.6 billion, making him Ireland's 21st richest man. The wedding was a spectacle of wealth with a Rolls-Royce Phantom for the newlyweds and a Bentley and three Chryslers for their top-table guests. One month later the family were back on the front pages, but this time they had less to celebrate. Police had discovered a plot to import cocaine and heroin into Weston on board Mansfield Snr's private plane.

Ex-boxer John Kinsella was arrested after he hired the plane and sent it on a round trip to Belgium. He'd been caught in a wiretap set up by Dutch police and focusing on a Scottish man who they suspected was a major drug dealer. He was quickly arrested and charged. Kinsella was on the Garda radar and had been working out of Weston. He owned a luxurious marble-floored, six-bedroomed house, which extended to 3,100 square feet, along with almost €3 million worth of property in Ireland and Thailand. Gardaí had noted that he was travelling all over the world and believed his speciality to be organising the transport of cocaine from Colombia and cigarettes from Asia. A Mr Fixit for some of the major crime gangs, the details of his wealth were laid out during a bail hearing where he vowed not to leave Ireland if he was released. He told the court that his computers and files had been seized and he had no way of chartering a flight if freed pending his trial. 'My children and wife are here. I don't want to be anywhere else but Ireland. If granted bail I would spend as much time as possible with my wife, whom I sorely miss and who could go into labour at any time,' he said. Despite his pleas, he was refused bail after the court heard he was a broker who chartered private planes and had many contacts with people in the aviation industry. Kinsella, the court heard, was also the beneficial owner of a private plane valued at about €390,000, which was in France at the time. He had a property valued at €1.3 million along with two other properties in Ireland and one in Thailand worth almost €400,000. When his home was searched, gardaí had found a number of what appeared to be forged driving licences.

In the days leading up to the bust, and while cops were listening in, there had been conversations recorded between the Scottish suspect and Kinsella, whose plane hire company ran out of Weston. Wiretap transcripts later read to a court revealed that Kinsella had mentioned arranging a 'bird' and repeatedly referred to the 'auld fella' without identifying him. Mansfield was forced to admit that the plane was his but said he'd known nothing about what it was to be used for and had simply hired it out. The incident did nothing to quash the rumours about Mansfield and his links to the underworld of drugs and crime, but it did mean one thing: his son Jimmy Jnr would have to be extra careful about his friends and associates so as not to bring any further disrepute on the family.

Junior had enjoyed the company of plenty of women since his marriage to Donna Cosgrave had collapsed when their children were very small. Despite the split, relations had remained amicable with Donna accommodated in a stately mansion opposite Tassagart House, with their children Samuel and Ingrid. With PJ settled down with his model wife, Junior couldn't seem to stop entertaining. While he wasn't noted for the charm or sharpness of his father, the multi-millionaire heir certainly knew how to throw a good party and he knew how to treat his guests to bottles of champagne, Cognac and fine wines, chauffeur-driven lifts to and from his home; and, of course, the famous jacuzzi on the roof of his country estate was always a good spot for a late-night dip. Many who knew him felt sorry for his on-and-off girlfriend, a beautician who was known for her loyalty to her man despite often being cast aside when his gaze shifted to a leggy model. In particular, he had an eye for Katy French, the blonde girlfriend of his pal Marcus Sweeney, a fitness coach who had come to work for his father at Citywest and who became a close family friend. In her early 20s, Katy was almost a celebrity model and her picture was rarely out of the papers. She was also a close friend of PJ's wife Andrea and often the whole group would go out for dinner and get together in Palmerstown House. In early 2007 Katy and Marcus fell out spectacularly when he found her draped across a table in his Il Pomo D'Oro restaurant on South William Street in Dublin, scantily clad and in the middle of a photo shoot for the *Sunday Independent*'s Life magazine. Sweeney had lost his temper and screamed and shouted at Katy to give him back his '50 grand' engagement ring before throwing the photographer and stylist out the door. In the aftermath, he'd sent her vile texts and broken off their engagement. The whole debacle had played out in graphic detail in the tabloid press as the dream wedding went up in flames and Katy moved out of their apartment in Citywest. Journalist Barry Egan would later write about the conversation he had with Katy about the events: 'She and Marcus's on-off relationship had been a staple of my column in the *Sunday Independent* and I had gained her trust. Hence the late-night phone call. We talked for nearly two hours. She read me the texts over and over, like a manic mantra. She wanted me to print them in my column without saying where they came from or quoting her. She appeared in the reception of the *Sunday Independent*. I brought her to an editorial office . . . Conservatively dressed, with her hair tied back, she looked like she was going sailing in the Hamptons with the Kennedys. It was almost the polar opposite to the breathlessly sexy woman who would appear on the cover of Life magazine a few days later. This is how it all started for Katy. It is at this exact point, appearing on that glossy Life front cover, that Katy's career went supernova. It began the Year of the French.'

And it had, indeed, looked like Katy's year, despite the breakup of her engagement. Months after Sweeney's outburst, Junior moved in to pick up the pieces and offered Katy one of the family apartments in Citywest to live in. He told her that his friend Lee Cullen would give her a car, a brand-new Range Rover, so she could make her own way around town if his drivers weren't available. Katy had been in the Mansfield social circle for years, but she'd never considered Junior to be such a charmer, nor had she been aware of his impulsive personality and ability to turn every day into a party. The couple got very close, very quickly, and one day he ordered staff to move his girlfriend out of Palmerstown House and into an apartment so he could entertain Katy there. He was an attentive lover and started to see Katy as possible second marriage material, even though he felt uncomfortable with the media circus that surrounded her. However, as a mark of his commitment to her, he invited her to private family functions, presented her to Jim Mansfield Snr and introduced her to his children.

While it might have been a whirlwind romance, nobody within his tight inner circle doubted that this was the most significant relationship he had enjoyed since the breakdown of his marriage. In Palmerstown House Katy must have felt like a charmed princess, she must have had to pinch herself to be sure it was all real. Everywhere around her were priceless antiques, stunning pieces of art, furniture worth more than her annual salary as a successful model on the Dublin social scene. And the Lord of the Manor was besotted – the party boy was finally tamed.

In August 2007, as their relationship started to become public knowledge, Anne Bullitt died in her nursing home, her collection of fine art and antiques from a life of privilege and travel still behind the closed doors of Palmerstown House, her couture dresses gathering dust in the basement, her financial advisors still trying to reason with Mansfield Snr and his son to let them in to gather her things. Details of her colourful life featured in obituaries, with her greatest legacy regarded as the papers she had collected, catalogued and given to Yale, which contained manuscripts of Sigmund Freud and poems collected by her mother, Louise Bryan, a journalist who was friends with Scott Fitzgerald and Eugene O'Neill. A small service was held at Rathmichael Parish Church, attended by a handful of those from the racing world and staff who had worked for her, and her remains were taken to Philadelphia for burial in accordance with her wishes.

As the year forged on, so too did the relationship between Katy and Junior, and she was regularly asked about it by journalists although she was often coy in her answers. It certainly was, as Egan described, 'the Year of the French', and she was riding the crest of a publicity wave. A string of TV appearances had upped her celebrity status and she was becoming the darling of the model set. With her 24th birthday party in October, it was decided to hold back the celebrations until December when filming was due to start on a new reality show she was set to appear in. She hoped that a glittering knees-up would be the night that she and Junior would finally face the cameras together, but as she prepared for the bash at Dublin's Krystle nightclub, a problem arose that she knew wouldn't sit well with her boyfriend. The call from the newspaper had been a shock, but Katy had managed to negotiate and offer up an interview about her cocaine use instead of the details of the three-day drugs binge they were planning to run, a story which was sure to ruin her career.

'I have no choice,' she told Junior. 'Please say we will be OK.' Junior touched her arm and brushed a strand of blonde hair from her face. Minutes later, as she sashayed out of City-west Hotel to where one of his drivers waited for her, he picked up his mobile phone and scrolled down the list of contacts until he came to 'Katy'. Then he hit delete. Like one of Robert De Niro's most famous quotes from the movie *Heat*, Junior always knew the secret to success was to be willing to walk out on anything in '30 seconds flat'.

That evening, Katy tried to phone but to no avail. She had hoped they would hook up for a drink and talk about her party and the publicity it was sure to attract. She wanted to reassure him that the interview she would do would discuss her cocaine use in the past tense and never touch on him or his Citywest properties. She wanted to tell him she had it all in hand. She rang again the next day and the next, but his phone was either off or rang out. She left messages, sent texts and even briefly worried that he had fallen ill. As the days dragged on, she swayed from utter devastation to concern until she finally got a member of Mansfield's staff on the phone. He told her Junior had travelled to Marbella for an annual holiday with the family and would be in touch when he got back. In the meantime she was to enjoy her birthday party and could go ahead with plans to film in Palmerstown House.

Katy wasn't stupid, she knew the writing was on the wall, but she still hoped it was all a ruse and that Junior had a surprise planned for her big night.

CHAPTER FIVE

THE CELTIC TIGER
PARTY ENDS

As the girl in the gold Gucci dress stepped out of the chauffeur-driven car, blonde hair cascading down her shoulders, her long legs toned and tanned, photographers grabbed their cameras and the only sound was the shuttering of lenses as she swooshed by. For Katy French, it was to be the defining moment of her arrival as the queen of the model set: her 24th birthday party at Krystle nightclub was a calling card to anyone who didn't already know that she was the girl who had it all. But, just like the world she inhabited, it was all just a glittering show. Beneath that perfectly groomed surface lay a truly flawed woman with deep insecurities, a complicated love life, and a secret and insatiable appetite for cocaine, a habit that would ultimately lead to her death.

Some friends say she had been taking drugs since she was 14 years old, a student at the posh Alexandra College in Dublin, where her looks already made her stand out from the crowd. From 17 years of age, Katy was socialising in some of the most talked-about venues in Dublin and hanging around with wealthy socialites in the likes of Lillie's Bordello, where she was a regular. While she attended UCD and completed a course in psychology, her looks meant she would always be drawn to modelling, a career where she could make her fortune. By 20 she was signed up to the Assets Model Agency and, like most, she started off by turning up on Grafton Street wearing bikinis and holding placards to promote products. It paid well, and with it came invites to parties and openings, lunches and suppers, fashion shows and corporate gigs. Cocaine seemed to be one of the perks of the job and it was available wherever and whenever she wanted it.

While most people dabbled, Katy was a heavy user and built up a huge tolerance over time. Two and a half years before she died, she was introduced to Kieron Ducie, an older hanger-on of Dublin's social scene who loved his nickname, 'The Wolf'. Nobody could quite remember how he got it and many who knew him reckon he'd given it to himself, but he revelled in the idea that there was a whiff of danger about him. A truck driver from Meath, who worked at his family's scrap waste centre, he had an absolute and bizarre obsession with celebrities. He was a rabid socialite himself, attending nightclub launches, product endorsements and talking his way into club VIP areas, where he spent most of his wages buying champagne for pretty girls who would stand in his company. For years he had hooked himself on to the fashionable hems of up-and-coming models, name-dropping his 'friends' in all the right places and promising photoshoots in glossy magazines. He was out every night of the week, in all the right places, buying rounds of drinks, smiling and lavishing compliments on girls, swapping his mobile number with anyone he could. He latched on to photographers, journalists, models and anyone he thought could do him the favour of naming him – somewhere, anywhere – as a Z-list celebrity. Most important, though, he knew how to source cocaine.

Ducie had undoubtedly seen the potential in Katy to get him recognised on the social scene, but she, too, cultivated the friendship, texting him constantly, meeting him on nights out and allowing him to introduce her to his extended circle of friends. When they first met, Katy was dating the perma-tanned Marcus Sweeney, who would later tell gardaí that when they first started seeing each other, she had a serious cocaine problem. He told officers that he was introduced to suppliers by Katy, who he described as a two-day on, one-day off user. 'She never wanted to come down off a high. I saw her getting panic attacks as a result of drug abuse. Katy had no limit when it came to coke, she never wanted to stop, always wanted more,' he told officers who investigated her death, even claiming that he once had to get a gun to protect them from dealers who were owed money.

While her love life had gone through peaks and troughs, Ducie was one man who had remained loyal, there for her through it all, and Katy regularly visited his home in Kilmessan, County Meath, and used it as a sanctuary away from the bright lights of Dublin. While Ducie worked hard to cultivate the illusion of importance, underneath he was simply a fantasist who enjoyed impersonating gardaí and had blue flashing LED lights fitted on his 4x4 so he could pretend he was a cop. The last seven days of Katy's life seemed to capture the highs and lows of the generation she had come to embody, with her meteoric celebrity career and the tragic and seedy way it ended – in a cocaine party for one at Ducie's home, which granted him his lifelong dream of making front-page news. Undoubtedly from the media event that was her 'official' 24th birthday celebration to her collapse in a dingy suburban house, Katy had lived the Celtic Tiger dream . . . and paid the ultimate price.

The beginning of the end started on the night of Thursday November 29th, 2007 when Katy began preparing for what was to be her crowning moment. Her birthday party in the impossibly cool Krystle nightclub on Dublin's Harcourt Street was expected to have all the style and glamour of a night at the Oscars. For years Katy had battled it out with models such as the Miss World winner Rosanna Davison and brunette Glenda Gilson to take the crown of Ireland's super beauty and be the most photographed of all – and now her moment had come. Katy put on her face, anxious and excited at the same time. She had spent the week telling journalists that super bands Stereophonics and Snow Patrol were going to be there and that they would mingle with the great and the good of the Irish celebrity scene. But when it came to it, the night wasn't quite as she'd wished. The one person she really wanted there, Jimmy Mansfield Jnr, had stayed away.

Ducie, however, did show up with his then partner Ann Corcoran, and together with journalists, liggers, and a handful of real friends, they made up about 200 in attendance with very few star pickings in the crowd. Katy was so paranoid about arriving at an empty nightclub that she'd called Ducie en route and asked him to make sure there were enough people there before her big arrival. She showed up in a limo with her mother and sister, clad from head to toe in gold. Champagne flowed all night and Katy smiled for the cameras, hiding her upset. Not only had her boyfriend failed to show, despite her hopes that his last-minute trip to Marbella was a ruse and that he was going to surprise her, but most of her friends from the modelling industry didn't come either. Many admitted they had prior engagements or other bookings that kept them away, and it was generally agreed that Katy was unlucky with the night she had picked to hold the bash.

In the early hours of the morning, as the party wound down, Katy returned to a hotel room at the Westbury with a couple of pals and spent the night sipping champagne. At 8.15 a.m. the following morning, she arrived at her mother Janet's home in Dublin and went for a lie-down. By lunchtime she was refreshed, and she drank some coffee and ate muesli before heading to the

sprawling Citywest complex where she'd been living on the gener-
osity of her absent boyfriend.

She had an interview scheduled with a journalist, so she
arranged to pick him up from the local Luas stop and drove him
to the apartment. The interview lasted most of the afternoon and
they'd plenty to talk about; there had been the very public row
with Sweeney, his demands for his ring back, her appearance on
Celebrities Go Wild and her recent quotes in a tabloid newspaper
about having used cocaine in the past. And, of course, the whole
purpose of the interview was publicity for the upcoming reality
show that Katy was due to co-host with PJ Mansfield's wife,
Andrea Roche, where the pair would 'model scout' while being
filmed, fly-on-the-wall style. The interview ended and Katy went to
bed, oversleeping her alarm the next morning for an appointment
with the TV crew. A little later than scheduled, the camera crew,
sound engineer and producer headed with her to Palmerstown
House, where Katy and a stylist conducted a mock discussion on
what clothes she should be wearing. The cameras rolled as she
got into her car, Lee Cullen's Range Rover, and stopped to buy
the newspapers, which were covered in stories about her birthday
bash, before dropping in to collect her pal Andrea at her home in
the Mansfield-built millionaires' estate of Coldwater Lakes. Then
the two made their way to Dundrum Town Centre to scout the
crowds for young would-be models. It was contrived, but Katy
and Andrea were assured that they were working well together
and at the end of the day they all gathered in a Thai restaurant
for food.

Later, Katy dropped Andrea home and then made her way to
her mother's house, but friends would report that she was feeling
down because the publicity her party had received had mentioned
the absence of Mansfield Jnr and many of her other friends. With
her sister Jill, she watched an episode of *The X Factor* and a

Saturday night chat show before telling her mum she was heading back to her own apartment for the night. She might, she said, drop in to see her friend Ann.

Katy never did go home. Instead, she did something that made her iconic for all the wrong reasons, and it would give gardaí a unique window into a seedy underbelly of a world where cocaine connected high society with gangland criminals.

Earlier that night, as Katy watched television in her mum's house, Ducie and she were in touch. He was heading out on one of his legendary benders and phoned her to see if she wanted to join him. She refused, telling him she'd call up to his house in Kilmessan and visit his partner Ann instead, but she wanted him to arrange a bag of cocaine for her. On her way she stopped off at a garage in Dunboyne where she met a drug dealer called Russell Memery and handed him €200 for a bag of cocaine. She spent the next five or six hours snorting the powder and chatting with Ann. When her mother, Janet, next saw her, she was hooked up to a life support machine. The snapshot of what was going on in the life of the famous model and the wealthy social set around her, along with a seedy underbelly that operated parallel to it, would be contained in the investigation file into her death.

It was almost 10 a.m. on December 1st when 'The Wolf' Ducie burst through the doors of the A&E department at Our Lady's Hospital in Navan with the body of Katy French in his arms. Both himself and his partner Ann Corcoran denied to doctors that she had taken any drugs at their home. Instead, Ann said she had consumed a large amount of champagne, vodka and Red Bull. Half an hour after their arrival, Andrea Roche was on the phone to Janet French breaking the bad news. From the outset, medics were trying desperately to save Katy's life, but from very early on they knew there was little hope, as her brain had been starved of oxygen.

On arrival, her heart wasn't even beating and she was immediately put on a cardiac defibrillator as doctors tried to resuscitate her until the team eventually got a rhythm. She was then hooked up to a full life support system and while they worked trying to save her life, medics attempted to get any history of cocaine use before she had come in, but neither Ducie nor Corcoran would offer any assistance. Eventually Ann conceded that Katy had not taken cocaine in front of her, but had been to the bathroom a number of times while they were together. As Katy's mother, sister Jill and father John reached her bedside, her condition continued to deteriorate, and a toxicology report from the National Toxicology Lab at Beaumont Hospital came back, the results showing that on arrival at the hospital her blood alcohol level was negligible but it was positive for cocaine.

On this news, her father decided to phone the Gardaí over his family's concerns about how Katy had arrived at the hospital, a delay they perceived may have occurred in getting her there and 'stories' told to the nurses and doctors that were incompatible with the toxicology findings. A full investigation got underway and a search warrant was obtained for the home of Ducie.

Later that evening, as the house was searched, no drugs were found, but a Garda ID card was. The badge, it emerged, had been reported missing four years earlier by an officer who knew Ducie and was convinced it had last been in his possession before mysteriously disappearing. After the search, Ducie and Corcoran were invited to Navan Garda Station to give their accounts of what had happened before they drove Katy to hospital, but the pair stuck to their story that the model had consumed a large volume of alcohol before having seizures. Two days after the interviews, on December 7th, two brain stem death tests were carried out on the model at Navan Hospital and at 3.38 p.m. Katy was pronounced legally dead.

Her father identified her body as she was moved to the morgue and the following Monday she was buried in her home town of Enniskerry. Her funeral, by invitation only, was attended by the then Taoiseach's aide-de-camp Captain Michael Tracey, reflecting the extraordinary national impact of the death of the young woman, who had been barely known two years before. In the background, senior Garda management were concerned that the investigation into her death and who supplied her the cocaine would be a thorough one. Her relationship with Jimmy Mansfield Jnr, coupled with the rumours that were still in the ether since the Mansfield plane was caught in Belgium loading drugs bound for Weston, meant that the supply chain for the cocaine that had killed her needed to be forensically analysed. Officers seized Katy's phone, along with a second phone with no SIM card found in Ducie's 4x4, as they started to unravel what had happened in the run-up to her death.

Tracing Ducie's movements, officers discovered that he had collected a friend in Swords, driven his Land Cruiser 4x4 to the Phoenix Park where he parked it and took a taxi into town, making his way to the Cocoon bar. He'd phoned Katy at 11 p.m. and a series of phone calls had followed between him, partner Ann and the drug dealer Memery, who had met Katy at 12.30 a.m. at a Statoil service station in Dunboyne, where she'd handed over the money for the cocaine. In the meantime, Ducie and a pal had picked up two girls and made their way to Lillie's Bordello nightclub, getting a taxi back to his friend's apartment in Swords around midnight. Statements collected from the group said that Ducie disappeared into a bedroom with one of the girls while his friend, a 49-year-old company director, chatted up the other who opened up her Bebo page to show him pictures of her burgeoning modelling career. The friend, in his statement to police, said that Ducie spread cocaine out on a coffee table and that the group snorted the drug. Ducie, he said, had left without telling anyone, but texted the apartment owner: 'enjoy'.

At 5 a.m. Ducie's phone showed he'd called Ann Corcoran, and at 6.30 a.m. he told cops he'd arrived back to Kilmessan to find Ann and Katy still up, saying he saw two bottles of empty champagne on the table and found the model close to tears about her boyfriend, her party and her struggle with the media. He claimed he spoke to her for an hour and a half, stopped her from driving home as she was drunk, and put her to bed in a room downstairs near the bathroom. He then claimed that he went upstairs to bed, but heard a loud bang and returned to discover Katy lying face down on the floor beside the bed. He told officers she was bouncing up and down off the ground and rigid. He said Katy's eyes were bulging, she was foaming at the mouth, and her teeth were gritted together. He told officers he screamed at Ann to get the keys of the Land Cruiser, picked up Katy and put her on the back seat. He said he rang 999 on the way to the hospital and spoke to ambulance personnel. Officers would later query and investigate a time discrepancy of more than an hour and a half in Ducie's version of events and the time he actually arrived at the hospital.

His phone told some of the story of what he had done before he phoned 999. Records showed that at 10.02 a.m. he'd phoned Russell Memery, the supplier of the cocaine. Memery would claim Ducie shouted down the phone to him: 'What was in the coke?' Four minutes after Ducie first called Memery, he dialled 999 and told personnel that Katy had banged her head. At 10.12 a.m. Ducie arrived at Navan Hospital denying to medics that she had taken anything except alcohol at his home. By 10.20 a.m. the first of several phone calls was made from Ann Corcoran's phone to Memery's phone, and at the same time Ducie phoned Citywest Hotel reception and asked to speak to PJ Mansfield. He was put through and the pair had a conversation. He next rang a photographer friend of Katy's and told him the story of hearing the thud and coming down to find her foaming at the mouth.

Two months after Katy's death, Ducie and Corcoran were arrested on suspicion of supplying drugs to Katy French. Ducie denied ordering drugs from Russell Memery or ever having anything to do with drugs in his life. He claimed he only phoned Memery the following morning because he was hitting buttons in a panic. He made no comment when asked if he 'cleaned' his house before taking Katy to hospital after a potentially catastrophic delay. Corcoran, too, denied taking drugs and cleaning the house before leaving for the hospital. She told officers that her conscience was clear. Memery was also taken into custody and questioned about selling and supplying drugs. He initially claimed Ducie only phoned him about work, but later conceded that it was to see if he had €200 worth of cocaine. He told Gardaí that the arrangements were made for the drugs by Ann Corcoran and he admitted the entire handover at the Dunboyne service station. He said he was regularly used by Ducie to supply 'Daz Automatic' and said that after Katy's funeral, Ducie phoned him with a concocted story, telling him: 'Deny. Deny. Deny.'

The investigation had unearthed a complex web of supply that included names that linked directly back to the major-league dealers based on the Costa del Sol, who were flooding the country with cocaine. Officers discovered that on the night in question, Ducie had first phoned a known cocaine supplier who was not able to provide him with the high-grade 'Daz Automatic', nor was he bothered to drive it to Meath for his model pal. The dealer, known as the 'Taxi Driver', was linked to a known cocaine dealer, 'Mr Big'. Ducie then made contact with another big dealer who told him he could have the drugs delivered to an arranged meeting point within the hour. Memery was only the footman, and the four crisp 50 euro notes he had taken from Katy went directly back up the supply chain, first to the dealer, and then on to Gary Hutch, to whom he owed a large sum of money.

Gary Hutch, the nephew of the legendary Gerry 'The Monk' Hutch, was at that point living between Dublin, Amsterdam and the southern coast of Spain, and he was a significant member of the Kinahan Organised Crime Group (KOCG). While the older generation, particularly the family godfather The Monk, cared about their image and tried to distance themselves from drugs, Gary and his brother Derek 'Del Boy' had grown up surrounded by a drug culture and had an ambition to get in on the action themselves. In 2000 Hutch had been jailed for his role in the robbery of jewellery and cash from a house in Malahide, during which a businessman and his wife had been put through a terrifying ordeal before a gang made off with €40,000 in jewellery and €8,000 in cash. In prison he'd decided to work for the Kinahans and invest anything else he got his hands on into the organisation.

The ease with which Katy's deal had been done and the way her money had ultimately made its way straight to the Kinahan mob was exactly what was happening hundreds of times every night all over the country, and it was what was making the Spanish-based group stunningly wealthy. Gardaí had been concerned for some time about how the Kinahans had been growing their power base on the Costa and how much control they were gaining over the drugs market in Ireland.

The knock-on effects of their growth at home and the spread of cocaine to the suburbs and deep into rural Ireland had seen escalation in the feuding gangs of Clondalkin, Finglas, Limerick and Crumlin as they continued to fight it out for turf. The same

year Katy died had been dubbed the 'Year of the Gun' for the ferocious greed that had turned childhood pals against one another,
pitted neighbouring groups against rivals, and created notorious
and vicious bosses who needed to cement their fearsome reputa-
tions or face elimination. In March 2007, Robbie O'Hanlon was
murdered as he played five-a-side football, the killing believed
to be retribution for setting up his pal Jonathan O'Reilly to be
killed some years before. In Finglas Eamon 'The Don' Dunne had
begun a killing spree since his dramatic takeover of the operation
run by his former boss Martin 'Marlo' Hyland. Under the tutelage of gangland mentor and convicted cocaine trafficker Eamon
Kelly, Dunne had moved quickly to stamp his authority on his
patch, ordering the murder of John Daly, a notorious career
criminal who'd telephoned a radio station from Portlaoise Prison,
resulting in the upturning of cells for weeks.

In January 2008 the frozen body of criminal John Paul Joyce
was found near the airport with gunshot injuries. 'The Don' was
also suspected of organising the murder of a Latvian woman,
Baiba Saulite, in 2006. The mother of two had been smoking a
cigarette outside her home when she was shot dead in a crime
that shocked the country. Just a month before Katy's death in
2007, Dunne, a prolific cocaine user, was arrested by undercover
gardaí in a Tesco car park in Kildare and subsequently charged
with conspiracy to rob almost €1 million from a cash-in-transit
van. But as he awaited trial, he'd been busy forging links with the
McCarthy–Dundon gang in Limerick and with the Irwin gang in
Sligo to supply them with guns and cocaine.

Limerick feuding was at its height and that year there were
100 shooting incidents, almost a third of the national figure,
and two murders, that of Noel Campion and Gary Grant.
Calls were being made to flood the city with police and put
the gangs under 24-hour surveillance in an effort to curb the

violence and put them out of business. That same year the McCarthy–Dundon gang had attempted to order an arsenal of weapons, including an RPG-7, a portable rocket-propelled grenade launcher. A joint Garda and UK Serious Organised Crime Agency sting had placed two undercover officers into the negotiations with representatives of the Dundons, who tried to order the lethal firearms.

The murder spree of the 'Fat' Freddie Thompson gang in Crumlin had not abated and 2007 saw a shocking double shooting of car dealer Brian Downes, 40, and innocent Edward Ward, 24. Downes was the target of the hitman but Ward, who was not considered a criminal, was shot dead because he was a witness to the execution. Downes had a history of providing vehicles to the Thompson gang, but he was targeted when suspicions grew that he'd become an informer, blamed for providing Gardaí with information about two major drug seizures.

In Galway the body of a 52-year-old was found in a walk-in freezer at the back of a fish shop. He'd been violently killed by a criminal associate. The remains of Patrick McCormack had been in the freezer for five years before the discovery, and a court would later hear that he was killed by Edward Griffin, who would receive eight years for manslaughter, in a row over drugs. When Roy Coddington was shot dead close to his home in Drogheda in County Louth, suspicion focused on a cocaine-fuelled hitman called Eric 'Lucky' Wilson, who officers believed had double crossed him. Wilson had worked for 'Marlo' Hyland in the past and had been contracted by him to kill a number of people, including a member of his own gang who had been caught with his cocaine. After Coddington's murder, Wilson had disappeared to Spain where he'd been offering his services on a freelance capacity to the Kinahan mob. There had been other murders too, 17 in total, linked to the drugs trade as sales of

Above: Christy Kinahan Snr.

Above: Christy Kinahan Jnr.

Below: The Burj Al Arab hotel, where Daniel Kinahan married in the summer of 2017. The wedding was attended by members of the European super cartel and a host of boxing stars.

Above: Daniel Kinahan.

Left: Eamon Kelly was one of the first convicted of cocaine trafficking in Ireland. He became a mentor to younger criminals but was shot dead near his Dublin home in 2012.

Photo of Eamon Kelly courtesy of Sunday World/Ernie Leslie
All other photos courtesy of Sunday World/Mediahuis.

Left: Johnny Morrissey fled to Spain after he was targeted by the Criminal Assets Bureau and in 2022 was arrested there after being sanctioned by the US Treasury and described as an 'enforcer' and 'involved in money laundering' for the Kinahan organisation.

Right: Martin 'Marlo' Hyland was a gang boss targeted under Operation Oak who was shot dead in December 2006 in a relative's house as he slept.

Left: Eamon 'The Don' Dunne was suspected of multiple murders after he took over from his assassinated drugs boss Martin 'Marlo' Hyland.

All photos courtesy of Sunday World/Mediahuis.

Above: International drug boss George 'The Penguin' Mitchell remained under the radar for 20 years until he was tracked down to Germany in 2015.

Left: James Mansfield Snr, who once declared his worth to be €1.6 billion.

Right: Katy French arrives for her 24th birthday party days before her death.

Photo courtesy of Gerry Mooney.

Left: Brian Rattigan was released from prison in 2023. His battle with rival 'Fat' Freddie Thompson was known as the Crumlin-Drimnagh Cocaine Wars and claimed the lives of 16 people.

Photo courtesy of Sunday World/Mediahuis.

Left: Keane Mulready-Woods was 17 when he was murdered in January 2020 at a house in Drogheda.

Right: Sean Little in the run up to his murder in May 2019. He lives a champagne lifestyle as an 'Instagram gangster'.

cocaine hit a record high, with experts estimating its value in the Irish market as more than €200 million per annum.

The number of shootings had been steadily rising for five years, jumping by 54 per cent, with cases of possession of firearms increasing from 373 in 2003 to 428 by 2007. Despite the risks from rival gangs, the dangerous characters who inhabited the underworld and the looming risk of a jail sentence, more and more criminals wanted to get in on the cocaine gold rush as Ireland and Europe increased its demand for the white powder. And still there were many who fancied cutting out the middlemen and trying, where others failed, to land their cargo themselves.

∽

Months before Katy French died, a 58-year-old bricklayer was found floating off the West Cork coast next to 65 bales of cocaine worth €440 million. Englishman Martin Wanden, who had an address in South Africa, where he had worked in construction, was picked up by a lifeboat crew after they were alerted to a rigid inflatable boat (RIB) which had got into trouble. The case would become one of the most infamous catastrophes for a drug gang in history when it emerged that the RIB had been loaded with 1.5 tonnes of cocaine from a catamaran named *Lucky Day* 30 miles off the Cork coast, but when one of its petrol engines was mistakenly filled with diesel, the RIB had floundered and sunk in unseasonably rough July waters. Wanden would later tell a court he had been left to die in the Atlantic by others he had tried to save. It was a farmer who had first raised the alarm when he found an exhausted man in wet clothes at his door begging him not to call the police. The man was later identified as Gerard Hagan.

Out on Dunlough Bay the farmer could see another man on a RIB in heavy seas. Among those picked up by police were

Michael Daly, an ex-drugs squad officer and his brother Joe, who insisted he was only in West Cork on a summer holiday and had nothing to do with the drugs; his brother Michael blamed him for getting them mixed up in the plot, saying he had only arrived to deliver a powerboat. Police killer Perry Wharrie, who was 58 years old and out on licence from jail, claimed that he had nothing to do with the drugs and was in West Cork on an arts holiday in the weeks before the cocaine was due to be landed on the coastline. The product had come directly from the Medellín area of Colombia, had a 75 per cent purity, and had been picked up off the Venezuelan coast on the *Lucky Day* and then sailed across the Atlantic from Barbados.

The incident proved that drug barons hadn't abandoned Ireland's coast as a route into Europe, and a year later, an even bigger haul bound for the UK came undone when it hit rough seas off Cork. A Costa criminal, 61-year-old John Brooks, who'd previously escaped jail on a jet ski, was the brains behind the *Dances with Wolves* plot to deliver one and a half tonnes of coke from South America to Liverpool. Police had been tracking the yacht as it made its way across the Atlantic before moving in when it got into difficulty 200 kilometres off the Irish coast in early 2008. Brooks, who'd lived a luxury life in Marbella, went into hiding while the crew, Philip Doo, 53, Christopher Wiggins, 42, and David Mufford, 44, were picked up and brought before the Irish courts. Each would later admit to possession with intent to supply, and all three were jailed for 10 years, while Brooks was eventually caught in the UK when he tried to sneak into the country to visit family.

In October 2009 the case against John Kinsella relating to the Weston plot concluded when he pleaded guilty to conspiring with others to import cocaine and heroin from Belgium through the Mansfield-owned airport, and he was sentenced to 12 years in jail. In court Judge Tony Hunt accepted Kinsella wasn't at the 'top of the Christmas tree' and that there was at least one person above him, referred to as 'the auld fella', whom he'd refused to name. But shortly after the case concluded, Jim Mansfield Snr moved to hit back at rumours that he had earned his fortune through the illegal drugs trade, blaming the gossip on jealousy. In an interview with the *Sunday Independent*, he said he wasn't bothered by the ongoing whispers about Weston, saying it had a spotless reputation and that he believed not one drug had ever passed through the facility. 'The people who are spreading these rumours are definitely liars, in my opinion, because they have no such proof and if they have then the police should know about it, or we should know about it. I have no doubt that if drugs came through Weston, they would have been found. Just look at the amount of drugs that have been found in other airports,' he said. 'I would love to get someone who could tell me directly, some policeman or someone else, about who is spreading these rumours about me and drugs, not for money or anything – but I'd love to take them out and I would bring them to court because there's no drugs in my business.'

Mansfield Snr went on to address his son Jimmy Jnr's relationship with the late Katy French: 'Katy French's death had absolutely nothing to do with me or my family. I felt very sorry for her and for the family. She seemed like a very nice person, but, other than that, it didn't affect me at all. I would have met Katy three times in my life. I thought she was a very nice girl and that her death was very sad. I suppose all those types of people take some sort of drugs, which is terrible really, and Jimmy, my middle lad, would have known her well, but not that well. He would have known her for two or three months through Andrea [Roche] because she would have held the beauty contests here in Citywest. I heard rumours that it linked back to Jim [Junior]. A few people said this, that and the other about Jimmy and the drugs, but maybe it was lucky he was away that week. He was in Spain at the time, and he came back afterwards . . . None of my sons have ever, ever taken drugs. I can sit here and honestly say that. I would never have had to talk to any of them about drugs in my life because they are simply not that way inclined. They're always too busy doing something else.'

Interestingly, Mansfield pointed to collecting antiques and the refurbishment of old properties as being among his hobbies in downtime. 'When I see all the people around who have lovely properties just lying there and don't bother about it, I do wonder if I am mad. When I get something I have to get it tidied. Palmerstown is now the most magnificent house in the country and it was falling to bits when I got it.'

Palmerstown may have looked better, in Mansfield Snr's opinion, since Anne Bullitt lived there, but efforts to tidy up her affairs hadn't gone so smoothly. It was 2009 before the High Court finally heard that the case had been settled and representatives of the William C. Bullitt Foundation could finally inspect the mansion. The case had opened briefly before Ms Justice Mary Laffoy and, in his opening, Bill Shipsey SC for the Bullitt estate described how by 1997 Anne was living in three rooms in the stately home and her bedroom was only ever lit by artificial light. He described her as an 'independent and determined lady', and when her advisors were negotiating for her they became aware that the 75-year-old had agreed to sell the house to Mr Mansfield for £10 million. Among the claims was that a deposit, which was allegedly to be paid by Mr Mansfield as part of the sale of the house, had been retained by a company owned by him and should be returned to the estate.

Robert Pennoyer, Anne Bullitt's US lawyer, made his way to Palmerstown House and spent 11 hours going through what things were there. A team from Adams Auctioneers were permitted entrance to the house and had only catalogued a quarter of the contents when Mansfield Snr argued about their valuations and then chucked them out. Worryingly, nobody could see either of the Picasso works and, in particular, a work which had been given to William Bullitt by the artist himself after Bullitt complained that he didn't like his Cubist paintings. On one visit, a member of the Bullitt committee was told that the Picasso had been placed in the boot of a Maserati car and hidden. Gone, too, were the George Washington pistols, which William Bullitt had said were stored in his daughter's bedroom. Despite their attempts, they never found 'Head of a Young Man' or 'White Clown' by Picasso, the two prized possessions of the Bullitt estate. Pennoyer said: 'I remember we went down to the house and Mansfield Snr was there. He was a thug. His son had a Maserati car parked outside. It had taken so long to get in we had no idea what should have been there or what was once there. But we never found the Picassos or the George Washington guns. They were the most important and valuable things ever in the collection but they never showed up. I think the politicians were afraid of him and the police were afraid of him. Everyone seemed to be afraid of him.'

In the following years, as Anne Bullitt's treasures were sold off at auctions, the investigation into the death of Katy French wound up with Memery pleading guilty to the possession of drugs with intent to supply in County Meath. Kieron Ducie and Ann Corcoran were both charged with conspiring with Russell Memery to possess cocaine with the purpose of supplying to another, and with intentionally or recklessly supplying cocaine to Katy and failing to get medical assistance in a timely fashion, which created a substantial risk of death or serious harm. In 2012 they both pleaded guilty to the lesser offences, but inevitably those higher up the ladder in the Kinahan organisation were so far from the actual deal that they remained untouchable and continued to flood the country with drugs from their Costa HQ.

CHAPTER SIX

DEATH OF THE FIRST
COCAINE COWBOY

Dessie O'Hare, the Irish Republican paramilitary dubbed 'The Border Fox', who was once the most wanted man in Ireland, stepped up to the altar of St Brigid's Church in Killester in north Dublin and looked out over the packed congregation. Small in stature but with a potent presence, the terrorist studied the mourners gathered to pay their respects to his friend Eamon Kelly. He laid out his scribbled notes on the oak ambo in front of him. Kelly's five surviving sons and two daughters had specially requested that their father's best friend deliver the eulogy on the cold December morning in 2012, after which they would lay him to rest with his best friend, his late wife Ann. The family sat in the front row, sombre and dressed in black, while within the body of the church a strong representation of the criminal underworld respectfully kneeled side by side with middle-class neighbours and law-abiding friends of the wider Kelly family.

Eamon had just celebrated his 65th birthday, which meant he was officially an old-age pensioner and entitled to a free bus pass when he'd been shot dead on a pavement near his home. Two years previous he'd survived a gun attack, but not this time. Kelly might have been older than the young thugs who were trying to extort money from him, but he was no pushover, and he'd made a point of showing no fear in the face of their brazen attempts on his life. After all he was a mentor to many, a boss of bosses of an underworld populated with increasingly violent, gun-toting gang leaders who went to him for advice and for sanction. In the end, Ireland's *capo dei capi* had made his day of reckoning easy for his killers, taking no precautions as he went about life as normal and spent his last afternoon, as he spent every afternoon, betting on horses at Ladbrokes in his native suburb of Killester. He might have come of age at a time of hold-up style bank robberies, when a generation of so-called 'ordinary decent criminals' robbed from the rich because they were poor, but he'd lived through the changes in the criminal landscape and, in many ways, had been the architect of the cocaine-fuelled modern era where his role as a mediator and a mentor had guided the careers of many.

As the mourners awaited O'Hare's speech, officers kept a watchful eye outside, as fears grew of a gangland retaliation of epic proportions. Kelly was far and away the most significant criminal killed in Ireland since Martin 'The General' Cahill had been gunned down in 1994. His death meant many things, not least the changing of the guard. The old rules would no longer apply.

The Border Fox drew a breath and held back a flood of emotion welling up inside him. Despite once confessing that he had murdered 27 people over a career that spanned Northern Ireland's Troubles, the shooting of his friend did not sit easy with him. He straightened his clothing and leaned into the microphone. Quoting the poet W.B. Yeats, he said that Kelly's death was part of the 'terrible beauty' of the struggle for freedom. 'British colonialism is wrong. It is morally wrong and it can never be justified,' stated O'Hare, who once kidnapped a dentist and chopped off his fingers as he demanded a ransom. 'Every self-respecting country has gotten rid of their colonial masters . . . Eamon's life was to achieve the same goal of freedom and peace.' And he continued: 'Eamon was a kind, courageous and loyal comrade who had done much work for others, in particular prisoners, and he had a real sense of justice that was matched by his integrity to do something about that injustice.' As mourners dabbed their eyes and the family comforted one another, O'Hare went on to compare his friend to Jesus, saying: 'On a more spiritual note, I would like to emphasise the sacredness of Eamon's life as a reflection of Christ's life. Eamon, as you know, had suffered. Jesus, too, was sent by his father to suffer.' And he finished his eulogy with the messianic words, albeit sinister in tone and directed at the Real IRA hit team who had carried out the daring murder of Ireland's Godfather of Crime: 'Father, forgive them, for they know not what they do.'

The irony of the entire event wasn't lost on the scattering of undercover journalists and police who attended the service to monitor the mood of the crowd and note those in attendance. Kelly and O'Hare had been a formidable duo who had struck up an enduring friendship while serving sentences together in Portlaoise prison, and despite the ten-year age gap, had become blood brothers with similar ambitions, beliefs and codes. In a way, the man giving the eulogy was a celebrity in Ireland's underworld, a criminal who had regularly been described as a psychopath and a serial killer, and one who had blazed a trail from the wild countryside of south Armagh right to the heart of Ireland's conscience, despite stiff competition from a rogues' gallery of paramilitaries whose crimes had left their bloody mark on a country steeped in war.

O'Hare had been first sent to Portlaoise in 1979 when he got seven years for firearms offences, but when he was freed in 1986 he set about raising funds for a Republican campaign and put together a plan to kidnap a multi-millionaire businessman called Austin Darragh. When his gang arrived at Darragh's home to find he wasn't in, they bundled up his son-in-law, John O'Grady, instead and, while holding him captive, hacked off his fingers with a chisel and left them in Carlow Cathedral alongside a picture of the stumps. For weeks Gardaí pursued the Border Fox across the country, but he lived up to his nickname, always keeping a step ahead of the law. O'Grady, a dentist, was finally freed when gardaí raided a safe house in Cabra. But, despite a gun battle, O'Hare escaped again while the country was put on a national alert that sparked school evacuations, woodland searches and general terror. He was eventually tracked down to Urlingford in County Kilkenny in 1987, and was shot 15 times in a standoff. In a scene straight out of *Pulp Fiction*, O'Hare survived despite the gunshot wounds and later turned to God, becoming deeply religious. He was jailed for 40 years, the longest sentence ever handed down for a non-capital offence, but at his trial he made an angry 10-minute speech calling for 'republicans' to turn their guns on the Irish judiciary, prison service, Defence Forces and Gardaí. He lashed out at the leadership of the Provisional IRA, and finished with a plea before he was cuffed and led down to the cells: 'May all my deeds reverberate until bloody war is waged against the British and their southern allies.'

Back in Portlaoise he met Kelly, an old prison acquaintance, and they bonded over their political beliefs, their relaxed attitudes to violence, and their loyalty to their wives. Years later, as Kelly enjoyed his role as a gangland elder and advisor to drug bosses, he sought advice from his pal about another paramilitary hardman who was trying to extort him for money. O'Hare knew exactly how the situation should be handled, as a man who'd often issued threats himself, and he told Kelly to hold his ground and show no weakness in his dealings with Real IRA leader Alan Ryan, saying he should give the same advice to the clients he mentored in the criminal underworld as there would be strength in numbers.

Ryan led a gang of terror thugs, who lurched from one cocaine mob to the next demanding a cut of their profits, while threatening bloodshed and the full might of the new paramilitaries on those who refused. He had his own brute force in Dublin, and anyone who thought they could fight back was soon warned of the army he had at his disposal in the North, armed to the teeth and ready for war. Publicans and club owners paid up rather than have their premises fire-bombed or their door staff attacked, but it was the profits being enjoyed by the cocaine dealers that he really wanted a slice of. While some dealers simply paid up, others didn't and, under the tutelage of O'Hare, Kelly told Ryan and his mob that he did not intend to buckle despite their warnings of pipe bomb attacks, beatings or kneecappings.

Higher up the ladder, the drug bosses from the bigger outfits didn't like Ryan and his thugs trying to muscle in on their business, and when they heard that his Northern comrades were becoming suspicious about the money he was handing over to their 'prisoners' funds' they saw an opportunity to remove their problem. Because of Ryan's status as the head of the Real IRA's southern command, even the the top dogs in Ireland couldn't go ahead and kill him without a blessing from on high, and so together they approached Kelly. In the seedy underbelly of drugs and crime, everyone has a place, and Kelly had earned his stripes as top dog. He had the ear of Ireland's highest-ranking overlords, from both the paramilitary and the criminal underworld, who held control of the fine balance of gangland. While he was a diplomat, he was also ruthless and knew that business came before loyalty.

Two years before, when his own student Eamon 'the Don' Dunne had been seen as a liability after a cocaine-fuelled murder spree, he'd sanctioned his murder in the Fassaugh House Pub despite having mentored him like a father for years. Previously, Kelly had done the same to Martin 'Marlo' Hyland and given the nod to Dunne to take his place. Months after the Don's murder, the Real IRA had come for Kelly, but the gunman's weapon jammed and he fled, leaving behind a car, it was in Kelly's interest to see the back of Ryan.

Neighbours who lived near Kelly in leafy Killester had heard the rumours, but found it hard to believe that the doting granddad was really a hard man of crime with contacts that spanned across drugs, racketeering, money laundering, weapons and right into the heart of the paramilitaries. To top off his impressive résumé of mentoring up-and-coming criminals and using his contacts to make connections, he was also in the unique position of middleman to the Godfather himself, the 'Dapper Don' Christy Kinahan. Kelly was respected and feared by most, and when Ryan's mob initially approached him, he'd thought they wanted his advice, but when they told him they were after his money, he'd confided in O'Hare. O'Hare assured him that he had far bigger players in his pocket than Ryan and the natural order would see to placing Ryan back in his box. But, instead of retreating, the Real IRA had strengthened their rackets across Dublin, Ryan even taking on the job of murder, killing criminals Seán Winters and Michael 'Micka' Kelly, aka 'The Panda', for money.

Ryan had been blooded young by a veteran Provo and had first come to Garda attention when they uncovered a paramilitary training camp in an underground bunker in Stamullen. He was only 19. He pleaded guilty to receiving training in the use of fire-arms at the camp and was sentenced to four years in prison. When he left jail, he'd started into the extortion racket, rising through the ranks of the Real IRA to become its Dublin leader. Although a portion of the ill-gotten cash was sent North for 'the cause', the rest was simply trousered, so when the plan was hatched to finally kill Ryan, his own were more than happy to let it go ahead. It was Kelly who gave the nod, with the backing of Kinahan and the paramilitary groups, for the trigger to be pulled. The end came swiftly and with the brutal precision of a professional hit. Ryan was walking along Grange Lodge Avenue in Clongriffin on a bright autumn afternoon when he was approached by a gunman who opened fire, then leaned over and shot him in the head as he lay injured on the pavement. The gunman had jumped into a silver Volvo, which was later found burnt out in a graveyard.

In the aftermath of Ryan's death, gangland in Dublin went into turmoil and Gardaí were braced for a major retaliation from the Real IRA commanders' mob, while also under pressure from the government after a deeply embarrassing show of gunfire by dissidents at his funeral. The assassin who carried out the hit quickly fled the jurisdiction, but Kelly was confident he was at arm's length from the killing and believed he had nothing to fear. He continued his daily routine of walking his dog and enjoying his retirement in his northside home, but behind the scenes, an out-of-control and badly managed Real IRA, being dismantled by the Northern command and under huge pressure from the Gardaí, was in turmoil. It was a perfect storm as members became desperate to avenge Ryan's death and prove they were still a force to be reckoned with, identifying Kelly as an easy yet significant target. Meanwhile he remained oblivious to the danger he was in and instead of being cautious began to relax now that Ryan was gone. He'd even taken to leaving his front door permanently open so that his dog could go in and out, and he fell back into regular meetings with associates in pubs.

It was shortly after 4 p.m. on December 4th as Kelly made his way home along Furry Park Road, when he was gunned down, but his murder was not seen as the coup the Real IRA had expected; it was viewed as a stupid and hot-headed mistake. Following the murder and the swift arrest of the suspected killer, the Real IRA continued to implode, with members fighting among themselves for control of the remnants of what was once a cash cow for the inner-city gang. By March 2013, Gardaí were on alert again when Declan 'Whacker' Duffy was released from jail in the UK and returned to Dublin, where he believed he could take over some of their rackets and move into the vacuum that was left behind. The long-running cocaine wars, which had created a new breed of incredibly violent criminal, coupled with a wave of unemployed dissidents looking increasingly to the Republic for work opportunities, made for a complex situation for Gardaí. The murder of Kelly and a move by some more senior gang leaders out of the country after the introduction of new tough anti-gang laws meant nobody seemed to be in charge or in control . . . but still the cocaine flowed.

∽

While many of those who plied the drug to a hungry public, getting fabulously rich in the process, were well-known criminals who were rarely out of the tabloid media, another class of dealer was also in on the action, proving that 'Daz Automatic' knew no social divide. Gangland criminals who went to war and were regularly delivered Garda Information Messages about threats to their lives were usually tough men reared hard in homes where organised crime was the family business, or where neglect had seen them drawn to gangs. But the drug bosses didn't all come from working-class estates or underprivileged communities, and one English businessman in particular showed that there were ways to run a cocaine empire with far more middle-class manners.

Neighbours in the exclusive Bawnogues estate in Straffan, County Kildare, believed bespectacled dad of two Philip Baron had made his fortune renting deckchairs on a Spanish beach until he pleaded guilty at Liverpool Crown Court to conspiracy to import cannabis and cocaine with an estimated value of €300 million. Baron, a former truck driver from Manchester, was a flamboyant big spender who mixed with high society, attending charity functions with his wife, Elaine, and educating his children at a private Dublin secondary school. But, all the while, he was leading one of the most successful drug-trafficking operations in Britain and Ireland, flooding the streets with cocaine and cannabis and dealing directly with Colombian cartels.

For 15 years he got away with an incredible double life as he ordered shipments of cocaine estimated at 52 tonnes and took a corporate approach to losses – that they were simply part of the risk of doing business. Baron had started out in the legitimate haulage business, but quickly spotted that there was nothing to rival drugs as a transport commodity and, together with a group of businessmen, created a non-violent and structured import firm where, like an ordinary business, losses were absorbed and there was a division of labour. The only similarity to the terrifying European mobs was that Baron's system involved a complex arrangement of couriers and money men who spoke only in code.

Baron, his sidekick Walter Callinan and their associates acted like a board of directors and their profits were divided like shareholders, while the consignments seized by cops around the globe were written down on the balance sheets as 'losses'. The extensive investigation conducted by the Gardaí and the Serious Organised Crime Agency (SOCA) uncovered unprecedented paperwork, logs of drug deals, and the massive profits being made by the traffickers. It also showed how Baron cruelly used his daughter Rachel from his first marriage, who lived in Manchester, while favouring his Irish children.

In one deal, profits were allocated and prepared for distribution and included a fee that was kept aside to pay for Philip Baron Jnr's 18th birthday party, which entailed match-day tickets and a private suite at a Manchester United game. Meanwhile, Baron cruelly exploited and manipulated Rachel into doing his dirty work, paying bills and laundering cash. When she had a child, his only grandchild, he sent over a Salford drug dealer with €200 for a cot and got her to launder vast funds for him, including having her buy a €100,000 Bentley convertible and a Range Rover on his behalf. When she was convicted and sentenced to three years in jail for her involvement in the conspiracy, the court was lenient, due in no small measure to the manipulation by her father. While his Irish children, Philip and Nicola, lived in luxury, his first daughter was surviving on benefits and the small crumbs from his proceeds of crime.

But it was all a house of cards, and echoing Al Capone's demise, it was the gang's meticulous bookkeeping that led to their downfall. Officers were able to link 'losses' in the ledgers with seizures of drugs by European and UK drug agencies. Baron's partner Callinan, who was the financial brains of the operation, also rented a property on the exclusive K Club estate in Straffan, County Kildare, through the Celtic Tiger boom years, and even used it to secure an AIB bank account in Mullingar, which was used to launder cash. But it was 'respectable millionaire' Baron who specifically dealt with the notoriously violent Colombian cartels for his cocaine consignments, which he transported from Costa Rica into Spain and then into the UK and Ireland. Eighty-nine people were arrested in the five-year investigation before Baron was targeted. It was discovered that he organised a network of 12 virtual offices across the UK, from Glasgow to Cardiff, from where he would arrange for parcels of drugs to be delivered by mainstream legitimate international couriers. He was finally caught when after months of police work he was recorded giving orders for drugs and arranging deliveries in code that matched up to consignments which were found in the gang's financial logs. Other phone calls linked Baron to 'Dapper Don' Christy Kinahan and his billion-euro Costa Cartel, with suggestions that both organisations co-operated to bring drugs into Ireland. In one coded phone call, Baron advised an associate to destroy mobile phones linked to Kinahan's Irish mafia in Spain. Baron, who was known as '4x' because of his love of Range Rovers, regularly attended English football matches and the Ashes test series, as well as attending black-tie balls. Despite investigations into an associate believed to have set up trust funds in Eastern Europe, few assets were ultimately found and Baron pleaded poverty as he fought extradition from Ireland to the UK in a case that went all the way to the Supreme Court until he eventually lost – but not before, he claimed, his wife, Elaine, pawned off a €250,000 ring to finance his legal bill.

Baron had loved Ireland and found it easy to hide his wealth in Kildare, where he attended race meetings, drove his Bentley and bought his children horses, which were stabled at their school. One consistent thing about the 'gentleman' dealer was claims from family members that they had all been left broke despite the vast wealth he was linked to. In an interview shortly after he was jailed, his son, Philip Jnr, who once believed he was heir to the multi-million euro 'deckchair' business, said he, his sister Nicola and glam mum Elaine had been left penniless since their father's secret life was busted by cops. 'We are broke, on our knees, we have nothing,' he told the *Sunday World*, saying that the family had been left destitute and they had nothing left to live on. 'I mean, look what my mom is driving,' he said, pointing to a six-year-old Peugeot in the driveway of the stunning home, complete with paddocks. 'She used to have a Range Rover for God's sake. We have nothing. Look at us!' Undoubtedly the mortgage on the home told a tale and while expensive cars, fur coats and champagne lunches had been part and parcel of the Barons' life, they had bought the home with a small €100,000 loan but remortgaged it to €400,000 while Baron Snr fought extradition proceedings to the UK on drug charges. 'The house? Sure, it's not worth anything,' Baron Jnr said. 'We have nothing . . . My mother didn't know [of his father's involvement in drug dealing]. She believed him. We all did. If there is money there, I wish they would send it our way. Trust funds? I wish. We are broke . . . Ruined.'

Baron ultimately admitted importing cocaine and cannabis and money laundering despite fighting extradition for almost two years. He was sentenced to 18 years in prison. Shortly after, Elaine opened a small hair salon in nearby Naas to make ends meet. Among her network of female friends was her 'VBF' Donna Cosgrave, the ex-wife of Jimmy Mansfield Jnr, who invited the Barons as guests of honour to the Mansfields' Christmas table. The Barons had first met the Mansfields when they moved to their stunning mansion in Straffan, and both families sent their children to the prestigious King's Hospital School, where they became close friends. Gardaí who had been drawn into the SOCA investigation were able to make further connections between the 'Baron of Kildare' and the Kinahan network, discovering that drug cartel members had met him to discuss a joint venture project to operate grow houses in the west of Ireland. Under surveillance, Baron had been connected in Garda intelligence files with accountant Matthew Dunne, the one-time brains behind Kinahan's money laundering, and with Brian Mahoney, a Finglas-based criminal. They had met with Baron in Straffan and discussed the project involving the establishment of lucrative grow houses, which never got off the ground.

The meeting took place while the CAB was in the process of a massive trawl through the finances of Dunne and Mahoney. Both had been identified during investigations into businesses in Ireland believed to have been used to launder cash for the Dapper Don, including gyms, dry-cleaning services and even hair salons, after the first major crackdown on the cartel. Dunne was named as one of the main targets for Spanish police in May 2010 after Operation Shovel, a multi-agency offensive against the Kinahan organisation, and his villa on the Costa del Sol was searched along with an apartment in west Dublin, where three Rolex watches and documents relating to his accountancy services were seized. Dunne was very close with the Kinahan family and was best man at the wedding of Christy Kinahan Jnr and Georgina Corish in 2007.

While the Dapper Don Kinahan had never missed an opportunity to make money, it's equally likely that he wanted to let Baron know he was watching him and knew what money he was making. Christy Kinahan Snr hadn't got to where he was by allowing anyone away with anything, no matter how minor or insignificant it might seem. For years it had been crystal clear to both the criminals and police that the Kinahan Organised Crime Group, headed up by Kinahan Snr and his two sons, Daniel and Christopher Jnr, were the premier league players in the drugs market. Since he had established himself, first in Amsterdam and later on the Costa del Sol, Kinahan had risen to become a powerhouse rivalling the mafias of Europe. By the mid-2010s he was on to a new part of his ambitious plans for world domination, and was in the process of handing over the baton of running operations to his son and heir Daniel so he could concentrate on expanding the logistics wing by elbowing his way into Africa.

Kinahan Snr had become bigger than anyone could have ever imagined since he first dipped his toe into the drugs market back in Dublin. A major supplier of drugs and weapons to a network of franchises across Europe, he was at times estimated to control nearly 90 per cent of the cocaine market in Ireland, but even at that Kinahan hadn't achieved his full ambitions. He wanted a strong presence in the African corridor, recognising its importance to the continued supply of drugs to a growing European market. Kinahan's wealth had escalated throughout the noughties, largely due to the never-ending supply of cocaine from Peru and Bolivia which he shipped in large containers into the ports of Antwerp and Rotterdam. Speaking a number of languages including Dutch, Spanish and French, and using his long-held skills as an accomplished fraudster, he'd managed to mix with business partners and bankers, and portray himself as a jet-setting and wealthy importer and property investor despite a list of serious criminal convictions.

In Spain, the headquarters of his financial behemoth, he'd linked up with Johnny Morrissey, the Mancunian who'd made Kinsale his home before being targeted by the CAB and plotting to kill its legal officer, Barry Galvin. Morrissey had a good knowledge of hiding money and was happy enough to be a frontman, setting up companies in the British Virgin Islands and Panama, including one which would act as an online exposé of rogue traders, criminals and terrorists called TheRatBook.com. For decades Kinahan had recognised the importance of politics when it came to surviving in the cut-throat world of drugs and weapons trading. He knew from early on that to run a successful operation you had to have police in your pocket and guarantees when it came to transport, which often meant bribing port workers or managers with weekly wages in return for their support and information.

Europol had first tried to stop his unprecedented growth in 2010 when they moved in under Operation Shovel after two years of undercover surveillance and intelligence gathering. The bust had undoubtedly rocked the foundations of the mob in Spain, the UK, Ireland, Cyprus, Belgium, Dubai and Brazil. It was reported as a shock crackdown by police, and had put forward a confidence in the face of the 750 officers involved in the searches, the 31 arrests and the follow-up raids. But Kinahan Snr had told the ranks to keep the faith and stay quiet, and behind bars at Alhaurín de la Torre prison near Malaga, he met with his lawyers and secured bail for himself, his right-hand man John Cunningham, and his sons Christopher and Daniel on strict bail conditions. All had to surrender their passports and sign on at an Estepona court once a week, but the criminal mastermind known as the Dapper Don was sure he'd outsmarted the law and was confident he'd beat any criminal charges.

One month after he secured his freedom, he lost an appeal against a conviction for money laundering in Belgium and was sent back to complete a four-year sentence. He'd been arrested there two years previous along with a Dutch business associate, with whom he had set up a real estate company in the port city of Antwerp with plans to convert an old gaming casino into an apartment block. Belgian cops had been watching him for some time and had established his connections with some of the most dangerous criminal gangs in Europe, including the Russian and Israeli mafias. The inquiry into Kinahan's money laundering had also established an extraordinary web of corruption involving the organised crime gangs, a local professional soccer club and members of the Belgian police, and following his arrest, local newspapers reported the case as one of the country's worst police corruption scandals ever exposed.

As he languished in prison in Belgium, a Spanish magistrate continued to pore over the sheaves of Shovel documents of recorded conversations and details of company set-ups which showed the links between Kinahan and a network of international criminals. The files detailed the Dubliner's extraordinary reach into legitimate and shell companies, which traded in crude oil, cement, fruit, vegetables, olive oil, grain and soya beans, and financial interests in Libya, China, Greece, Panama, several Caribbean islands, the Cayman Islands, the United States, Switzerland, Liechtenstein and Latvia.

Greenland Securities, Daniel Kinahan's property firm in Spain, caused one of the major delays for the investigation as documents were sought from Brazil regarding land transfers and purchases. A tapestry of criminals featured in the files, including Gary Hutch and Freddie Thompson, who had led one side of the ten-year cocaine war in Crumlin and Drimnagh against arch rival Brian Rattigan. Both were described as underlings of Daniel Kinahan, with roles organising drugs and weapons shipments. Links were established between the group and Brian Wright, the mastermind behind the doomed *Sea Mist* and her cargo nabbed off Cork in 1996, and mass race fixing in the UK.

In its early stages, Operation Shovel promised it would destroy the Irish mafia and it concentrated on suspicions of drugs and weapons trafficking along with murder. As the fire of Shovel went out under an avalanche of paperwork, red tape, bum steers and dodgy deals, and as Christy Kinahan Snr finished his prison term in Belgium, a magistrate dropped the more serious charges in Spain and instead decided to focus on money laundering. By September 2014 Kinahan Snr landed himself a UK passport under the name Christopher Vincent Kinahan and packed up on the Costa for good, leaving his son Daniel behind to manage his interests. Finally, he was ready to move on to the next part of his career plan, with the aviation industry firmly in his sights and the trade route through Africa top of his agenda.

∽

Back in 2012, the same year Kelly died in a hail of bullets, the US government had produced a paper for the Office of National Drug Control Policy that gave an interesting overview of the demand and supply of cocaine in the US and Europe, estimating that 849 metric tonnes of powder left South America that year alone. The export figures marked an increase in production estimated at 18 per cent, particularly from Peru and Bolivia, which were the two main countries that supplied Europe. Commercial ships were the most popular form of transport, the report noted, and the 'principal cocaine trafficking threat' to Europe, with Africa listed as the most popular entry route. Guinea-Bissau had by then been identified as one region that had swiftly been taken over by traffickers looking for a backdoor route into the booming European cocaine market, when members of its military organised a coup and seized power to protect it as a transport hub. Mozambique, Nigeria, Ghana, Kenya and South Africa had also been identified as places of government-sanctioned smuggling where traffickers found corrupt ruling systems open to bribes, and terrorist organisations like Hezbollah and al-Qaeda became involved in the lucrative money spinner.

While the US had made some modest efforts to curb the fast-accelerating African problem, the business brain of Kinahan could easily weigh up the risk versus the gain. He knew that ownership of the transport routes was so significant a role in the cocaine trade that it was second only in importance to those who controlled its production. For Kinahan Snr, reinventing himself in aviation was just another face of many that he had portrayed to the world since his early days in Dublin, when he fenced for criminal gangs and blaggers like The Monk's brother Edward 'Neddy' Hutch. For the Mensa-listed Kinahan, it was easy to take on any role, in any language, and change his background with the flick of a switch. After all, he had left behind Dublin, his ageing mother and two sisters knowing he'd never be able to go back as he followed a career path to the very top of organised crime on the Costa del Sol, so a move to Dubai to establish himself as a 'legitimate businessman' in the United Arab Emirates was not going to be a challenge. Along with his partner Nessy Yildirim, a Dutch national of Turkish origin, and their two young children, he'd moved lock, stock and barrel to Dubai, the ultimate destination of the super-rich where luxury yachts bob in the immaculate azure waters of the Persian Gulf, and the crime bosses of the world mix with oil-rich Arabs desperate for their money.

Kinahan quickly felt comfortable around the marina area, surrounded with fine-dining restaurants and designer shops, but paranoid about being placed under surveillance again, he regularly moved between suites in the Grosvenor House hotel in a waterfront area just like Puerto Banús in Spain, and the H building where he rented a number of apartments.

His choice of Dubai wasn't a unique one, nor was he blazing a trail. He was simply following a path first discovered by another cocaine boss, Robert Dawes, almost two decades earlier, and Dawes had only recently lost his battle against being handed over by authorities in the UAE. If anything, Dawes had proved that money could buy loyalty high up in Dubai. The UK crime boss was on the Costa del Sol with other gangsters around the end of the 1990s, but he had slowly become a more frequent visitor to the fast-growing skyscraper metropolis of Dubai. He set up some businesses and led the way for others to realise that if they shared the wealth with Emiratis, and identified them as major shareholders in any venture, anything was possible. Dawes was one of the first to discover the underground secret banking system called 'hawala', which was built on trust and where money could be moved across the globe with no paper trail. The hawala system is an ancient Middle Eastern practice in which 'hawala-dars' transfer money between each other like a bank would, using agreed passwords to know who and who not to trust. While the system was legal in Dubai, nobody had to register. Between 2008 and 2011, Dawes had even used Dubai's archaic legal system to his benefit, bouncing a cheque to guarantee himself three years in prison as Spanish authorities sought his extradition for a massive cocaine shipment. During that time, he co-ordinated a two-tonne shipment of cocaine into Antwerp along with the Dutch crime lord Gwenette Martha, a former associate of Kinahan Snr, who would later be murdered in Amsterdam in a takeover of his business linked directly to Daniel Kinahan. Dawes was eventually returned to Europe in 2015 just as Kinahan Snr was finding his feet in his new home. Since the purchase of properties opened up to foreign buyers in 2002, many other criminals had followed Dawes to Dubai and, particularly, those in the top tier of organised criminals. Christy Kinahan Snr was certainly one of those and, under the searing Gulf sun, he settled in, opened his laptop and started to reinvent the wheel.

CHAPTER SEVEN

THE FALL OF THE HOUSE OF MANSFIELD

They were probably the closest thing to royalty that Ireland had ever seen, but when 60 booted and armed officers burst through the doors of the Tassagart House family mansion in Dublin in January 2015 and searched other significant premises connected to them, it was clear that the fall of the house of Mansfield was almost complete. In a few short years, the private plane, helicopters and Rolls Royces were all gone, and the business empire that had made them the richest family in Ireland had folded. Now their belongings and papers had been packed into boxes marked 'evidence' and taken away for examination in specialist Garda units dealing with money laundering, antique theft and organised crime. For more than a decade, the late Jim Mansfield Snr, and in more recent years his son and heir Jimmy Jnr, had batted away allegations that they were connected with common criminals or had anything to do with drugs. Mansfield Snr had dismissed rumours after his plane was caught up in an attempt to smuggle heroin and cocaine from Belgium and the boxer John Kinsella had pleaded guilty to his role in the conspiracy, refusing to name who 'the auld fella' he referred to was. Senior had come out fighting, saying that no drugs had ever come through Weston and that none of his businesses were involved with anything untoward. He'd defended his son Jimmy Jnr after the cocaine-related death of Katy French, dismissing unfounded gossip that he'd been with her on the night. Jimmy Jnr, too, had laughed off suggestions that he had been issued with a Garda Information Message that his life was under threat from criminal associates of slain gangster 'Fat' Andy Connors, or that he had been a close friend of the CAB target, dodgy car dealer Lee Cullen. But the dramatic search of Tassagart by armed officers from the Organised Crime Unit, along with colleagues from the Criminal Assets Bureau and Revenue Investigators, which yielded boxes of documents, antiques, paintings, guns and ammunition, suggested otherwise.

As was the family way, in the aftermath of the raids and the media frenzy around them, Jimmy Jnr came out determined he'd been wronged, this time in the form of a letter of complaint written to the then Taoiseach Enda Kenny about the heavy-handed tactics of the gardaí who he said had terrorised his elderly mother, Anne, and who had the audacity to search through his things and the private homes of senior management of businesses owned by himself and his children, Ingrid and Samuel. The raid had happened on the first anniversary of his father's death, he complained, and details of it were leaked to the media, who he would later say were present at the family home in Saggart with gardaí during the searches. Apart from the 'blatant intimidation', he wrote, the raids were designed to 'destroy' the Mansfield family. Later, Jimmy Jnr issued legal proceedings against the Garda Commissioner, the Taoiseach, the Criminal Assets Bureau and the *Sunday World* over a series of articles linking his father to organised crime. A submission was also drawn up for the European Court of Human Rights suggesting that the Mansfield family had been illegally deprived of €1.5 billion in assets by a conglomerate of government, the Central Bank, the Irish justice system, the Gardaí, banks and the liquidators who had been appointed to his father's estate.

The fall of the Mansfields had been nothing short of spectacular, but the efforts by Jimmy Jnr to suggest that it had been the fault of others would go nowhere, and the denials of father and son that they had anything to do with dangerous criminal gangs, cocaine traffickers and paramilitaries would come back to bite them.

In the years before the raids, an extraordinary set of circumstances had created the ultimate collision of the underworld and the high-society lives of Ireland's one-time wealthiest family who'd got filthy rich under a patriarch with a questionable past. It had all started to go wrong, in the same way it had for so many, at the dramatic end of the Celtic Tiger dream when Ireland went under in a tsunami of debt, repossessions and shattered dreams. An overextended banking system, excessive Irish property values, and an overreliance on the construction sector had come together in a perfect storm after the collapse of the Lehman Brothers bank, and the ripple effects it had across the world. Ireland had become the first eurozone country to officially enter recession in September 2008, with the Celtic Tiger declared dead a month later. In an interview at the end of the year, the then Taoiseach Brian Cowen had said many people still did not realise how badly shaken the public finances were.

Years later, a court would hear how Jimmy Mansfield Jnr was still partying long after the collapse of state revenues and warnings from the International Monetary Fund predicting the most severe economic distress in post-World War II history. In Citywest, his father was worried, but on the day after Good Friday in 2009, Jim Mansfield Jnr, aged 42, woke up with a hangover, opened a suitcase stuffed with cash, and joked that he could even make money while he was drunk. There were two suitcases, in fact, filled with €4.5 million in notes belonging to Daniel Kinahan and Thomas 'Bomber' Kavanagh – the two most significant and feared criminals on the international scene – and they'd been delivered to Tassagart House in a white van. Good Friday was always a big one for Mansfield Jnr, as it was the one day where dated laws meant nobody could get a drink unless they were resident in a hotel. Given he had his own hotel, he simply opened the residents' bar to his pals and partied all night, and he'd been enjoying himself so much that when two men showed up at reception looking for him, he'd sent his security officer instead.

Martin Byrne had worked for Mansfield Snr since 2005 as the in-house security director of Citywest Hotel, and he was like family. He would later say the men waiting for the younger Mansfield were criminal kingpins Freddie Thompson, representing Daniel Kinahan, and Kavanagh, who were offered and who accepted VIP treatment and hotel rooms for the night. The following day, Byrne would claim, Mansfield asked him to let a white van onto the grounds of Tassagart House, and that the suitcases had been handed over as payment for four townhouses being bought by the Kinahan Cartel in a bid to launder their drug money. The money sloshed around the Mansfield coffers, but in the chaos that became the next few months, nobody did the paperwork and the houses – five-beds in plush Saggart Court Lodge – remained on the company books and were never transferred. As the financial news got worse, unemployment soared and the National Assets Management Agency (NAMA) was established, Mansfield Snr slowly realised that he had overextended himself with massive borrowings into assets predominantly in the shrinking property sector. He fought to get a number of projects off the ground which he believed would keep him afloat, including an international college he hoped would attract rich

Saudis, but it was too little, too late, and even a giant of business like his own couldn't hold back the tide.

Just over one year after his son took the Kinahans' money, his Citywest Hotel, conference centres and golf complexes were placed into official receivership by Bank of Scotland. Mansfield Snr was flabbergasted and he went into denial about what the future might hold, trying first to fight back through the legal system to hold onto his assets, but to no avail. Apart from the Quinn Group, headed up by another patriarch, Sean Quinn, there would be no bigger loser from the crash. Mansfield Snr, unlike Quinn, couldn't afford to sit back and launch protracted legal battles. He knew he was sick and that his health would fail over the years to come. He also knew that he had many debtors who simply would not wait for the wheels of justice to turn or for his big comeback of the future; he urgently needed access to funds to pay off some of the country's most violent criminals because they had lost control not only of his legitimate debts, but of the dirty money ones too.

For decades, Jim Mansfield Snr had mingled with a network of criminals and paramilitaries who regularly used him to wash their money through his huge construction projects and interests. He'd managed to finely balance a seesaw between the underworld and the politicians, police, diplomats and celebrities who he hosted in Citywest for years, but the Bank of Scotland now threatened it all. Mansfield Snr had been careful who he had let into his circle of trust, and he preferred the old-school crooks, gangsters and forgers who respected him and his rules. But in the years leading up to the crash, his son, Jimmy Jnr, had been less considered about who he'd done business with, and Mansfield Snr knew that a long queue of ruthless cocaine lords and underworld heavies would be coming looking for their investments back.

The extent of the problem was far worse than he could ever have imagined, and he soon realised that his son had mixed business and pleasure with the undesirable figures from Crumlin and the inner city whose faces and names graced the tabloid press and who were known for their ruthless nature and lack of understanding on financial matters. His friend Lee Cullen, who'd given the Range Rover to Katy French, had provided the introductions and, in the years that followed, an infestation of figures from the criminal underworld would swarm the family home like vultures as the great ship Mansfield went under. Cullen had been targeted by the CAB under Operation Tie in 2007, and he was hit with a massive tax bill over outstanding debts and VAT payments from his Exclusive Cars company which he couldn't pay back. He'd been the car dealer to the rich, but he'd also networked with criminals who had seen the potential in the industry to transport their product and hide their money. He regularly brought his drug-dealing pal Christopher 'Git' Russell into Jimmy Jnr's company and had even used Tassagart to store cash and meet with suppliers. He'd introduced Mansfield Jnr to 'Bomber' Kavanagh, to the Byrne brothers from Crumlin and their mob and, ultimately, to Daniel Kinahan, who along with his brother Christopher Jnr had become regular visitors to Citywest any time they were home on business.

Mansfield Snr drew up a list of who needed to be paid and at the top of the pile was Daniel Kinahan and his violent sidekick Kavanagh. Among those shouting for money was 'Fat' Andy Connors, a neighbour and the leader of a burglary mob who terrorised the countryside and had got filthy rich from drugs, stolen antiques and extortion. Senior criminal figures living outside the State, who'd pumped money into properties over the years, were also caught up in the mess.

A second list laid out the plan for the future of his family and the legacy he had hoped to leave. His portfolio had been valued at €1.7 billion at its height in 2008, and included the City-west Hotel, Weston airport, the Palmerstown House estate, and lands in Kildare, but by 2011 the High Court had given Bank of Scotland judgment of €214 million against his companies. HSS, Jeffel and Parke, and NAMA had moved in to seize anything else that was left. On paper it was a fiasco, but there was life in the old dog yet. Despite a diagnosis of the rare multiple system atrophy (MSA), which caused symptoms similar to Parkinson's disease, he felt he could still play his way back into the game. The family patriarch was determined to put a brave face on his predicament; he knew that you never showed any weakness. In his last public interview to the media, he'd insisted: 'The one thing I would never do is worry over money. Money means nothing to me.' Asked about the collapse of the Celtic Tiger, he'd told the *Sunday Independent*: 'Everybody was in it. The government was there and the Minister for Finance was there, the Regulator. Why didn't any of them do something about it? Wouldn't somebody have to say one day "sure this can't last . . . you can't build a house for €200k and sell it for €1 million". I bought into it to a certain extent myself: we built houses too and they'd be greatly reduced in price now, in comparison to the price we expected to get for them. That was part of it though. The banks were giving out the money too handy. If people were to start getting jail sentences for what happened, there wouldn't be enough jails in the country to hold them. If they jailed one, they'd have to jail everyone.'

While to the outside world he appeared resilient and reflective, behind the scenes Mansfield Snr was trying desperately to come up with a solution. There was a new intensity to his living arrange-ments with his estranged wife, Anne, who for years had resided in a private mansion at nearby Coldwater Lakes, but was then back living in Tassagart. Jimmy Jnr, forced out of Palmerstown House, was back with the parents too. It seemed like a lifetime ago since Mansfield Snr had done the deal of his career with Anne Bullitt for Palmerstown House and estate, but he was still being pursued for missing items her executors claimed had mysteriously vanished from the house. Mansfield Snr knew he needed a clever plan, and in the last of his business brilliance before his illness totally took over, he formulated a complex buy-back scheme with the help of an old friend. Concentrating on what he had left to bargain with, Mansfield discovered he retained control of three pieces of land around the family home, which he called 'ransom strips' and which were key access routes to Citywest Hotel and other properties that he insisted were worthless without them: one was the main entrance to the hotel, another was on the left-hand corner of the convention centre, and the third was attached to part of the golf course. Without them, the lands were useless, he believed, but with them he was still in the game.

He spoke to an old pal, Kevin McGeough, a Dundalk businessman, and asked him to help negotiate a claw-back of three key assets from the receiver. McGeough agreed to buy the assets and sell them back to Mansfield Snr when he'd raised the funds. The deal came with strict deadlines for the repayment of McGeough and any investors he brought in or they'd be entitled to keep the assets themselves. The properties were significant: 30 townhouses and 100 apartments at Saggart Court Lodge – which included the properties sold to Kinahan and Kavanagh, Finns-town Castle Hotel, and Paddy Reilly's Field. The latter was a parcel of prize land which Mansfield Snr always believed was the jewel in his crown because of its location and development potential. The site, once valued at €30 million, ended up being sold to the Newry builder Gerry McGreevy, brought in by McGeough as an investor, for €800,000. Known as a shrewd businessman, McGreevy saw the potential gain should the Mansfields miss their payback deadlines.

The entire agreement was a lifeline to the family, but before anything was concluded, Mansfield Snr's health began to fail and the mantle was passed over to Junior. As is often the way of the world, what the father had in cunning, the son lacked, and the carefully balanced attempt to rebirth the empire began to stumble as he missed payment deadlines and began to fall out with McGeough and McGreevy. Many felt sorry for the predicament that the younger Mansfield had found himself in and the layers of problems he had to face, which were a far cry from the privileged upbringing he had enjoyed. He was already in financial bother himself, with a judgment order granted to AIB for €6.32 million against him and three other businessmen over loans it had advanced between 2003 and 2009 in connection with the purchase of a site at Duleek in County Meath. Jimmy Jnr had appealed the decision, claiming he'd signed a document by mistake as he couldn't read. Criminals will always find weakness and they could almost smell it off of Junior: while some were looking for money they had invested, others were seeing opportunities in the mess that had been created. Jimmy Jnr began to panic and fire-fight underworld debts and the running costs of the extraordinary lifestyle he'd been accustomed to. As the pressure got to him, he hired Real IRA thug Alan Ryan to protect him and to represent his interests with his father's friends. Jimmy Jnr believed that Ryan's reputation as the man who'd taken on the cocaine dealers would keep the wolves from his door.

Everyone seemed to have their hand out looking for money from him, and none more so than 'Fat' Andy Connors, who was insisting that he was owed a million euro and would take it in land around his property which backed onto Coldwater Lakes, the most exclusive of the Mansfield-built housing developments in the area. The debts just seemed to keep mounting, and despite being hired in to help, Ryan only added to the problem. Ryan alone was on a wage of €2,500 per week and his sidekick Nathan Kinsella was using Tassagart as a meeting place for Real IRA business. Other forces, however, came to bear, and when Ryan was murdered in September 2012, Kinsella took over the job, befriending Jimmy Jnr and his inner circle. A month later Kevin McGeough was listed as a director of Finnstown Castle Hotel, a first step to return it to the family if the deal could be honoured.

It was into this mess that James 'Fat Boy' O'Gorman arrived as a fixer, who promised to come up with ways to keep the show on the road. He was a friend of Connors, who had recommended him as a business genius who knew how to find holes in the system and ways of exploiting it. While his involvement was going to mean another large salary, Jimmy Jnr hoped he was going to be his saviour by coming up with ways to create an income to match the outgoings of the estate. O'Gorman was 43 and a convicted fraudster who once had links to drug dealer 'Marlo' Hyland, and who listed a serious array of old-school Provos as his backers and friends. He told Jimmy Jnr he would bring in investors to help fund the buy-back and make McGeough and McGreevy see sense about the handover of the assets. He also promised to come up with ways to make enough money to pay off the criminals, which was all music to Jimmy Jnr's ears. He needed at least €8 million to get out of his immediate problems and at least €20,000 a week to pay the basic household bills.

O'Gorman moved his offices into the family mansion, where Mansfield Snr was now bed-ridden and had moved himself into the apartment out-houses on the grounds where loyal security guard Martin Byrne and his family had lived for years. O'Gorman put together his finance plan, which he promised would see Jimmy

Jnr rise from the ashes, but not everybody was happy with his presence – particularly Kinsella, who'd survived a kneecapping and who was facing charges of membership of an illegal organisation. True to his promise, over the course of a few months, O'Gorman convinced a number of criminals to invest millions with him. As pressure came on to repay a debt, he drew in other investors, including a drug dealer closely linked to George 'The Penguin' Mitchell, and used their funds to keep the show on the road. He developed a proposal to build a fishing village in lands at Brittas Lake, which had gone undeclared by Mansfield Snr, and he convinced the Wall gang, known for robberies, to invest €5 million into the plan. To help with the monthly bills, he also established a VAT fraud scam which netted up to €12,000 per week in the scramble for funds.

O'Gorman's brainchild involved setting up a company that hired out staff to the hotel industry and creamed millions from the exchequer by collecting 23 per cent VAT on top of every euro it charged, despite not being registered. O'Gorman had been spared a four-year jail term for fraud eight years previous when he handed out €60,000 in compensation to his victim. He had been found guilty of dishonestly obtaining almost €55,000 from a company director after he had approached him at his business premises and offered him a deal on a sterling exchange. The court heard that O'Gorman and two accomplices had taken a suitcase of cash from the man, but when he repeatedly asked them to adhere to their end of the bargain, he refused to co-operate. He told the court that during one meeting, the company director heard O'Gorman ask, 'Where is the Beretta?' At the time he said he did not know it was a type of firearm. On another occasion, O'Gorman had told him, 'I am a member of the biggest organisation in Ireland and I am not referring to the GAA.'

O'Gorman was not low profile and his presence in the middle of the Mansfield fiasco didn't go unnoticed. Security companies linked to him had previously been raided by gardaí investigating the laundering of funds from organised crime, including money made by the murdered drug lord Hyland, so suspicions grew and they began to investigate what was going on behind the walls of Tassagart.

In January 2014, Jim Mansfield Snr lay down to die as the vultures circled the home he'd spent a lifetime filling with price-less antiques and works of art. On the ground floor, O'Gorman had his feet firmly under the table, but his presence had only intensified the chaos. Just weeks earlier, on New Year's Day, he'd been assaulted by Nathan Kinsella, who had jammed him into a wall with a Louis XV table. O'Gorman, afraid of the Real IRA thug, had called in his own reinforcements from the INLA, and soon Gareth 'Red Gar' Byrne, a convicted terrorist, was living next to him in the outbuildings, while his sidekick John Roche spent his days patrolling the grounds of Finnstown Castle Hotel and Tassagart.

Any signs of trouble were well hidden when the family lined out to remember the giant that was Mansfield Snr, who had won and lost it all during his lifetime. At his funeral he was remembered as a 'unique and special patriarch'. Speaking at the ceremony, his daughter-in-law Anita, married to Tony, described him as a loving father who enjoyed taking his family on holiday to watch Grand Prix motor racing at Silverstone in England. The parish priest, Fr Enda Cunningham, praised his business prowess and his pride in being part of the local community. 'I've met some in this parish who would forever swear by Jim Mansfield and people are deeply grateful for a helping hand in a time of need.' Mansfield was buried in a cemetery across the road from the church to the strains of Frank Sinatra singing 'My Way'.

Obituaries told the story of his rise to riches, about the Falklands machinery and the building of Citywest.

Days after the funeral, the Special Criminal Court issued a bench warrant for the arrest of Kinsella, who a detective inspector said hadn't been seen since before Christmas and had failed to answer his phone. On February 20th, Kinsella was arrested in a gym in Cabra and two months later pleaded guilty to membership of an unlawful organisation. But things were looking up somewhat, and in May 2014, five months after his grandfather's death, Samuel Mansfield, then 20, was listed in the Companies Office as a director of Finnstown Castle Hotel, the first green shoots of a family decimated by the recession.

While Finnstown was back, the disagreements in relation to Paddy Reilly's Field and the houses had only intensified, as had the difficulties with 'Fat' Andy Connors who was increasingly threatening for his money. In August the Traveller mob boss was at his home with his wife, Ann, and four of their six children when a gunman burst in and shot him dead in front of his family. The finger of suspicion immediately fell on the INLA. A murder investigation was launched and officers discovered the semi-automatic pistol used in the killing in a burnt-out white Opel car nearby. Reports at the time detailed that the Garda line of inquiry was that Connors might have been killed over a money dispute with a high-profile south Dublin businessman. Jimmy Jnr was issued with a Garda Information Message to warn him that his life was under threat, but in October 2014 he gave an interview to the *Irish Independent* saying he wasn't worried, and that it was news to him that anyone would want to see him dead. 'Is my life in danger? I'd pay no heed. I haven't done anything on anybody,' he said. The murder of Connors, the intensity of the paramilitary activity around Tassagart House, and the presence of O'Gorman fast-tracked the Garda investigation into what was going on around Citywest, and officers knew they needed to move in when they would be least expected.

A year to the day after he died, Gardaí carried out heavy-handed and co-ordinated searches of the late Jim Mansfield Snr's Tassagart home, along with Finnstown Castle Hotel, apartments in Citywest, offices of solicitors and accountants linked to him, and they seized papers, paintings, antiques, money, guns, ammunition and what they suspected to be a Picasso original drawing. In the outbuildings they discovered O'Gorman and the paramilitary figures who were staying there. At number 10 Coldwater Lakes, a property listed in the name of golfer Christy O'Connor Jnr but which had been the home of Anne Mansfield for years, they discovered the boxer Matthew Macklin, who had founded the MGM gym and boxing promotions company in Spain with his best pal Daniel Kinahan. The raids were detailed as being part of a money laundering probe and when officers were finished, they went back to their specialist offices to start a massive examination into what had been found.

There was pandemonium at Tassagart, but Jimmy Jnr was more incensed that his home had been searched and that he had been treated like a common criminal. As he sat down to write to Taoiseach Enda Kenny, tensions among some of the older staff and the new blow-ins on the Mansfield payroll rose. A year after Connors' murder and with investigations still firmly focused on the INLA, three six-foot marble statues of Jesus Christ, Mary and Joseph were winched by a giant crane across the graveyard in Wexford to where 'Fat' Andy lay. In life he'd bullied, intimidated and terrorised his way through the homes of the elderly and vulnerable he robbed, and he had pocketed a millionaire's fortune through drug dealing and loan sharking. But in death little had changed, and despite a lengthy standoff with one brave parish priest, his wife eventually got her way and erected the giant marble epitaph to the fallen thug, a huge headstone that cost in the region of €50,000, and placed it on his grave at St Michael's Cemetery, Gorey. The work, completed just in time for his first anniversary, made Connors' grave one of the most ornate in the cemetery, with a five-plinth tomb complete with a carved verse, a prayer to Padre Pio, urging mourners: 'Don't remember me with sadness, don't remember me with tears, remember all the laughter we had throughout the years.' In the months since her husband's death, Ann Connors had moved her family out of the large family pile where the shooting took place and employed the services of criminals Martin 'The Viper' Foley and Troy Jordan to represent her interests with the Mansfields, insistent that she was now owed the €1 million that her husband had been demanding. Despite her regular social media postings showing flash cars and family gatherings, Ann had her own problems too, and the CAB, who'd been a long time putting together a case against her late husband, now focused on her.

'Fat' Andy had bought up a lot of land around the Saggart and Tallaght areas of west Dublin and placed much of it in Ann's name. But there was more to come, and by summer the tensions at Tassagart would explode with the oddest meeting of worlds ever seen. With the Real IRA gone from the picture, the INLA had settled in but were charging huge money for their services, and Jimmy Jnr decided he wanted a full clear-out and a change of the guard, this time with security provided by the legendary 'Border Fox' Dessie O'Hare. If anyone was going to scare away unwanted visitors, Jimmy Jnr wagered, it was Dessie. His only problem was that his father's trusted security man Martin Byrne didn't agree, and when he brought him to meet O'Hare and his sidekick Declan 'Wacker' Duffy, he'd warned them off, telling them that there were already representatives of the INLA in place and that they were not needed. A second meeting was arranged, but this time it was Byrne who was told he was no longer needed and he was bundled into a car by the terrorist pair and their mob and dragged to Tassagart where he was told to clear out his home and be on his way. John Roche was cornered and assaulted and things quickly got out of control. In the middle of the incident, a Garda car pulled up to the gates of the property and Byrne was allowed to talk to the officers as would be normal, but he managed to indicate to them what was going on and they called for backup. Once they realised they'd been busted, the terror team Duffy and O'Hare fled across fields, while the Garda helicopter followed.

By the time the incident came to court, it would be clear that it had all gone on under CCTV cameras, which had captured the assaults and kidnap. Other footage would show Byrne and Jimmy Jnr leaving Finnstown Castle Hotel in a black Audi A6 earlier that morning. In a show of his lack of cunning, Jimmy Jnr had requested Patrick Byrne, Martin's brother and an employee at Finnstown, to destroy the images, but he had kept a backup. In his naivety, Jimmy Jnr had made the fatal mistake of believing in his own position as his father's beneficiary of the loyalties of everyone around him despite the chaos he had created, and he had definitely underestimated Byrne, a loyal employee to the last, who had cared for the dying Mansfield Snr and who knew where all the bodies were buried. If he thought the raid on his family home was an abhorrent act of the State, he had far more humiliation to come, and he was soon to find out exactly what it meant to be a common criminal.

CHAPTER EIGHT

A WEDDING, A COCAINE SUPER CARTEL, AND A VERY UNWANTED GUEST

The Burj Al Arab hotel couldn't have been more perfect for the nuptials. Listed by Forbes as the best hotel in the world, it boasted a Viennese Opera-style ballroom on its 27th floor, which promised to give a regal touch to any occasion. For Daniel Kinahan, his wedding to Dubliner Caoimhe Robinson was going to be more than just a romantic occasion, it was his day to cement his position at the very top of Europe's cocaine trade and to show everyone just how far he'd come. The guest list was a jaw-dropping mix of the people who now made up his new life in the Gulf, where he had moved after packing up and leaving Spain for good. A few more had travelled from Dublin and his old stomping ground around Oliver Bond flats, which were regularly raised in the Dáil due to the high levels of crack cocaine dealing in front of the children who lived there.

It was May 2017 and the temperature was beginning to rise as the end of the Emirates winter gave way to the searing 40-degree heat of the summer months. Daniel Kinahan knew he had a lot to be grateful for; after all, he had survived two shooting attempts in recent years and outwitted gunmen on another occasion. It was his father's coaching in countersurveillance training and obsession with security that had stood to him each time, but he had been clever too, getting out of Spain just weeks after the Regency Hotel attack, which saw members of his own organisation turn on him in spectacular fashion, and just before the cops moved in on his business. In Dubai he'd initially rented a two-bed apartment on the 14th floor of the Iris Blue building in the Marina with his brother, but he'd moved on while Christopher Jnr stayed put, happy with the central location and the security around the tower. Daniel wanted a proper home, so he'd bought a villa on the world-famous Palm Jumeirah, an artificial island stretching out into the Persian Gulf that had been dubbed a playground for the world's wealthiest people. He'd bought an office too, which he shared with his father: 115 square metres of opulence with stunning views at the Jumeirah Bay Tower 3. There were other properties: offices in the Boulevard Tower and a penthouse apartment in a skyscraper, Elite Residence Tower, in the Dubai Marina. The lads had followed soon after: Bernard Clancy and his cousin Ian Dixon had moved into a house at Arabian Mansions, then came Sean McGovern. It was a fresh start after the nastiness with the Hutch crew and their loyalists had spilled into a full-blown feud. They had done what they knew how to do and set up a company under the name Haizum General Trading to trade clothing, pasta, sugar and cooking oil, which was incorporated in a special tax zone with the help of a UAE national in order to comply with local laws. They also set up Ducashew Consultancy to hide their real activities in the Gulf. With everything established, Caoimhe Robinson had moved out to join him, giving up her life in Dublin to be with him, and he'd organised schools for their children and started to plan the wedding.

For those who knew her background, it was clear that Caoimhe Robinson was the ideal partner for Daniel Kinahan and was no stranger to the uglier side of his business dealings. She was already a gangland widow; her previous partner, Michael 'Micka' Kelly, had been shot dead in a hail of bullets outside their home. Kelly, nicknamed 'The Panda', was a notorious figure on the Irish gangland scene throughout the 2000s and was suspected of being behind six murders himself. At 6 feet 4 inches, he was an imposing character who supplied drugs to a number of gangs across the country, and he gained a terrifying reputation when he employed the hitman Eric 'Lucky' Wilson to kill his former boss David 'Babyface' Lindsay and Alan Napper in 2008. Kelly owed more than a million euro to each and to teach him a lesson they'd had his friend shot dead. Less than a week after the killing, Kelly had plotted an extraordinary double-cross, promising to pay back the money he owed, but instead bringing Wilson with him to kill the pair. While their bodies have never been found, it is suspected that they were dismembered and buried. Kelly had worked with Eamon 'The Don' Dunne and was suspected of carrying out hits for him, but over the years he'd holidayed in Spain with Caoimhe and the couple had mixed with Daniel Kinahan and his crew. He was known to be fearless, but when he refused to pay Real IRA boss Alan Ryan and his gang, he had unwittingly signed his own death warrant.

Caoimhe was at home with their newborn baby on the day he was killed. She'd heard the gunshots as his assassins pumped six bullets into him and then reversed their car over his body to ensure he was dead. She'd run outside to find him dead on the pavement, his head pulverised and a silver Lexus screeching off down the road. One witness would later describe seeing her screaming for help outside the apartment complex. At the funeral, Fr David Lumsden warned mourners to give up drug dealing. 'Desist from any activity that will lead to you ending up at the front of a church in front of your parents, partner or your children in a coffin. I do not judge anyone who comes into this church alive or dead. I would appeal to anyone in this congregation involved in this lifestyle today to pull back and get out,' he said. Later, Vincent Ryan, the brother of Alan, was charged with having a gun on the day of the murder, September 15th, 2011. He would die himself in a hail of bullets shortly after the Regency Hotel attack.

Bereft, Robinson had literally been left holding the baby and with no insurance policy as the CAB moved in on Kelly's wealth, seizing a house and two cars, but it wasn't long before she was back holidaying on the Costa del Sol where she'd caught Daniel Kinahan's eye. He was soon secretly visiting her Dublin home and, despite trying to keep their relationship under wraps, it became gangland gossip that Kinahan had moved in on The Panda's girl. When she moved out to join him in the UAE, they'd become official. The deal was sealed when they announced the wedding, which was to take place at the Al Falak two-tiered ballroom in the Burj Al Arab, bedecked in millions of Swarovski crystals and complete with thrones for the loving couple and a 10-tier cake surrounded with hundreds of white roses.

As they prepared for their big day, Kinahan had plenty on his mind. While he was at the pinnacle of his career on the international stage and had much to celebrate, he had been repeatedly denied the one thing he wanted more than anything: the scalps of his one-time close friend James 'Mago' Gately and the older Hutch brothers, Gerry and Patsy. Things hadn't been going so well back home for some time and, more than a year into the high-profile feud with the Hutch organisation, there had been 11 murders, but he was frustrated with the calibre of victim as no big targets had been taken out. To make matters worse, a number of Kinahan's valued hitmen were in custody or on the run, and despite throwing never-ending resources at the problem, he had consistently ended up with egg on his face.

Just a month before he was due to get married, a major plan had come undone that left Kinahan and his sidekick, Sean McGovern, vulnerable on many levels. The pair had spent months planning what they believed would be the perfect hit on Gately after receiving information on where he was living in Northern Ireland. They'd used their encrypted phones to plot the kill from Dubai with Thomas 'Bomber' Kavanagh, who had formed a blood bond with Kinahan after the Regency Hotel and vowed to pump his own resources into the bloody retaliation that had followed. Kinahan had personally organised for the international hitman Imre Arakas to be flown into Ireland to carry out the job. The Estonian with the striking blue eyes and James Bond looks had built up quite a reputation as a celebrity gangster on the Costa, but Kinahan was sure that the Gardaí were too busy and too stupid to work out who he was, and believed he could float in and out of the country like a ghost without anyone knowing what had happened.

Heading for his 60th year, Arakas had a very colourful past and had spent a lengthy period in a Soviet prison, known as a gulag, where conditions were notoriously bad. In the early 1990s he had joined an Estonian organised crime gang and had taken part in a feud with a Russian outfit that killed over a hundred people. By the late 1990s he was in Spain where he was part of a large network of Eastern European criminals who worked as freelance professional killers, and he had a reputation for getting physically close to his victims, which meant that he rarely, if ever, missed. From their Gulf paradise, Kinahan and McGovern had plotted and planned the fine details of the hit, giving the job of heading up the murder cell to Douglas Glynn, a loyal lieutenant from the Hardwick Street area of Dublin. He was to join forces with Bomber's top man Peadar Keating to make sure nothing went wrong and to ensure that no intelligence would leak to the Gardaí. But Kinahan had made one huge error in judgement – he had no idea that Arakas was under surveillance and being tracked across Europe by a network of police forces. Two years earlier, Deimantas Bugavicius, nicknamed 'Diamond' and a leader of an organised crime group in Kaunas in Lithuania, had been shot dead in front of his celebrity girlfriend Vita Jakutiene, a Barbie lookalike from the girl group New Puppets. The publicity around the case had put pressure on police and ensured it was prioritised, and the Lithuanians had called in the help of the Estonians who, through their network of informants, came up with three names as those responsible for the murder, one of whom was Arakas. Co-ordinated by the Europol and Eurojust platforms, the investigators had been liaising with other jurisdictions as they mapped Arakas' movement and when he was booked on a flight to Dublin, the Garda's Drugs and Organised Crime Bureau were alerted.

Kinahan was excited as he awaited news in the Emirates. Arakas, disguised as a fisherman, had boarded a bus to Dublin city centre and walked around for two hours, oblivious to the fact he was under surveillance. The killer had even visited the north inner-city area, which had been the epicentre of the feud for more than a year. He'd walked past Champions Avenue where Patsy Hutch lived and observed the Garda car that had been a permanent fixture outside since February 2016. With his rucksack on his back, Arakas had wandered up to Avondale House where Gareth Hutch had been shot dead by Kinahan killers the previous May, before he turned towards the Sunset House pub where Eamon Cumberton, on the Kinahan payroll, had worn a Freddy Krueger mask when he killed barman Michael Barr. After his tour, Arakas went back towards O'Connell Street and into a gift shop where he purchased a wig, and later, as he stood outside Barry's Hotel, undercover officers had watched as a van embla-zoned with 'Blakestown Tyres' pulled up and he got in. Driver Stephen Fowler was 60 years of age and well known to Gardaí, and his son Eric was listed as an associate of the Kinahan organ-isation. At the Fowler home, Arakas had settled down for the night on a camp bed set up in the sitting room unaware that the property was being surrounded, and the following morning he'd found himself joined by gardaí as he rose to dress for the day. The BlackBerry phone he had been using the day before was on the couch beside him, as well as a piece of paper with Estonian writing on it and the name 'James Gately . . . in Newry' scrawled in English. When the Estonian from the note was translated, it read: 'Eight row, second picture visible'.

Kinahan was raging. He'd spent a fortune on the encrypted BlackBerry phones, which were password-protected devices that had been handed out to all his operatives on the ground. The contents were supposed to be impossible to access and could be deleted remotely, but the Gardaí had been quick and photo-graphed the thread of messages that were open on it. Kinahan and McGovern had spent the previous day messaging back and forth with Arakas under their user handles 'Bon' and 'Knife'. They'd sent instructions about the building where Gately was living and details about his car, a champagne-coloured Toyota Avensis. Arakas had responded with his plans, requesting a silencer for the 'dog'. 'So far, in case I'm totally alone it seems it's possible to take him down when he comes out of the car . . . Also there is a trick that won't allow him to close the front door behind him and I could follow him to the corridor . . . I see there what I can do. Best regards,' the texts read. The final message from Kinahan's 'Bon' phone to Arakas' device read: 'We have a tracker on his car so my idea is when he goes out in car we know he is coming back we tracks him live when he is heading back to his apt when he is 10 minutes away he get in position and he parks in the same space always so then you have him.' The arrest of Arakas was bad enough, but the others caught up in the plan meant that heavy prison sentences awaited some of his key men.

Kinahan was furious with nobody more than Gately, who'd dodged a bullet again and, in a final push to make his wedding day even more special, he'd paid hitman Caolin Smyth to take on the job. He'd got to Gately and shot him five times as he sat in his car at a petrol station, but Gately had survived and Smyth had been caught. Newspaper reports from Ireland had detailed how an injured Gately had refused to make a statement, but from his hospital bed had shouted that the feud wouldn't end until Daniel Kinahan was dead.

As the big day arrived, Kinahan managed to put his troubles behind him. He stepped out with a smile plastered across his face, met by the huge gathering of guests from across the globe. It was everything the couple had expected when it came to style and class in the seven-star venue, and world boxing champion Tyson Fury, who Kinahan was secretly advising, was even there for a touch of celebrity. Kinahan's boxing friends stuck together, including coaches and pals from Spain where he had first founded his MGM club along with his friend Macklin. Scottish business-woman Sandra Vaughan, who had just been announced as the new owner of the MGM company, was there with her husband, Danny, a boxing coach and friend of Kinahan. The guests were an international bunch; there were Emiratis – in particular, a member of the royal family who Kinahan had befriended – along with South Americans, Dutch, Belgians, Italians, Bosnians and a good scattering of accents from the UK. Johnny Morrissey and his wife, Nicola, enjoyed a seat at a prime table having travelled from Spain, and they mixed with the UK contingent, which included Richard Cashman, the notorious business partner of the infamous John 'Goldfinger' Palmer – the timeshare gangster once reported to be worth £300 million, who had been shot dead in the back garden of his Essex home in June 2015. 'Dapper Don' Christy Kinahan and his partner, Nessy Yildirim, sat at the top table with Christopher Jnr and his young partner from Dublin, and a scattering of children from all three Kinahans' various relationships. Members of the Robinson family sat separately with friends of the bride from back home.

While he showed off his wealth and his status to the ordinary guests, Kinahan had business that day too. What he didn't know was that the DEA were also secretly in attendance, thanks to top-of-the-range intelligence technology, and that back in the Netherlands a chain of events had begun which would bring down his house of cards. The sudden interest by the Americans in the Kinahan nuptials was no coincidence; they suspected that he had formed an alliance with underworld mobsters in Spain, creating a European cocaine super cartel which had made him and others phenomenally rich. In fact, since his arrival in the Gulf in 2016, he had gone from millionaire to billionaire, such were the profits from the European cocaine market. As undercover officers using the latest surveillance technology watched the proceedings, they could see Dutch mobster Ridouan Taghi arriving. He was one of the top men of a brutal Dutch–Moroccan gang in the Netherlands that had been involved in a vicious gang war, which had broken out in 2012 over the theft of a large cocaine shipment which had entered Europe through Antwerp and was destined for the UK market. Sixteen murders had been linked to the feud, which had culminated in one so grisly it had shocked politicians across Europe: a decapitated body was discovered in a burning car in Amsterdam and later a severed head was left on the pavement outside a shisha lounge on the busy Amstelveenseweg Street. The remains were those of Nabil Amzieb, a known gang member and rival of the outfit headed by Ridouan Taghi.

Taghi had fled to Dubai followed by a blaze of publicity as he became the Netherlands' most wanted man. Beside him at the wedding table was drug trafficker Ricardo Riquelme Vega, aka 'El Rico', who was known in gangland as the most dangerous Chilean in the world. It was suspected that he was key to the purchase and transport of drugs across the globe as well as being behind many of the gang murders in the Netherlands, including that of the dismembered Amzieb. He was also suspected of putting together a daring plan to try to break out his business partner from an Irish jail. Naoufal Fassih, known as 'The Belly', had been picked up during a Garda search of a Kinahan safe house in Dublin in 2016, and he was being held pending his extradition to the Netherlands on murder charges. When intelligence filtered through about a plan to help him escape, he had been moved to the top-security Portlaoise Prison and the military had stepped in to ensure it didn't happen. 'El Rico' Vega had been based in Dubai since 2015 and was suspected of operating under a number of passports, including those issued in the UAE, Chile and Holland.

Italian Raffaele Imperiale mingled with the Dutch mobsters too. He had swapped the picturesque town of Castellammare, overlooking the Bay of Naples, for Amsterdam when he went there to run a coffee shop and legally sell cannabis, but he had quickly expanded his business to organising massive shipments of cocaine for the Camorra, earning him between €15 million and €20 million a year. Put on trial in Naples, he had relocated to Dubai, which had no extradition treaty with Italy. The last of the big fish picked up by DEA officers at the wedding was the Bosnian Edin Gacanin, the leader of the Tito and Dino Cartel, also known as a 'European Escobar'. He had been involved in shipping cocaine to Europe and onwards to the Balkans regions where he'd been recruiting enforcers, couriers and dealers, while also laundering funds throughout Europe, Slovenia, and Bosnia and Herzegovina.

The fact that all four were in attendance was a start for investigators probing their links, but their presence alone wouldn't be enough to prove the business relationship between the group, who were suspected of controlling almost a third of Europe's €10.5 billion yearly cocaine market and believed to have been working together since around 2014.

Around that time, El Rico was suspected of making a power play by ordering the murder of rival mob boss Samir Bouyakhrichan, nicknamed 'Scarface', who was shot dead in Spain. Piecing together the details of what had gone on, officers from Ireland and the Netherlands believed that it was the murder of Scarface that cemented the partnership between the Dutch and the Irish on the Costa. At the time of the hit, Scarface, Europe's biggest cocaine lord, was in a restaurant with Fassih, who placed his arm around his shoulders minutes before a gunman ran at them and opened fire. Officers even suspected that Kinahan had provided the hitman as the two groups saw their opportunity for a ruthless takeover of the cocaine market. Fassih had fled the Costa and remained in hiding until he showed up in Dublin.

It was at that same time, just days before the Scarface murder, that things had turned sour in the Kinahan organisation and when Gary Hutch made a first attempt on the life of Daniel Kinahan, which had resulted in boxer Jamie Moore being shot at his villa in Estepona. Days after the Scarface hit, Dublin drug dealer Gerard 'Hatchet' Kavanagh was shot dead in a Marbella bar, a murder believed to have been sanctioned by Kinahan and 'Bomber' Kavanagh, with whom he'd worked. By the time Daniel Kinahan had got married, the extraordinary relationship between the Dutch Mocro-Maffia and the Irish was being linked to at least 16 murders in the Netherlands, four in Spain, and the 11 assassinations at that point in the Irish feud.

∽

In the months prior to the wedding, events outside the gang's control meant that the secrets of the blood pact had started to emerge and spurred the DEA to place a major surveillance operation on Kinahan's big day. It all started in early 2017 when a Dutch gang member identified as 'Nabil B' handed himself in at a police station in the Netherlands saying his life was in danger, that he'd been threatened and wanted to talk to police about underworld killings. He told officers that he was involved in organising murders on behalf of his boss Taghi, and in one case the wrong person was killed, setting a powerful crime family against him. Nabil B said he was left with two options, die or start talking, so he decided to go to the cops. Between January and May of 2017 he made a series of statements linking Taghi, El Rico, Fassih, Imperiale and Kinahan.

At the same time Nabil B was talking, Dutch investigators were making serious inroads with a number of probes into encrypted phone networks, which had been sparked by the assassination attempt of Peter Raap in Holland in 2015. Raap had been driving when he came under attack, not realising that his enemies had a tracker device on his car and had been following him. Thinking quickly, he swerved his car over to the side of the road and miraculously survived a hail of 35 bullets by jumping into a river and staying submerged until the attackers fled. Unknown to the gang, headed by Fassih, police had bugged their getaway vehicle and later arrested suspects, retrieving two mobile phones enabled with Pretty Good Privacy (PGP), an encryption system for emails and texts. Fassih went on the run and wasn't discovered until he was found in Dublin with seven phones, three of which were PGP-enabled devices. Gardaí sent the phones, which were linked to the Ennetcom network, to the Netherlands, and six months after the failed assassination attempt on Raap, Dutch police arrested Ennetcom owner Danny Manupassa on suspicion of money laundering, and they filed an urgent request to Canada where they believed the servers were held. In the months that followed, a Canadian judge had authorised a search on an address in Toronto where officers found the server, and the data was given to the Dutch, who had worked out how to decrypt the 3.6 million messages. While it remained to be seen if the information could be used in a court prosecution, they were able to use Nabil B's information and look through the messages for back-up. Sure enough, they found evidence that the Dutch trio had, indeed, teamed up in the world of cocaine smuggling and in underworld killings. Coupled with the information garnered from the Burj Al Arab wedding, the process to dismantle the cocaine super cartel began.

As cocaine continued to move across the world and Kinahan and his cohorts enjoyed the fruits of their labour, a massive international operation involving the co-operation of police forces in Europe and the US got underway. First to fall foul of the operation was El Rico, who was dramatically arrested in Santiago in October 2017, just months after the nuptials. He had just returned to Chile from Dubai and was kept under surveillance in the days before his arrest, carefree days which he had spent with a female companion oblivious to the huge sting that was about to nab him. While he was in custody in Chile, Dutch authorities sought his extradition, saying they wanted him for controlling a major drug gang, trafficking narcotics, money laundering and ordering murders, including the beheading. Extradition papers were issued and El Rico was soon returned under massive security to the Netherlands, where Fassih had been handed down a life sentence for the murder of political dissident Mohammad-Reza Kolahi Samadi, allegedly on behalf of the Iranian government, and 18 years for the failed assassination of Raap.

In a warning sign to the cocaine cowboys of Europe that their phones would be their undoing, a key piece of evidence that convinced judges of Fassih's guilt was a watch found in the Dublin apartment where he'd been arrested in April 2016. He was in Ireland when a PGP account with the handles 'Dirty' and 'Big Head' had sent messages via the Ennetcom network ordering the hits, but the same account had ordered an Audemars Piguet Royal Oak Offshore Michael Schumacher wristwatch, which had been in his possession and seized by gardaí. Given El Rico's botched plans to bust Fassih out of Irish prison, Dutch authorities took no chances with him in the Netherlands, placing him in an extra secure prison and always transferring him to and from court in an armoured car for fear he would escape.

Facing drugs, weapons and money laundering charges, his arrival in court in Amsterdam was akin to a scene from the Netflix series *Narcos*, with a helicopter circling overhead and masked policemen with machine guns securing the streets. The court heard that officers were using encrypted communications from the Ennetcom server to piece together any involvement he may have had in directing his gang 'missions', but said they were still examining the technology. In an edition of *Panorama* magazine, one of the best-known publications in the Netherlands, El Rico was profiled as the son of a refugee who came to the Netherlands after the Augusto Pinochet coup of 1973. In the 1990s his father was arrested and sentenced for drug trafficking, and El Rico soon followed in his footsteps, becoming a close associate of the notorious Amsterdam crime boss Gwenette Martha. In 1999 he was caught in Germany trying to sell cocaine to undercover officers and was sentenced to 11 years in prison. On his release, he returned straight to the Amsterdam underworld and *Panorama* pointed out that Martha had been shot dead in Amstelveen just three months before Scarface died in Benahavis, clearing the way for El Rico's move to the top of the cocaine ladder.

While individual trials moved through the justice system, the Netherlands was ultimately preparing for a large case against Ridouan Taghi and up to 16 of his loyal servants, who it was decided would go on trial together for a number of murders and other criminal activities. Taghi was on the run and had gone to ground in Dubai, but the events that followed were to be a wakeup call to Europe about just how dangerous drug gangs had become and how they, like their Mexican cartel partners, had ultimately morphed into narco terrorists prepared to take on the very foundations of the State to save their businesses. Just like Pablo Escobar had done in Colombia decades before, the Mocro-Maffia went to war with civil society like never before.

First came the murder of a man known as 'Reduan B', the brother of the then state witness Nabil B, who'd agreed to give evidence in exchange for the halving of his own sentence for his involvement in the murder of a rival. The killing, understood to have been ordered by the exiled Taghi, had a chilling effect on the legal system, which was reliant on Nabil B and his evidence in forthcoming trials. Then, on the morning of September 18th, Nabil B's lawyer, Derk Wiersum, was shot and killed near his home in Amsterdam. The father of two was a well-known advocate who had built his career in criminal law and had worked as a deputy judge, focusing on organised crime in the years leading up to his death. The news sent shockwaves across Europe. Never before had a criminal lawyer been targeted in such a blatant way in an effort to disrupt the court process, and the murder forced the Netherlands to provide extra security for up to 30 people closely involved in what became known as the Marengo trial, including judges and prosecutors.

In December 2019 Taghi was finally arrested in a luxury villa by Dubai police in what was described as a joint operation with authorities in the Netherlands. He'd been living like a virtual hermit at the property and had tried to flee as soon as he saw the cops. Taghi had become the most wanted man in the Netherlands since the two murders he was suspected of ordering from his desert outpost, and Dubai authorities immediately sanctioned his expulsion. He was brought back by Dutch military under intense security and placed in isolation in the Vught maximum security prison for terrorists to await trial.

Marengo opened at the beginning of 2020 in a specially modified bunker courtroom with extraordinary security, but the emergence of the COVID-19 pandemic caused massive delays due to the number of lawyers, solicitors, police and prosecutors who needed to be there for the 16 defendants, not to mention the media interest. A social distancing nightmare followed as the trial limped along every time there was a window of opportunity for a hearing.

In the meantime, one of Fassih's cohorts, described as 'Muhammed S', went on trial and evidence was given that he'd visited Dublin while the Moroccan hid out in the Kinahan safe house. Dutch authorities said the pair ran a 'well-oiled machine' shipping cocaine in containers and then using wet bags to dump their product in the North Sea, where they were picked up by fishermen using tracking technology, the methods unveiled through the Ennetcom trawl. Evidence heard Muhammed and his co-accused used the specially purchased BlackBerry phones to organise the shipment of cocaine on large container ships and then sent co-ordinates of where the contraband was dumped for collection. A fisherman, the court heard, was threatened by the narco terrorists when he was shown a picture of his child and instructions on what to do. At the same time, in a separate court in Amsterdam, judges heard that the Netherlands Forensic Institute had not finished its research in the case of El Rico, and while he had been convicted on money laundering and other charges, he was still under investigation for his role in a number of murders. Prosecutors told the court that whether he directed murders using phones was also still under investigation. One of the communications cited to the court involved a murder plot in Dubai. 'Two ninjas are ready,' said one message sent to El Rico's phone. Others showed requests for contacts with the Medellín Cartel.

As the Marengo trial continued in fits and starts, a curious detail emerged about a surveillance operation in Dubai that had almost led to the arrest of Daniel Kinahan back in the summer of 2019. As the Dutch worked with the Emirates under the codename 26CapeCoral to find where Taghi was hiding, two lawyers had been placed under surveillance as police suspected they were heading to the Gulf to meet their client, Taghi. When they landed in Dubai, they were picked up by undercover police who followed them to the lobby of a hotel where they met with one client and then another man who was initially believed to be Taghi. But as police considered moving in on the man, they realised it was not the target at all but was, in fact, his lookalike Daniel Kinahan. They pulled back and let the meeting resume.

Across the world, the focus on the takedown of the Super Cartel continued with a level of co-operation between police forces never seen before. In Colombia Taghi's right-hand man, Saïd Razzouki, was arrested, and President Iván Duque Márquez signed an extradition order to return him to the Netherlands. A reward of €100,000 had been placed on his head, but still it had taken two years to track him down and arrest him in Medellín. Details of his arrest showed the commitment of the DEA in the process, as they had facilitated a lengthy undercover operation involving agents staying in two safe houses for months to determine his location.

Marengo proceeded with evidence of intercepted messages showing the ruthlessness of Taghi when it came to death. Prosecutors told the trial that killers were told 'no matter what time or morning or night light, if it sleeps, you will be well rewarded.' They were told to carry out hits 'calm and stylish'. Taghi and Razzouki were the leaders of the gang, the court was told, who set out to ruthlessly stamp their mark on the Dutch underworld and anyone considered a threat was put on Taghi's death list, including innocent people he feared could provide information to the police. He micro-managed some killings, ordering the hit teams to put three bullets in the head of one victim.

But even behind bars and facing a life sentence, it seemed he wasn't prepared to give up without a fight. On July 15th, 2021, the Netherlands' most famous journalist and campaigner Peter R. de Vries was walking out of a television studio of RTL Boulevard in Amsterdam, where he had appeared as a guest on a show, when he was approached on the busy Lange Leidsedwarsstraat and shot in the head. As he lay on the ground, a video was recorded of him appearing to struggle for breath before his hands fell to his side. In the months previous, the 64-year-old had been working with the Crown witness Nabil B. His death sparked a wave of condemnation across Europe and beyond. Dutch Prime Minister Mark Rutte, who would later be placed under 24-hour security, said the shooting was 'shocking and incomprehensible' and King Willem-Alexander and Queen Maxima said that journalists 'must be free to carry out their important work without threats'. The President of the European Council, Charles Michel, called it an attack against journalism, saying: 'We will relentlessly continue to defend the freedom of the press.' The International Federation of Journalists called the murder 'another tragic blow to press freedom in Europe'.

Behind bars, the former street dealer turned cocaine million-aire Ridouan Taghi became the chief suspect and efforts to work out just how he could order such a killing from a high-security jail and while on trial began. But still, despite the outrage, the grief and the despair, cocaine continued to flood in through Rotterdam and Antwerp like never before, as an insatiable demand for the white powder drove tsunamis of the drug through the borders and pushed the European market value over the €10 billion mark. That cocaine had become the fuel powering a whole new world of organised crime was just becoming clear.

CHAPTER NINE

DECRYPTING THE COCAINE MOBS

Vincent Ramos had bigger problems on his plate when the Irish Criminal Assets Bureau officer arrived at the San Diego jail where he was being held after his business, Phantom Secure, an encrypted phone company, had been the subject of a massive FBI sting. It was just months after Ennetcom data had fallen into the hands of the Dutch investigators probing the existence of a European cocaine super cartel, and Ramos was facing a lengthy jail term for facilitating serious crime. He had been quizzed by police from the US, Canada and Australia about biker gangs, drug cartels and transglobal crime networks who had purchased his BlackBerry phones and used them to do their business under the radar of law enforcement. Phantom Secure was a business plan dreamed up in 2008 by the middle-class marketing executive with the pretty wife and two children, but the start-up which offered PGP-enabled phones had attracted a far from legitimate customer base and Ramos had got in deep. He took the form from the CAB officer and signed it off, indicating he was agreeable to the Section 4a order under the Proceeds of Crime legislation that handed dirty money over to the Irish exchequer. Just 10 months after identifying funds of more than €500,000 in two Irish bank accounts, and a number of companies used by Ramos in Dublin, a judge in the Irish High Court brought down the hammer on the CAB's case against Phantom Secure and announced that it was case over, deal done, and probably one of the quickest turnarounds in the Bureau's history with a nice bit of pocket change for the Irish exchequer.

Ramos had never even been in Ireland; he'd simply used it as a stop-off point to wash his dirty funds, moving them around time zones and banking territories, until he could get his hands on them as supposedly 'clean' earnings. He had established the accounts after using a totally innocent company to help set him up as a 'businessman' in Ireland, to whom he spoke in person over the phone, registered his address with their city centre offices, and filed documents with the Companies Registration Office in Dublin. His story seemed legitimate, his demeanour businesslike, and nobody had any reason to suspect that he was a vital cog in the wheels of the top end of organised crime.

The takedown of Vincent Ramos and his Phantom Secure company was the start of an intriguing plot which resulted in the creation of ANOM: the FBI's own futuristic network which promised drug dealers and killers security to talk freely but trapped them in the process. It also marked a significant step for law enforcement across the world, who'd been dealing with an incredible cocaine gold rush for more than a decade, which had empowered the mighty cartels and sent street gangs into gun battles as everyone fought for a piece of the action. The fact of the matter was that while officers were trying to fight crime with their usual methods of intelligence gathering, tip-offs and expensive surveillance operations, the criminals had been chatting away on their bullet-proof phones secure in the knowledge that they could do business without being bothered.

Phantom Secure had been set up innocuously, much like Ramos had done business in Ireland, and had been registered in Richmond in Canada. On its first website, Ramos described himself as the CEO and wrote: 'I truly believe in our right to privacy and like many internet users, I have always had a concern with the security of my email storage and communications.' Phantom not only used a version of PGP, but also locked down BlackBerry devices so they had no camera and couldn't work as an ordinary phone. There was a remote delete feature, which meant that Phantom Secure could wipe the phone on demand. Servers were located in Panama, and sales were at first limited to Canada but later spread to Asia, the US and Australia.

It was an FBI field office in San Diego that had first started to investigate the phones and who was using them. When local law enforcement made an arrest and found one of the phones, they decided to strip it down and realised it had no function other than communication within a closed-loop network. This resulted in the FBI and the US Attorney's office getting together to conduct the investigation to target Ramos and his top executives. They discovered that 20,000 phones had made their way across the criminal landscape, from the Middle East to Europe, and even into the hands of members of the Sinaloa Cartel. During the investigation, the FBI turned an insider, who said he was working on the next generation of the encrypted devices, into one of their own operatives and set him to work secretly for them on the system called ANOM. Ramos wound up pleading guilty to the charge of racketeering conspiracy in the US and was sentenced to nine years in prison. Danny Manupassa met the same fate in the Netherlands when he was eventually convicted of purposely facilitating crime and sentenced to four and a half years. Neither Manupassa nor Ramos had backgrounds in crime; rather, they were tech forerunners who saw the benefits of selling encrypted phones to people who wanted to stay in the dark, but there were others eyeing up the new technology with a far greater reach into the underworld.

∽

George 'The Penguin' Mitchell undoubtedly had the criminal calibre to become a salesman to gangland and his little black book of contacts reflected his globe-trotting career as an international cocaine and ecstasy dealer. So, when he decided to move into the area of encrypted phone networks, he found himself wire tapped through a huge German police investigation into just what was going on in a huge Cold War bunker in the sleepy town of Traben-Trarbach on the River Moselle. The extraordinary story, which resulted in a lengthy trial in Trier and the jailing of a number of operatives from the bunker, gave the first proper insight into Mitchell's vast criminal empire, but it also showed how the encrypted phones were game changers for everyone – from the violent drug tsars of the Medellín Cartel to the Hells Angels biker gangs. Mitchell, at almost 70, wasn't the first criminal that people would have expected to invest in such complex and modern technology, but bad health had left him nervous and he wanted to ensure that when he passed on, he could leave a legacy to his extended family – and the more legitimate his last will and testament the better. A great-grandfather, he was known for his old-fashioned approach to staying out of trouble, but that didn't stop him seeing a good investment for €500,000 into the new encryption provider, which his pal Herman Xennt was developing at an underground bunker in Germany. The service, just like Ennetcom, was to exist in the unregulated but legitimate world of secure communications offering total privacy to customers, complete with a 'panic button' so messages could be deleted in an emergency. The plan was to sell expensive €1,200 a unit BlackBerry phones, coupled with a €3,000 secure app for communications, with an annual service fee that guaranteed customers they would not be bothered by the authorities. The system, developed in Warsaw in Poland, was to be marketed as the most secure in the world, and Mitchell was going to get his friends to buy it. As luck would have it for Mitchell and Xennt, just as they got near to completing the technical details on their system, Danny Manupassa and his Ennetcom company were shut down, leaving a huge opportunity in the market.

Mitchell and Xennt were an odd coupling and they had met first in Amsterdam, where the Dubliner had moved in the mid-1990s after an ecstasy factory he had built in Ireland was discovered by Gardaí. He'd settled near Schiphol Airport in a modest house so as not to draw too much attention to himself, and at that point specialised in the supply of ecstasy and heroin to the Irish market. But in 1998 he was caught in the Dutch capital unloading £5 million sterling worth of stolen computer equipment from an Irish truck. During his trial, he said he was involved in an 'import-export company' and insisted he was a legitimate businessman, but he was jailed for a year. After his release, he expanded his drugs business greatly and began dealing directly with major Colombian drug cartels – who'd placed operatives on the ground in Amsterdam, with the Russian mafia, and with Afghanistan's heroin producers, through Turkish agents. Around the same time Mitchell became a close friend and acquaintance of Xennt, a computer-obsessed odd bod who had purchased an old Cold War bunker where he had set up Cyberbunker, a web domain company he was hoping to develop. In 2002, when there was a fire at the premises, an ecstasy-making factory was discovered in an underground area and Xennt and others were investigated, but his company later dissolved and the eccentric Dutchman went to ground.

Mitchell became increasingly low profile and stayed on the move around Europe, basing himself between the Netherlands and Spain's southern coast, where he kept a nondescript two-bedroom apartment and a small three-door car. Until 2015, when he was tracked down by the *Sunday World* newspaper to Traben-Trarbach in the Moselle Valley in Germany, nothing had been heard of the notorious Penguin in decades, but his presence there with Xennt raised the interest of local police. Xennt had purchased another bunker in the hills above the town, an ugly cast-off from the Cold War, and registered it as a data centre in 2013, promising politicians that he would create employment. But when police realised who he and the small, portly Irishman with him were, they decided to investigate further.

Over the following two years, Mitchell was the subject of wiretaps as police sent undercover officers into the bunker to find that it was a dark-net superhighway where the encrypted phone service had been under development. Warrants for the wiretaps submitted to the courts lifted the lid on the scale of Mitchell's extraordinary criminal network and his direct deals for cocaine shipments with Colombians. They showed how as part of his sales pitch, he had shipped sample phones to customers in Bogotá and Medellín. The warrants revealed that he was suspected of smuggling cocaine, along with Glock weapons, from the Netherlands to Northern Ireland; shipping cocaine, three tonnes at a time, from North Africa via Spain and Portugal to the Netherlands in containers of oranges; and that, in November 2016, was the owner of a 283-kilo cocaine seizure in Brazil headed for Europe. When 1.4 tonnes of the compressed drug was discovered on a shipment from Colombia to Valencia in December 2015, cops also said it belonged to

Mitchell. German police admitted they lost sight of Mitchell in 2017, but before they did, they had placed him under surveillance as he travelled around Europe and even met with a Hells Angels president from one of the German chapters in France and later in Frankfurt in Germany. It was there in a café that Mitchell was recorded trying to tempt him with an unbeatable investment opportunity in Ireland, a €4.5 billion project, which he said was a 'lumen' energy -saving solution at an 'unreal profit margin'. Mitchell ended the conversation by naming an individual in Ireland suspected of being a money launderer.

Later, officers realised that the Hells Angel was using the encrypted app after he sought an email address for registration and, weeks later, they were listening in when the contact told him his Hells Angel associate – believed to be the notorious Frank Armin Hanebuth, the alleged leader of the Hells Angels in Europe – would meet him in Ibiza. Hanebuth, cops realised, also had Mitchell's app. Under surveillance they were seen back in Germany with Xennt at a meeting to discuss the Hells Angels group taking on the BlackBerry phones and using the app. By the end of the summer, Mitchell and his contact travelled again to Ibiza on a Eurowings flight from Cologne, with the Penguin picking up the tab.

Back in Germany, at the small airport of Weeze on the Dutch border, Mitchell was observed getting a taxi with one of the workers from the bunker and, a month later at the Delicious restaurant in Berlin, Mitchell, accompanied by his 'Minister for Finance', conducted another meeting where he agreed to meet Hells Angels representatives in the Hyatt Hotel to discuss the encryption technology. At the Hyatt, monitored phone calls registered after the meeting picked up Mitchell telling a contact to buy cheap android phones from China for the app, saying that the meeting went well and he would be furnishing a computer and ten phones to the Hells Angels representative. There would be another meeting to secure much larger sales, he concluded. The Penguin later phoned his partner, Khadija Bouchiba, and told her: 'It went well, the project will be larger than that in China.' More meetings followed, with Mitchell remarking: 'Don't push them or they'll think they have power, wait until they call.' According to the investigation files: 'BlackBerry phones are encrypted using the Cyberbunker. Mitchell provides contacts with the international scene. Bandidos bought several devices in the Netherlands. Mitchell is currently in contact with **** (Hells Angels confidante).' The papers say that while investigators cannot make factual conclusions, they believe that Mitchell also sold the system to customers in Bogotá and Medellín.

At one point during the probe, prosecutors had applied to have 16 of Mitchell's phones tapped, but despite the amount of time and resources put into the operation, police were hampered by the secret language and codewords used by The Penguin, which had been developed over years at the highest echelons of organised crime. In one conversation overheard on the wiretap, Mitchell spelt out that he would only talk when he sent the other person a secure phone with an encrypted app: 'It's the only way. All my friends use it, everybody.' In another call, police heard Mitchell talking about the 'boxes of oranges in Malaga' and discussing how to get to a bank to pay for them. He tells an unidentified caller that 700 'boxes of oranges', his codeword for cocaine, should be in the warehouse but a third party 'will still need 800 boxes'. Over the course of the investigation, the wily Mitchell never let his guard down and talked about 'parking at Starbucks', his 'children going to nightclubs drinking champagne', 'dumping money' and meeting 'Colombian people' in Malaga. Associates were referred to by nicknames like 'Uncle', 'Slimeball', 'Pigeon Man', 'Paco', 'Mo' and 'Crazy Horse'. Talking about encrypted phones, he said: 'There will be no problem. A very large company is currently using it. And someone is trying to get them into the Tunisian government. Right now . . . we urgently need programmers, but the outlines are top notch. Because everyone can make an app, but it's very, very complicated.'

Rhineland police culminated their investigation in a spectacular raid in 2018 during which 650 armed police surrounded the bunker and seized control of it. The Penguin's business partner Herman Xennt was among more than 10 people arrested, and he was later jailed for his role in making illegal platforms in the bunker, but Mitchell was long gone. In court papers, however, the wire taps and files painted a picture of the life of an international cocaine smuggler always on the move: to meetings in Majorca and Ibiza, to see clients in Scandinavia, the Netherlands and Spain. Mitchell talked at one point of 'Paco' who he said had flown to London, Cork and then back to the Netherlands in one day. Paco is 'useful', he remarked. Mitchell swapped his phones constantly: a German number one day, a Spanish number the next, and then a Dutch one. He rented cars, arranged meetings, got picked up at airports by a network of chauffeurs, talked of luring investors with big profit promises, and lent money to a close circle. Along with his 'Finance Minister', an unidentified associate living in Malaga, he talked about investing in various projects including €700,000 in the Traben-Trarbach data centre. Files detail how the pair discussed investments in servers in Venezuela, wastewater in Canada, and gold in the United Arab Emirates, Laos, Dubai and Katra in India. They chatted about investments in platinum in Belgium, oil in Colombia, respiratory masks for health authorities in China and Indonesia, road machines in Nigeria, blue-chip stock in the City of London, and swimming pools in Asia. While Mitchell managed to waddle off to the sunset, his pal Xennt faced trial for dark net activity. But it was the next big bust on an encrypted phone network that would rock the world of organised crime to its core.

∽

The massive EncroChat phone hack was a first for policing and one of the most sensational takedowns of organised crime groups ever. For officers involved in the massive cross-border probe, which began when French police started investigating phones using the EncroChat platform, it was wearing an invisible cloak at the top tables of organised crime. EncroChat gave itself away in its marketing, with its website proudly boasting tamper-proof handsets, live customer support, remote message destruction, rapid 'panic wipe', and the ability to masquerade as a normal android phone. Cameras, microphones, GPS functions and data ports were all removed.

Over a period of years, the French had worked with their Dutch counterparts and somehow managed to crack into Encro-Chat, listening in live for months before moving in on hundreds of criminals, stash houses and weapons factories. The encrypted platform had been particularly popular in the Netherlands, Belgium, the UK and Ireland, and users had no idea that the police were eavesdropping until the service pushed out an SOS message on June 13th, 2020 alerting them that the system had been breached and urging them to throw away their phones. At that point, as police moved in, in the UK alone 746 suspects were arrested and £54 million was seized along with 77 firearms and two tonnes of drugs. Several suspected corrupt police and law enforcement officers were also identified in the operation, which was codenamed 'Venetic'. The Dutch launched a wave of drug raids and arrests, uncovering 8,000 kilos of cocaine and 1,200 kilos of crystal meth while dismantling 19 synthetic drugs labs and uncovering a torture chamber hidden in a shipping container, complete with a dentist's chair. For months law enforcement had been picking off drug dealers and firearms importers and muscling in on plots to kill, with criminals unaware that their communications platform was causing the problem. The NCA described the hack as the equivalent of breaking the Nazis' World War II Enigma code, while the Metropolitan police said some of those arrested were serious criminals who operated without being known to them.

Trucker Thomas Maher was the first criminal to lose his freedom after the hack, pleading guilty to conspiring to import Class A drugs into Ireland. The demise of the greedy trucker would be a lesson to all criminals that nothing is above the law, not even an encrypted communications system that was supposed to be impenetrable. For two decades, Thomas and his wife, Joanna, enjoyed an enviable lifestyle as a 'haulage company boss' and a 'hair salon manager'. Instead, they were milking it from criminal gangs who needed to transport their goods in the same way ordinary businesses do. He proudly told neighbours that he had worked hard for everything he had, but underneath the veneer of a family man was a gangland fixer who provided a vital service to drug mobs, one which literally keeps the show on the road. Maher had an insatiable appetite for money and took work from warring criminals, including both sides of the Hutch and Kinahan feud. He was known as a tight-fisted facilitator who linked drivers with drug mobs, but who always made sure he got his cut. He regularly commanded payments of as much as €3,000 for making a phone call and putting a long-distance trucker in touch with lower-ranking members of gangs who had been charged with handling cocaine and even guns for transport. His EncroChat handle was 'Satirical' and he talked freely with pals, though he used codenames for places, like 'flat' for the Netherlands, and for the drugs that he was arranging to transport. He whinged about lockdowns but boasted that he could wait until things returned to normal: 'I'm at this game the last 20 odd years pal. I'm not an overnighter so I know the way of plays.' Messages intercepted by police, and which firmly linked him with the incriminating texts, included photos of his feet, which he had sent to show how unwell he was and how difficult he found it to walk.

Even though Maher had come on the police's radar after he sold a truck which was later driven by Maurice Robinson when 39 migrants were discovered dead in the back of it in Essex, he continued to trust the phone and never thought his messages could be read by police. A criminal fixer and two money launderers who worked with Maher were the only three EncroChat arrests in Ireland, despite the fact that Gardaí received the live intelligence along with their UK counterparts. A decision made by Garda management at the time not to release the information or pass it on to local units shocked European partners on the operation. The Maher-linked arrests were only made as Gardaí were operating in tandem with officers from the NCA, who had intelligence that he'd arranged for the movement of the cash.

In the UK Peter 'Fatso' Mitchell washed up in the EncroChat wave. He was once king of the Costa del Crime until the Kinahan mob turned on him and he was forced into hiding for more than 10 years, finally showing up in Yorkshire working as a driver for a cocaine gang. A murky gangland story involving double crosses, greed and paranoia lay at the heart of Fatso Mitchell's journey to a prison cell in Wales where he was locked up for 10 years for his role in the 'Avengers' coke gang. Mitchell, the last member of the notorious John Gilligan gang, had been secretly building his wealth by flooding South Wales with cocaine before his EncroChat phone exposed his criminal operation, and the criminal once dubbed 'the one that got away' by Gardaí was eventually forced to do porridge.

Mitchell was lucky to escape with his life when Christy Kinahan Snr had sanctioned his murder, weeks after he was arrested in Belgium for money laundering and police corruption in 2008. Fatso shut up his Paparazzi bar outside Puerto Banús, which had become an HQ for international gangsters, and ran for his life after miraculously surviving a daylight shooting six months after his pal Paddy Doyle, a hitman, was set up and murdered by the mob. A Kinahan hitman, who would himself fall out with the mob, is suspected of carrying out the botched shooting, which failed when the assassin stumbled. Fatso had established a thriving business between Peurto Banús and Amsterdam after slipping the net of the Veronica Guerin murder team. With partners in Liverpool, over the years he had often worked with George 'The Penguin' Mitchell and was in regular contact with John 'The Coach' Traynor, who was moving between the Netherlands and Margate on the UK's south coast. Traynor was another member of the Gilligan gang who had slipped the net, but was suspected of being the 'contact' of Guerin who had set her up by passing on information about her court plans to his boss.

Fatso Mitchell had cemented his status as one of the top dogs on the Costa when he purchased the Paparazzi bar and held a grand opening, promising good-value food and late-night entertainment. But it was really a meeting place for drug dealers, including the Kinahans, who brokered deals with their customers from all over Europe and regularly arranged to pool their resources and purchase in bulk directly from the producers – all under the guise of having ordinary business lunches. Neither Kinahan Snr nor his right-hand man John Cunningham liked Mitchell, so any business done between the two organisations was brokered through Daniel, who was regularly spotted meeting Fatso at the bar.

On February 4th, 2008, Fatso's pal Paddy Doyle was murdered while he was sitting in a 4x4 with Gary Hutch and Freddie Thompson, and while investigators initially suspected the Russian mafia, who they had been told Doyle had fought with during a night out, they quickly realised he had been killed by his own and that his childhood friend Hutch had set the trap, despite returning home to carry his coffin. Two months later Spanish cops raided Paparazzi bar and shut it down over 'licensing irregularities', and when a month after that the Dapper Don Christy Kinahan was swooped on by cops in Antwerp, he blamed Mitchell for his arrest. Daniel Kinahan went to see his father in prison and agreed to take control of business in Spain while his mess was sorted out, and officers suspect the same meeting sealed Mitchell's fate.

In August 2008 Fatso had been sipping a drink at the El Jardin bar when a hitman in a balaclava ran at him with a gun. When he dived for cover, the gunman slipped and managed to hit his target just in the shoulder and leg, while two other people sitting nearby were injured. In hospital Fatso realised his days were numbered and put his home and bar up for sale; soon after, another bar replaced Paparazzi as the meeting place for criminals. This time the proprietor was Daniel Kinahan and the bar was called the Auld Dubliner.

Two years after he disappeared, Fatso showed up in Amsterdam where police discovered him when they raided an apartment being used by John 'The Coach' Traynor. Fatso fled again, this time going further into hiding and leaving the Netherlands behind. He stayed completely dark until a Welsh court heard that he was part of a gang that had trafficked more than €2 million of cocaine into Swansea in just five months. Unknown to him and his gang, they were being watched by police using information secured during the EncroChat phone hack, which had harvested communication with dealers in

Colombia and arrangements for the packages shipped to Swansea to be stamped with the Avengers superhero logo as a way of identifying them.

Hundreds more across the UK and Europe were caught up in the hack: drug dealers, enforcers, logistics experts and money launderers are expected to be processed through the courts for years to come. The window into the underworld was a grim exposé for officers working the organised crime beat, but the next communications network was already in the sights of law enforcement.

As the ripple effects of EncroChat were still being felt across the criminal underworld, Belgian, Dutch and French police cracked another encrypted messaging service in March 2021, when they announced they had listened live on the Sky ECC service for three weeks, decrypted half a billion messages, and got a frightening insight into the amount of cocaine flooding into Europe – including the incredible markup on a kilo from €4,000 in Colombia to a staggering €50,000 on arrival. During the small window of the live hack, they had read 80 million messages over the shoulders of criminals, foiled numerous hits and torture sessions, and uncovered a level of corruption in policing, ports and government departments that was staggering. Seizures of more than 90 tonnes of drugs with a street value of €4.5 billion, and proceeds of crime worth almost €60 million, were some of the incredible figures put out in press releases in the aftermath. However, the big takeaway for those working in law enforcement was the sheer torrent of cocaine making its way through the ports of Rotterdam and Antwerp, and the payoffs to port workers, transporters, politicians and police that went with it. The real underbelly of the criminal underworld and how it operates left Belgian and Dutch police with a conundrum: they simply didn't have big enough forces to deal with all the intelligence they had gathered, and it would probably take years if not decades to follow up the leads. For criminals it seemed that there was some safety in numbers.

The Sky ECC hack was by far the biggest and had started in Belgium where police managed to track a server to northern France and worked with officials there to gain access. At first, they could only see the nicknames of the users but not the messages that were flying over and back across the world, but when an international team of hackers broke through they got an unobstructed window into criminal activities in Belgium and the Netherlands, the gateways into Europe. Messages and photos showed the confidence criminals had in their phones as they shared pictures of mountains of cocaine and graphic images of those who had been murdered because of it, along with revelations of new methods of transport like soaking the drug into plastics and soda drinks shipped from Colombia.

The US, under its powerful RICO laws, moved in to apprehend the bosses of the company who had defended their position as legitimate. 'It was as if we were sitting at the table with the criminals,' the executive director of Europol, Catherine De Bolle, said in a statement. A blizzard of arrests followed and, like EncroChat, are expected to last well into the future, but as the criminals dumped their Sky ECC phones, yet another encrypted service was ready to step in to fill the vacuum – but this time it was the FBI-created ANOM, which had been the future generation of Ennetcom.

More than 6,000 SKY ECC users switched immediately to the ANOM platform, walking right into the hands of a joint US and Australian honey trap. Hot on the heels of EncroChat and SKY ECC, the top brass lined out again, one after the other, with powerful statements for the gangs and kingpins involved in organised crime with news that the ANOM network, co-ordinated by the FBI and Australian law enforcement partners, has seen

800 arrests, the seizure of 32 tons of cocaine, cannabis and meth, 250 firearms and $48 million of dirty money. 'This is a watershed moment in global law enforcement,' said Jennifer Hurst of Australia's Federal Police. Calvin Shivers, the FBI's Assistant Director, told how the San Diego branch developed ANOM in 2018, working with its Australian partners, and planted it within organised crime by purporting to be a 'legitimate' encrypted communication company. 'Encrypted criminal communications platforms have traditionally been a tool to evade law enforcement and facilitate transnational organised crime. The FBI and our international partners continue to push the envelope and develop innovative ways to overcome these challenges and bring criminals to justice,' he said, adding: 'We've turned the tables.'

Europol, too, had been part of Operation Trojan, and at The Hague policing figureheads stood on a podium to announce their success. Headed up in Europe by the Dutch and Swedish, but supported by all the other countries involved, ANOM, the press conference heard, had grown to service more than 12,000 encrypted devices and 300 criminal syndicates operating in over 100 countries, none of whom knew they were using a network developed and controlled by police. Over 18 months the forces sifted through 27 million messages. Linda Staaf, Sweden's Head of Intelligence, described it as 'the most important strike ever against organised crime'. She went on to describe the takedown of EncroChat as a 'game changer'. Taking to the stage, Janine van den Berg, a police chief from the Netherlands, declared 'we've done it again'.

As the press conference got underway, a map on a screen in the corner detailed the 16 territories involved in the most sensational of all battles against criminal networks. Highlighted in a bright turquoise was the lead nation of the US and 16 other participating coalition nations of Australia, New Zealand, Austria, Canada,

Denmark, Estonia, Finland, Germany, Hungary, Lithuania, the Netherlands, Norway, Sweden and the UK, including Scotland and Northern Ireland. Each speaker on Europol's stage sang the same song – that the only way to police organised crime in the modern world is to work together and hit back with shared intelligence and co-operation. But Ireland didn't feature on the map. Having failed to react to EncroChat, the Crime and Intelligence Division had been left off the international stage.

CHAPTER TEN

CHAOS BACK HOME

As the cocaine super cartel was being targeted by international police forces and the Kinahan cell structures in Ireland were being dismantled by the Garda's Drug and Organised Crime Bureau, a complex and chaotic situation developed in gangland due to a lack of governance and a changing of the old guard. Feuds involving violent cocaine mobs erupted with shocking results, a new breed of Instagram gangster emerged with an unrivalled confidence, and others, who were older and longer in the business, saw their opportunities to quietly step into the shoes of the embattled Kinahans and take over their turf. A vacuum in the criminal underworld will often result in an explosion of violence as the finely balanced order tips and mobs move in to take their new positions, but what happened after the fall of the Kinahan organisation in Ireland was, as former Taoiseach Charles Haughey said of the circumstances surrounding the arrest of double killer Malcolm MacArthur, grotesque, unbelievable, bizarre and unprecedented. As the Mocro-Maffia were coming undone in the Netherlands, resulting in new waves of violence against the State, the Kinahan downfall saw Irish mobs turn on one another in a torrent of murder that would cross new lines.

At age 23 Zach Parker was pretty much unknown when he was blasted in the head and chest by a lone gunman in January

2019 as he sat outside a gym in north Dublin. His murder would mark the first of five killings linked to the inability of the embattled Kinahans to collect their debts. The murder was the first of the year and those charged with investigating it, who were well used to a gangland roll call peppered with long-established family names, hadn't a clue who he was, and Parker certainly hadn't come on the radar of the larger units dealing with organised crime who could usually give a quick summary of the background of a gun victim.

Two years prior to his murder, the young barber with pale skin, black-rimmed glasses and lots of tattoos, had been convicted of drug dealing when he was caught with just €3,000 worth of cocaine, an amount so small it never got past the District Court and resulted in him getting a short few hours of community service as punishment. But by the time his remains were cordoned off for forensic examination at a crime scene, he was clearly a far bigger player than that and had all the trappings of what would be considered a mid-ranking player on the cocaine scene. Parker drove a BMW, he'd holidayed in Dubai, and he had €25,000 stashed away in a bank account for a rainy day – not a bad amount for a young man with wardrobes full of designer clothes, lots of jewellery, and expensive artwork all over his body. He clearly had money to burn. Those who knew him only suspected he'd dabbled with drugs, but they never considered that he'd wind up dead, and they certainly didn't realise he was mixed up in a debt owed to the Kinahan Organised Crime Group. Just like many of his young friends, it seemed that Parker had got so caught up in the cocaine superhighway that he had no idea how close to the black heart of gangland he had got and that the quick money could come at a price. What soon became clear was that he had fallen into a chain of debt which nobody wanted to pay.

If those close to him didn't know the extent of his dealings with organised crime, his funeral would certainly have been an eye opener to just how deep he'd got into a game of snakes and ladders that went from the streets of Coolock all the way to Dubai. For other observers, interested in seeing what was happening on the front lines of the fight to take down the mob, it was clear that his death marked a change of respect for the Kinahans, who were fast becoming a fading force in Ireland, one whose foot soldiers could be taken on and taken out on a whim with no concern of retribution.

One of Parker's best friends and another young and prolific cocaine dealer was Sean Little, 21, who was so shocked by his pal's murder that he took to social media to lament his passing with pictures of the two, which he described as 'brothers' enjoying themselves on fancy vacations all over the world. 'Words cannot describe it. I'm heartbroken brother,' he wrote. 'My right-hand man true [sic] thick and thin, absolute gentleman, pleasure to call you my best friend.' Little was the leader of a small crew of underlings under the umbrella of the so-called Gucci Gang, a north Dublin outfit linked to the Kinahan Cartel who had in turn been mentored by a violent hitman called Trevor Byrne. Byrne had been quizzed about the murder of the Monk's brother Eddie Hutch, and he had a fearsome reputation as one of the Kinahans' key lieutenants and enforcers in Dublin. Little was also a very close associate of a junior member of the Byrne organisation, who had essentially operated as the Dublin branch of the Kinahan Cartel for years. It was that link that had instilled in him a sense of untouchability among his peers. Only a few steps down the ladder, Parker believed that he, too, had protection from the Kinahan leadership and that his pal Little was a capo in waiting. Unfortunately for Parker, and later for Little, that ship had sailed, and the respect the Kinahan OCG had once commanded in Ireland had faded as each key member was jailed for plots to kill, money laundering, drug dealing and murder. With more than 60 significant players in the wider cartel locked up in Dublin, the youngsters still had the swagger they believed came from the Kinahan name, but the underworld had swiftly sensed the storm clouds on the horizon for the mob and, for the first time, decided to hold their ground.

Parker's funeral was a sight to behold and the floral tributes displayed the names of the expensive fashion labels he loved to wear: Canada Goose, Moncler and Louis Vuitton. Another was shaped like a Rolex watch with a moving face and adorned in flowers sprayed in rose gold. For those who couldn't make the funeral, a lengthy video of the memorials was posted on Instagram, featuring close-ups of the tributes and panning back to show the volume of them that were set to be piled high on his grave. But more interesting for the officers who mingled in the crowd were the youngsters who came to mourn, who lined up in Colmcille's Church in Swords wearing the uniform of the Kinahan Cartel: a black fitted suit, pale blue shirt and black tie. Shoulder to shoulder with Parker's best pal Sean Little, theirs was an attempt to show supremacy, a declaration of war, a vow to avenge their fallen comrade, and to show those who'd ordered his death that they had taken on the might of a drug-dealing army.

The same attire had been worn some years before by hordes of young men who lined out to back their mighty drug bosses during the funeral of David Byrne at St Nicholas of Myra Church on Francis Street in Dublin 8 following his shooting at the Regency Hotel in February 2016. For a mafia, the funeral of a fallen colleague is all about a show of strength and a message of its contempt for society, but while the opulence at Byrne's funeral, coupled with the presence of Daniel Kinahan and Thomas 'Bomber' Kavanagh front and centre, had been a chilling warning of the bloodshed to come, no such message was sent out at Parker's funeral. In fact, as he was lowered into the ground, many were online and mocking those in uniform, taunting and threatening them about more to come.

Sean Little was known to his pals as 'Cha', the big-spending, party-loving fitness fanatic who lived fast and who died young, aged just 22, and less than a year after Parker went out in a hail of bullets. Little loved bottles of champagne, luxury sun holidays and Louis Vuitton man-bags, and he had never worked a day in his life save for selling cocaine and collecting debts for the Gucci Gang. The money he was so desperate for, his status as a wealthy drug dealer and the Rolex watch on his wrist seemed almost ludicrous as images of his body covered in tarpaulin appeared on news reports. Little had died on a quiet country road in Dublin as he stood beside his car, likely talking to whomever he'd gone to meet. His bullet-proof vest, a uniform of sorts since Parker's demise, lay at home. For a young man used to the high life, the last thing he saw was undoubtedly the view down the barrel of a gun – it couldn't have been pretty and he must have known what was coming. He'd seen so much violence in his short life: the murder of his best pal and the shooting of another friend, Lee Boylan, the previous April, who had been left with permanent life-altering injuries and whose survival had been called nothing short of a miracle.

Part of a new generation of cocaine cowboys dubbed the 'Instagram gangsters', Little had played out the few years of his adult life on social media with a permanent smile fixed on his face, his teeth veneered and dazzling white. His accounts were filled with photographs of his travels to far-flung destinations such as north Africa and Thailand, and just before his murder he had enjoyed an exotic trip hiking in the Atlas Mountains after he'd got serious about his fitness. City breaks with his designer-clad friends featured heavily in hundreds of photos of an enviable lifestyle akin to something enjoyed by a successful dot.com millionaire. There were cocktails in Ibiza, fillet steak meals in Michelin-starred restaurants, a collection of expensive watches and, in one picture, he even managed to hug a tiger on a safari ranch.

By the age of 18, Little had known exactly what he wanted to be in life and it involved bucketloads of cash that only one product could provide. 'Money can't buy happiness . . . but it's more comfortable to cry in a BMW than on a bicycle,' he had posted in 2015. When he drank vodka, he chose Grey Goose, one of the more expensive offerings on the market, and his prosecco choice was Valdo but he preferred champagne, a Moët & Chandon where possible. By 19 he was dressing head to toe in Hugo Boss and enjoyed his first proper holiday abroad with pals, no expense spared. In Ibiza he had partied hard in five-star luxury with his own outdoor jacuzzi and pool. In the pictures his pal Lee Boylan posed beside him and they began their adventure by enjoying a drink at Dublin Airport.

Months after their Ibiza trip Little and Boylan were back on their travels again, this time to Koh Samui in Thailand where they'd spent Christmas on the beach. Little had spent thousands of euro getting his teeth veneered by then and he was happy to show them off for the camera, with pineapple cocktails on Chaweng Beach, a snap which spurred Liam Byrne to message his young protégés: 'Love it boys, fair play'. It was December 2016, just ten months since Liam's own brother, David, had been shot dead at the Regency Hotel, taking a bullet for Daniel Kinahan, who had escaped with his security detail.

Little's elevation to a top dog in the Gucci Gang was swifter than it should have been. Although he was one of the younger members of the Finglas-based mob run by the criminal nicknamed 'Mr Flashy', Little had pedigree, in the form of his cousin Nathan 'Biggie' Little, who had been identified by the CAB as a low-level member of the Byrne Organised Crime Group by virtue of his close friendship with Liam Byrne's son Lee. Summer 2017 had kicked off for Sean Little with a weekend at the Forbidden Fruit festival along with the 'brothers', including his cousin Nathan and pals Lee Byrne and Lee Gibson, who had also been named by the Bureau as a member of the Byrne OCG. The alignment of the Gucci Gang and the new generation Byrnes from Crumlin, south of the city, was cemented, and they wanted to make sure that everyone saw the pictures that proved it.

Next stop was Croatia where Little and friends became regulars at the famed Papaya club at Zrće beach, and after a week of partying it was back home for the Longitude festival before jetting off again to Ibiza, this time with members of the young Byrne mob. On the sun-soaked island, Little and his crew became daily communicants at the VIP tables of Ocean Beach Club, at the cost of almost €1,500 a pop. The rest of the year was made up of photo after photo of Little and his pals posing on nights out in new clothes, sporting expensive watches, and then at a party for cousin Nathan's 21st, a lavish affair complete with a specially designed Rolex watch cake. April 2018 was marked by a trip to Barcelona with Zach Parker, who posed bespectacled, happily sipping a champagne cocktail, oblivious to the fact that he had just months to live. For Little, the only concern on his mind was his weight, which had been creeping up with all the partying and eating out so, after another trip to Ibiza in July 2018 and a few jokes that he had become a 'baby jumbo', he employed the help of a personal trainer.

Taking time out from his fitness regime to attend the McGregor fight in Vegas, he looked as if he had dramatically decreased his waist and spoke about a fresh start in 2019 which was going to be all about healthy living and travel, he said. Instead, it was an *annus horribilis* for Little. First there was the death of Parker, then the attempt on the life of Boylan, who was sitting behind the wheel of a Volkswagen van at Blakestown in West Dublin when a gunman opened fire. While it was a miracle that he hadn't died, he had been left confined to a wheelchair. Weeks later there was a third tragedy when Keith Foster, the 20-year-old son of Kinahan money launderer Darren Foster, died. Little turned out for the funeral and the mob-style commiserations afterwards. His last posting on Instagram came from Morocco: 'Halfway up Toubkal mountain. Great Experience with the boys,' he wrote. And then he was gone off social media for good.

As the two murder inquiries began, one aspect of Little's murder stood out: the 22-year-old had been stopped previously by cops while driving around the north Dublin area and it had been noted that he was wearing a bulletproof vest, but when his body was discovered on a back road that led from the townland of Walshestown to the M1, he was without it, pointing to the fact that he likely knew and trusted who he was meeting. After Little was shot the car was then set alight, with a member of the public sounding the alarm by ringing for the Fire Brigade. As his friends gathered the following morning at the spot where he died, media lenses picked up a stranger with black teardrop tattoos on his face; out of place among the young 20 somethings, the older man had been identified as an Iranian who had been working as a driver for Little. Less than 24 hours after Little's murder, his close friend Jordan Davis was shot dead as he wheeled a tiny baby in a pram. He had posted a tribute to Little and a picture of the two of them together with the words 'Rest in paradise, you were a gent' on Facebook, and less than 15 minutes later he had been shot dead himself. While Jordan's death was not linked to the Little and Parker murders, the speed with which it was carried out and the ruthlessness of it immediately suggested another cocaine dispute was to blame. Later, gunman Wayne Cooney would be jailed for life for the shooting, hired, it was believed, over a drug debt Jordan was alleged to have owed.

Less than a week after he was killed, associates of Little had zoned in on the fact that he had likely known his assassin and that someone in his close-knit gang had betrayed him. They wanted swift retribution and all eyes fell on Hamid Sanambar, the 41-year-old Iranian odd bod with a seemingly colourful past. Since his arrival into the middle of the Gucci Gang some months previous, Sanambar had been the subject of much gangland gossip and was rumoured to be a professional hitman, trained by Isis, an expert in torture techniques and sent to Ireland by Daniel Kinahan as his personal assassin. Given Kinahan had already sent an Estonian hitman to the country, it wasn't totally unbelievable, but while Sanambar wore facial gang tattoos, suggesting that he had killed twice, he was known to Gardaí as only a small-time crook and had been living in the country far longer than the terrorist organisation Islamic State had even existed. Involved in fraud and robberies, he had begun to hang out with the younger Gucci Gang members as they tried desperately to collect money owed up the ranks to the Kinahans, and the stories around him being trained in torture and beheading would have suited the group's narrative to those who they were trying to get to pay up. At the same time, Sanambar seemed perfectly capable of making up the stories himself and always appeared dark and brooding in their company.

One of the groups who owed money was a young mob just like the Gucci Gang, working under notorious crime boss Cornelius Price, who had a frightening reputation for violence. All the groups had been watching as Trevor Byrne was arrested in November 2019 and put behind bars on firearms offences. Byrne was the Kinahans' main lieutenant in Finglas and had mentored Mr Flashy as well as younger members of his gang. Flashy had in turn mentored Little and some of his crew but with Byrne off the scene, any last shred of respect or fear of the young guns died off. Sanambar had been noticed with the gang a number of times as rumours of his sinister past grew legs, but for those who scratched the surface, the stories about him never stacked up; it was discovered that he had in fact been in Ireland since at least 2007 and had been living hand to mouth on the fringes of criminal gangs. At one point he was arrested in Cork after robbing a brothel and he had other previous road traffic and drink driving offences. Around 2015 he was living in Longford and had links with a Traveller mob, but he'd tried to sell information to the *Sunday World* newspaper and had been dismissed as a spoofer by the veteran investigative journalist Eamon Dillon.

As much as Parker's death had shocked the group, Little's murder was a huge challenge to their power and they quickly pinpointed Sanambar as the most likely one to have turned against them. When he arrived at the family's Coolock home to pay his respects, as the body of Little was laid out in the sitting room, he was shot dead in cold blood in the garden. Images of his body lying on the newly paved driveway were recorded and uploaded to social media, yet nobody witnessed a thing and Gardaí started an investigation into the fourth murder within the small grouping in less than a year, this one put down to house-keeping. As officers dug deep into their underworld touts, they heard that Little, Davis and their pal Parker had all been accused of heavy-handed approaches to drug dealing and collecting debts, and of dismissing rival groups due to their 'association' with the Kinahan Cartel. As tensions grew in the areas of Finglas and Coolock, everyone tried to cement control and the Gucci Gang and their leader Mr Flashy engaged in a number of local feuds with other violent drug gangs, creating an extremely fluid situation that was hard to keep a handle on. There was a standoff on debt payments and, despite their insistence that they were 'cartel', the Guccis were told that nobody answered to them anymore.

The bold move to take out Little set off a second catastrophic train of events that resulted in more than six different groupings emerging in Coolock. Eoin Boylan, 22, was one who tried to make his mark and, despite surviving previous attempts on his life and being told by Gardaí to leave the area, he stayed put. Boylan's murder in November 2019 in the garden of his home was complicated, as there were a number of reasons he could have been targeted. Top of the list was the fact that he'd made derogatory comments about Little on social media and had been seen in the company of Sanambar moments before he was gunned down, but he had also been approached by convicted drug dealer Robert 'Ru' Redmond for money. Redmond was a volatile gun-toting criminal who was known to take an enormous amount of cocaine and had miraculously survived a number of hit attempts himself. He, along with his sidekick Bernard Fogarty, would later be jailed for life for the murder of Barry Wolverson. Redmond was also suspected of being the debtor behind the murder of Jordan Davis.

The complicated, entrenched feud was almost impossible for police, and gangs turned outwards and inwards in rows over money and cocaine turf. The Gucci Gang would go on to split and turn against one another in a second tranche of feuding that would result in another murder. The only sure thing in the chaotic situation was that it could all be traced back to the Kinahan Cartel debts and the pressure put on Little to get them paid back, but even at the upper end of what was rumoured to be owed, €200,000, it was hard to compute that being worth so many lives.

At the time, Europol had valued the cocaine market at €10 billion, a 60 per cent increase in just a few years, but as the rewards increased for the gangs so did the number of people trying to muscle in on the profits. In a 160-page report, the agency said there was 'grave concern' in the increase in violence around cocaine importation and cited the Kinahan and Hutch feud. It also stated that a 'service industry' including professional hitmen was developing in Europe to facilitate gangs.

∽

The two protagonists from the other shocking gang war that raged in the immediate aftermath of the Kinahan and Hutch feud and subsequent dismantling of key Kinahan cells were even more savage than anything that had gone before them, and for the first time the epicentre was a town outside the estates of Dublin. The Drogheda feud, centred on the commuter town of Louth, was one that peaked when, on April 4th, 2020, the body of Robbie Lawlor lay in the front garden of a terraced red-brick house in Ardoyne, a Republican stronghold of north Belfast. Hours later his arch rival, Cornelius Price, raised a glass of Captain Morgan and smiled into the camera as he drank to Lawlor's brutal demise.

Ardoyne is a rabbit warren with its rows and rows of iden-tical terraced houses and giant murals commemorating the Easter Rising of 1916 and those killed in the Troubles and the famine. The Irish colours of green, white and orange seem to be spray painted everywhere with messages about 'saluting the men and women of violence' and supporting the IRA. Trico-lours hang outside houses and graffiti reminds those who don't know that they are in nationalist Belfast. Just two hours of motorway separates Belfast from Dublin, yet the murals of Ardoyne tell a tale of two vastly different cities: one where a war raged over decades and the other which knew peace and looked the other way.

By 10.30am Robbie Lawlor arrived at Etna Drive, parked his car, and made his way to the door of a home owned by the grandmother of a low-level criminal known as Adrian 'Aidy' Holland. Within minutes he was dead, a hitman was on the run and, shortly after, three members of Limerick's notorious Dundon gang were arrested as they made their way to the border at Newry. Lawlor had been a dead man walking for a long time, but he wasn't the first person who sprang to mind when the first familiar crack of gunshots cut through the morning quiet in the Republican stronghold. As the men in white suits with cameras cordoned off the house, neighbours came out to investigate what had gone on and who was lying dead beneath the crime scene tent in the garden. Initially, it was suspected that it was Holland, but when he was spotted in the area later that theory was ruled out.

Nobody was quite sure who Lawlor was, his name initially wasn't an eyebrow raiser like it was on the other side of the border, but the people of Ardoyne had heard the story of the teenage boy, Keane Mulready-Woods, who'd been kidnapped, tortured and dismembered some months before, his legs left in a holdall bag and his head in a car boot. Very quickly the news started to seep out that the man under the tarpaulin was the one responsible for what was without doubt the most brutal murder in gangland history. The story had not only shocked Gardaí but had made headlines across the world because of the savagery of Mulready-Woods' grotesque death in his hometown of Drogheda.

The PSNI moved quickly and brought a number of people into custody for Lawlor's murder. In a car stopped in Newry, they arrested Ger Dundon and his nephew Levi Killeen, the son of the notorious John, along with another associate, Quincy

Bramble. A notorious Belfast criminal called Warren Crossan was also arrested near the scene, but very quickly all were let go, Killeen unconditionally.

Lawlor's death was hugely significant. He'd been on the run since the previous January when Keane Mulready-Woods had been reported missing by his mother Elizabeth. The family had last seen the 17-year-old the day before and, with Drogheda in the grip of a horrendous gang feud, the worst was feared. The youngster was typical of the teenage boys both sides, known simply as the 'Maguire' faction and the 'Anti-Maguire' faction, had recruited to do their dirty work, and unfortunately for him he was suspected of having a foot in each camp. The feud had started in 2017 when the drug gang headed up by gang boss Owen Maguire and his sidekick Cornelius Price had split. Two ambitious brothers and another young thug called Paul Cosby decided to go it alone, albeit under the direction of veteran criminal Richie Carberry. Carberry was Lawlor's brother-in-law, and a major drugs trafficker who'd moved out of the north Dublin suburb of Coolock to a new base in a seaside town in County Meath some years before. From there Carberry had supplied Maguire's former protégés with drugs and guns and, seeing the potential of the drugs market in the largest commuter town outside Dublin, with a population topping 100,000, he had groomed them hard to win turf and shut down the old order. The more success they had, the richer he would get, and Carberry craved both wealth and power.

Maguire, who was a member of the Traveller community, had deeper roots in Drogheda than Carberry, and he lived with his extended family on a State-built halting site on Cement Road. He'd forged a long-time connection with Price, who lived at a compound at nearby Gormanston. Price was known for his vicious temper and was feared by his contemporaries, but when he was convicted at the Dublin Circuit Criminal Court in February 2017 after evidence that he had driven a car at a garda, he'd been jailed for three years, leaving Maguire to face the threats from his rivals alone. Arson attacks and assaults intensified, culminating in the shooting of Maguire at Cement Road in the summer of 2018. Maguire survived the attack but would be confined to a wheelchair for the rest of his life, and many believed that the gunman Robbie Lawlor had meant to finish him off as he lifted his balaclava and showed him his face before trying to pump a final shot into him which failed.

By the time he discharged the six bullets into Maguire, Lawlor was working as an enforcer for Carberry, but was also on a personal spree of violence which had terrified an innocent family and pitted him against one of the most powerful criminals in Dublin. Months before he brandished a gun at the cowering Maguire, Lawlor had shot dead Kenneth Finn, a hitman and close friend of the powerful criminal known as Mr Big. Finn was in a car outside his house at Moatview Gardens in Coolock on February 25th when he was approached by a gunman and shot in the head. He was on life support for two days, with a bullet lodged in his brain, before he died. At his funeral mass he was remembered as a loyal friend whose death would not be forgotten, and although Mr Big didn't attend the ceremony, his presence was felt during the proceedings. Finn had kept interesting company in life. He was a close pal of the recently murdered Hutch gangster Jason 'Buda' Molyneux, who was suspected of carrying out a botched attack on volatile underworld figure Derek 'Bottler' Devoy in which the target escaped, but his sister, mother of five Antoinette Corbally, was shot dead along with her pal Clinton Shannon. He was also pals with murdered gangland gunman Jamie Tighe Ennis, who had been shot dead on the same estate just months earlier.

It wasn't unusual that Finn kept the company of killers, as he had a fearsome reputation himself as a hitman for Mr Big and he was a suspect in a number of gangland murders, including the 2012 slaying of the Real IRA boss Alan Ryan. Known as an experienced and cunning criminal, Mr Big was a powerful force in the underworld who had long had the backing of the Kinahan Cartel and was close to Daniel. He was known to Gardaí as a strategic and opportunistic criminal who had risen to great heights in the shadow of the Kinahan organisation, and who had become increasingly powerful since their demise. Those who knew him were sure that Mr Big would not do anything rash, that he would simply take his time and plan his revenge. Carberry had been accused of supplying the weapon used in the gun attack on Maguire and of failing to pay a debt of €700,000 to Mr Big's mob, putting his life in double jeopardy. While Carberry was aware of his troubles, he felt safe with Lawlor's terrifying presence as a gun-toting loyal follower capable of targeting anyone who might cross his boss, but Lawlor wasn't functioning in an organised fashion. He was on a path of destruction with his mental health breaking down due to a heady mix of cocaine and steroids. Many noticed the constant twitching in his face and the shocking mood swings that saw him elated one minute and angry the next.

Two months after killing Finn, Lawlor had turned his sights on his ex-partner, Rachel Kirwan, her new boyfriend, Derek Mitchell, and Mitchell's innocent mum, Fiona. Furious that she had moved on with her life and that Mitchell was close to his children, he had embarked on a terrifying assault on his love rival and his mum.

When Brendan Maguire was shot in February 2019 at a supermarket car park, he survived and managed to drive himself to a police station, leaving his injured brother, Owen, even more incensed and intent on ending the threat before it ended his family. The following month Richie Carberry survived a gun attack outside his home in the seaside village of Bettystown in County Meath, and he later installed bullet-resistant windows at the property. In August 2019 Keith Brannigan, an associate of Carberry, was shot dead at a caravan site outside Clogherhead. The popular holiday site was full of families at the time and the horror of the broad daylight gun violence sparked one of the most senior figures in the Catholic Church to appeal to those involved in the feud. The Auxiliary Bishop of the Archdiocese of Armagh, Bishop Michael Router, condemned the violent killing at the Ashling Holiday Park in Clogherhead, but his words were to fall on deaf ears in a feud in which more than 70 separate violent incidents had already been recorded.

A month later Gardaí caught up with Lawlor and charged him in relation to the attempted murder of Fiona Mitchell. In prison he knew he was in the sights of Cornelius Price, out to get even over the shooting of his business associates, the Maguires, and there were many people that Mr Big had behind bars too. A month into his remand he was stabbed in Cork prison after Price reached out and shook his hand, in what was known as a Judas shake, to give the nod for the attack. But, surviving the attack, Lawlor was confident that he could handle himself and that nobody would go near him again. He'd spent his days in the gym working out frantically and building muscle to big himself up, and he'd employed the protection of the Dundons in the prison, getting close with the youngest, Ger, who was serving a sentence alongside him. Outside, Gardaí prepared to bring Lawlor to trial on the attempted murder charges in the hope that they could remove him from the streets on a long sentence, which would leave them with one less violent criminal on the streets of Drogheda.

With Lawlor in prison, however, the Drogheda feud escalated, with arson attacks, bullets sprayed at houses, the use of
firebombs, and reports that young men were being abducted
and tortured over small debts or perceived misdemeanours
against their drug bosses. In October the killers came again
for Carberry and this time shot him dead outside his home
at the upmarket Castlemartin Drive in Bettystown, County
Meath. It later emerged that he was so fearful for his life that
he had been planning a move to the UK and had just found an
apartment in Manchester. Behind bars Lawlor went berserk,
vowing to beat the charges that could see him locked up and
personally finish the feud no matter what he had to do. He
was even recorded by prison intelligence on a phone call to
an associate in Louth stating that he held Mr Big responsible
for the murder as the Carberry gunman was suspected of
being another young thug groomed this time by his mob. The
teenage hitman had skin in the game, as he was an associate of
another murdered man, David 'Fred' Lynch, believed to be one
of Lawlor's earlier victims. Lynch had been shot in the head
with a 9mm semi-automatic pistol in 2009 in Coolock, leaving
behind a young son.

As Gardaí prepared to bring the case against Lawlor, they
tried a number of times to have it heard before the three-judge
Special Criminal Court, largely used for trials in gangland
cases, but they were refused on the basis that the crime was
deemed domestic. Gardaí feared that Lawlor and his associates could potentially get to jury members or intimidate or
cajole witnesses to change their statements. When the case
came to trial in December 2019, their fears were realised when
his ex-partner, Rachel, suddenly decided she could remember
nothing and refused to tell a jury about the threats she had
earlier informed police about. Lawlor was found not guilty by a

jury of the threats to kill, the attempted murder and possession of a gun, and of killing Fiona Mitchell's pet dog. It was a stunning result and a sense of foreboding hung in the courtroom as Lawlor looked over at the jury and whispered 'thank you'.

Immediately Gardaí issued a security bulletin as Lawlor was whisked away from outside the Criminal Courts of Justice in an Audi car, knowing he would go to war with Mr Big, Maguire and Price. The bulletin, issued to all Dublin garda stations, advised officers to exercise extreme caution when approaching him but, unsurprisingly, the same sense didn't filter down to the younger criminals working in the Mr Big network, who had no such problems. When they came upon Lawlor in the city centre shortly before Christmas, after he'd emerged from one of his daily gym sessions, they surrounded him. The video footage, which was uploaded onto social media, was crystal clear. It showed a tussle and Lawlor dropping his gym bag so he could fight back against the group as he shouted threats to the young mob. Then the camera captures the scene as he is punched and warned: 'That's only the start of it. That's only the start of it, Robbie!' And with that, someone picks up his gym bag. What would be regarded as a stupid and childish row in ordered society was a far different chapter in gangland, and it would lead to one of the most savage and disturbing retributions in the history of organised crime in Ireland. Following the incident, a photo was uploaded to social media of an individual wearing the flip-flops that Lawlor had in his gym bag, and the scene was set for the gruesome death of Keane Mulready-Woods.

On January 16th horrifying images began to circulate online purporting to show the teenager's body parts being chopped up with a chainsaw and knives. They featured dismembered legs, feet and a head, and included chilling threats to carry out revenge attacks with similarly brutal violence. The pictures were meant to goad Maguire, Price and Mr Big, and while Gardaí said at the time that they were unverified and urged the public not to share them, it was hard to imagine why someone would mock up such a scene.

Hours after Mulready-Woods had been reported missing, the first body parts were discovered in a sports bag, along with a pair of flip-flops, at Moatview Gardens and Moatview Drive in the Coolock area, a stronghold of Mr Big's mob. DNA results matched the remains to Mulready-Woods, but a day later when Dublin Fire Brigade responded to a call about a burning vehicle near Croke Park, they discovered a severed head in the boot. Hours later officers sealed off a scene at a house in Rathmullan Park in Drogheda and began a massive forensic analysis, but the torso was still missing and searches didn't discover it until after the funeral in early April, three days before Lawlor was wiped out in Belfast.

Despite being released from custody so quickly into the murder investigation, the Dundon mob would days later be implicated in a double-cross when two women were arrested having collected €50,000 in bank notes from a Maguire associate. Lawlor's lieutenants fled to Spain while Price went to Rochdale in England where he released the video celebrating the murder. Raising a glass of Captain Morgan rum, he smiled into the camera and said: 'Cheers to Robbie Lawlor, rest in peace. He's not even meant to rest in peace but fair play to you, Lee. There you go boy . . .' In Coolock the same young men who'd stolen his gym bag were videoed celebrating at a garden party complete with loudspeakers and boxes of alcohol.

Lawlor was buried just three graves away from his brother-in-law, Carberry, in Laytown Cemetery. Just 15 relatives and a handful of friends attended the ceremony, including his parents and his sister, Eileen. On the road surrounding the cemetery,

Gardaí, including members of the Armed Support Unit, manned the entrances in case there were any more murder attempts, a testament to the violent life and death that was being remembered on the day.

Days later, in Darndale, a young man was treated in hospital for stab wounds after he was attacked in broad daylight and accused of attending the funeral. A group of crack cocaine dealers, including the younger associate of murdered Fred Lynch, had set upon him. The teenager, suspected of being the hitman who killed Carberry, had survived a shooting attack himself the month before Lawlor's murder. He had spent a number of weeks being treated at St Vincent's Hospital for his injuries, including damage to his liver, and was discharged just on time to celebrate the Ardoyne killing, but the murder and the violence was not to stop there.

In the North, just months later, Warren Crossan was killed outside the home of his mother, Ann. He was suspected of supplying the getaway vehicle in the Lawlor killing. Of all the shady and violent characters in the cocaine-fuelled feud, Price probably had the most unexpected end of all. While in exile he had continued his involvement in organised crime in the UK and took part in a blackmail plot where two brothers were kidnapped and told they would be shot in the head if a £300,000 ransom was not paid. The brothers were tied up, blindfolded, fed sleeping tablets, made to wash with Dettol spray and forced to call their relatives for money before armed police rescued them. One of the victims was found lying on a mattress in the back of a van driven by another Irishman, Darren McClean, who was later convicted in relation to the incident. Cornelius Price was also charged but never stood trial as he was diagnosed with a rare brain condition and hospitalised. His condition deteriorated and he died in hospital in Wales surrounded by family and friends, as well as a Christian preacher who was brought in to help get him to 'heaven'. In a final twist in the double-cross of Lawlor, it would eventually emerge that McClean was, in fact, Ger Dundon, the 'friend' he had been with before his death but who had changed his name.

Back in the Republic, Paul Cosby pleaded guilty to facilitating the murder of Keane Mulready-Woods and was jailed for 10 years. His associate Gerard Cruise, 49, was also locked up for seven years for assisting in the teenager's death. The two had lured the 17-year-old to a house where he was tortured, killed and chopped up. At their sentencing hearing, Elizabeth Woods wrote a statement to the court in which she said she wished she could see her son one last time and hear him say: 'I love you, Mam.' She said she prays for justice for her son's inhumane, violent and barbaric death, and described it as 'one of the most brutal, tragic and horrifying murders in the history of Ireland'. But despite a mother's grief, the murders, the violence and the chaos, demand for cocaine continued to grow and a never-ending stream of ambitious newcomers made moves on the market. As one dynasty fell another was always waiting to take its place, and some who had been written off as yesterday's news were even tempted to make a comeback.

CHAPTER ELEVEN

THE COMEBACK KINGS

Brian Rattigan had spent almost all his adult life in jail, but he still managed to organise assassinations and drug deals and to terrorise communities while behind bars at the high-security Portlaoise Prison where he enjoyed his reputation as king of the wing. As a teenager he had gone to war, first with his arch rival Declan Gavin and then with the man who'd taken his place, 'Fat' Freddie Thompson. He'd lost his beloved brother, Joey, his sister Sharon's partner, Shay O'Byrne, and seen the collapse of his relationship with the mother of his children as he settled into a life sentence behind bars. A string of hitmen, enforcers and lieutenants had also lost their lives in the 10-year cocaine war he started in the Crumlin and Drimnagh areas with the murder of Gavin in 2001, yet Rattigan had continually managed to set his sights on his future in the underworld. When he'd been first brought into custody for the murder of Gavin, he'd received a four-year sentence while awaiting trial for shooting at a patrol car while he was being chased by gardaí. He was later convicted of Gavin's murder and while serving that sentence was found guilty of running a drugs operation from Portlaoise Prison after Gardaí seized €1 million worth of heroin and linked the drugs to Rattigan. He was jailed for 17 years, but in 2017 he got an unexpected bit of luck when his murder conviction was sensationally overturned and two years later, as he faced a second trial, he pleaded guilty to manslaughter and got nine years, paving a path to freedom once he completed the drugs sentence.

As meetings were held behind bars to consider his suitability to go back into the community in the autumn of 2021, he did the unthinkable and claimed that he had forgiven his brother's killer. Ironically for Thompson, he was only beginning a life sentence – for the Hutch and Kinahan feud murder of David 'Daithi' Douglas – as Rattigan's fortunes began to turn. As Thompson arrived at Portlaoise Prison to begin his sentence, his rival made it clear to prison authorities that his old foe was welcome on his wing and would have no trouble from him. Rattigan told the High Court the same and insisted that there was no bad blood between them and that he was a changed man who wanted to live a law-abiding life, while Thompson said their 'feud' was merely a media invention. Prisons are very unusual places where dominant inmates often hold the power over others. Those who control the supply of contraband also gain status, and those who play the game with prison officers, agreeing to represent the convicts and keep them in check, will often be asked if they give their sanction to new inmates. For Rattigan's part few were under no illusion, and assumed that his attitude to Thompson was purely for his own gain and that their bitter hatred for each other would follow them to their graves.

In August 2021, sporting a beard and long hair hidden under a hat, Rattigan re-emerged from the prison for the first time as an adult and quickly became one of the main crime figures in Dublin and a top target for officers. In the Basin Street area Rattigan had managed to hold his own despite being locked up, and within months of his freedom detectives believed his gang had stepped up to be one of the main players in the capital's drug trade, pushing out of their safe zones and into neighbouring territories in a power grab. Two murders were also quickly linked to Rattigan, including that of Tony Dempsey, whose body lay undiscovered in a city flat for more than a week while people came and went to take drugs. An associate of the crime boss was suspected of carrying out the assault on the 28-year-old addict over a drug debt and as a message to anyone that King Ratt was back. Rattigan's gang also found themselves under investigation for the murder of criminal Gary Carey, 41, a long-time rival of the crime boss who had survived a number of assassination attempts before he was shot outside a Kilmainham hotel, dying weeks later from his injuries. While Carey was being treated at the scene in June 2022, less than a year after Rattigan's release, he told emergency responders that Rattigan was to blame, although he was not suspected of direct involvement. With Rattigan back striking fear in the communities of the south inner city and west Dublin, he began to move in and out of Ireland, spending long periods in Alicante where his old mentor, John Gilligan, had lived for years and where he still had a network of high-end contacts in the drugs world.

If it was a surprise that there was still life in Rattigan after such a lengthy time behind bars, Gilligan's path back to crime was even more eyebrow-raising. Gilligan may have eventually lost Jessbrook Equestrian Centre and his family home in Kildare after a two-decade battle with the CAB, as well as surviving a serious assassination attempt, but that didn't stop him trying to get on the crime ladder well past his pension age. He was first arrested in the North and placed in Maghaberry Prison on remand while he faced charges relating to cash he was caught with at Belfast Airport, but it came to nothing and he beat the rap. However, when Spanish police moved in on him at his home in Alicante in October 2020, they discovered a Colt Python gun hidden under the patio and cannabis and prescription-only sleeping pills wrapped and ready for postage to the UK and Ireland. Back with his pal 'Fat' Tony Armstrong, suspected of being the criminal who organised the double murder of the Westies back in 2003 after they tried to rip off Gilligan's mob, he was caught red-handed with the drugs in his living room. A Spanish National Police spokesman at the time said officers had intercepted four postal deliveries in which four kilos of marijuana and 15,000 pills had been hidden. While Spanish police initially believed the gun was the one used to kill Veronica Guerin, Irish officers were more sceptical, believing Gilligan would never have held on to an item that could link him to the crime. Although Gilligan was acquitted of ordering the reporter's murder in 2001, he was convicted of importing two tonnes of cannabis resin worth £32 million and had been sentenced to 28 years in prison, which was reduced on appeal. Ballistics tests soon revealed that the gun was not the same, but Gilligan remained on remand on the drugs charge.

Around the same time Rattigan was released in Ireland, Brian Wright tasted freedom in the UK. Despite telling a court that he would die in jail, Wright was released just halfway through his 30-year sentence and went straight from jail to a run-down London bail hostel and later reunited with his son Brian Jnr, who had also been released having spent 16 years in jail for his part in his father's drugs network. On social media many celebrated his freedom and posted old photos of Wright in his heyday. Despite the wealth he had accrued during his time as a top-tier cocaine smuggler, a confiscation of assets hearing after his conviction had heard he was broke. At the hearing Customs and Excise demanded that he pay back £45 million, but Wright refused to attend court. 'His position is, he has nothing and no matter how much he says it, that will not be accepted,' his barrister told the court. 'Everything he had was paid for in cash and rented. The approach the Crown has taken is so unrealistic that it is pointless to engage and he takes the view that it almost doesn't matter. He is nearly 62 years of age and is serving 30 years. He will not see the light of day.' Alluding to the death of Wright's wife the previous year, the barrister said that if Wright was so wealthy he wouldn't have allowed her to live out her days in a rented flat. His plea was successful and the Court told him to hand over just £2.3 million within 12 months, or have his sentence increased by an additional ten years. The drug lord had paid up.

∽

While some crime lords have the pressure of supporting the lifestyles of their families, others have the hopes of future generations to support them and to carry on a lineage built on fear and greed. The Dundon organisation of Limerick had been signed off as finished when brothers Wayne and John joined their brother Dessie Dundon in jail, all serving life sentences for murder following their brutal reign, but that didn't mean they hadn't left behind blooded youngsters who could carry the name of the organisation on their shoulders in the years to come.

One such underling of the brothers emerged on the scene in recent years threatening long-time rivals of the family gang and terrorising many with his natural predisposition to violence. During 2023 Gardaí staged a number of raids on the family homes of the brothers on Hyde Road, which were the headquarters of the Dundon gang during two decades of feuding, claiming the lives of 17 people. There they seized a cocaine press and large quantities of white powder, indicating that the notorious brothers have not gone away.

Despite the massive resources pumped into Limerick to crush the gangs, fears are growing that they are lining up once again to show their muscle and that the unstable young Dundon

214

associate is emerging as a fearless protégé. Gardaí believe that the teenager has been involved in criminality since he was a young child and has been feared by those who know him since he was at least 12 years of age. He was just a small child when Wayne and John Dundon wreaked fear and chaos in Limerick City, when they went to war with rivals in the Keane and Collopy gangs. Together with the McCarthy faction, they joined forces to wipe out their criminal rivals, but both wound up with life sentences for the murders of innocent feud victims Roy Collins and rugby player Shane Geoghegan. However, a fallout caused by a Garda crackdown in the city resulted in the McCarthy and Dundon factions turning on one another. When Ger Dundon was arrested in Belfast along with his associate Quincy Bramble and young nephew Levi Killeen, a son of John Dundon and his partner Ciara, it was quickly suspected they had carried out the daring murder of Robbie Lawlor. However, all three were released after being questioned, Killeen unconditionally, and were able to cross the border back into the south in the wake of the shooting in Ardoyne. The barrister Joe Brolly, who represents a man charged in relation to the murder, would later tell a bail hearing that he believes Killeen was the triggerman and that Ger Dundon and Quincy Bramble were key in the double-cross. All three were able to make their way back to the South after they were released, but Dundon was later arrested with Cornelius Price, who had gone on social media to celebrate the Lawlor murder.

Gardaí in Limerick are closely monitoring the activities of the key players in the feud, which turned the city into a war zone and whose activities saw a €100 million regeneration project on key areas of the city, including Southill, Moyross, the Island Field and Ballinacurra Weston. The estates are within a kilometre of the city centre and still scattered with abandoned and board-ed-up houses. All the feuding factions have remained in the city and have homes in the areas, making them an easier target in the future for officers who have intelligence files on their movements, associates, and even the type of violence they favour.

The Dundons and their rivals are hardened criminals who have never fitted into the ordinary society which buys their drugs and makes them rich. They stick together, would never make it into the pages of *Hello!* magazine and they stand out as the brutish thugs they are. Equally, the younger Instagram gangsters who get rich quick by selling cocaine and splashing their cash on designer clothes, fancy holidays and fast cars look like drug dealers and act accordingly. But since the arrival of cocaine onto the drugs landscape, many others have managed to slip into the underworld largely unnoticed by the public or, at the very least, denying they were doing anything wrong.

Disgraced businessman Jim Mansfield Jnr eventually found out what it was like to be the common criminal he fought so hard to deny he was when he was sentenced to two years' imprisonment at the Special Criminal Court for perverting the course of justice relating to the kidnapping of his late father's former employee, Martin Byrne, by terrorists Dessie O'Hare, Declan 'Whacker' Duffy and a gang of their heavies. The entire Mansfield family were in court for the verdict including his brothers, Tony and PJ, ex-wife Donna Cosgrave, son Samuel and daughter Ingrid along with their partners. Jimmy Jnr's secretary Sally Anne Browne, who got a special dispensation to attend the court during the trial, was also there as the sentence was read out. Jimmy Jnr had been found not guilty of the more serious kidnapping charge, but his trial taking place in a court used for serious gangland criminals and terrorists, and the evidence that was heard, was sure to damage for good any reputation he might have had left. Martin Byrne was signed into the Witness Protection Programme following the kidnapping and gave evidence during Jim Mansfield Jnr's trial, which painted a picture of chaos within the family home. Mansfield was even described as having a 'mild' intellectual disability during his defence team's plea to the court for leniency and as a carer to his elderly mother, Anne, who the court heard he shared a home with, a far cry from his playboy days at Palmerstown House. Mansfield was an early school leaver, the court heard, and a psychological report submitted by his legal team cited him in the lower range of intellectual ability with difficulties in day-to-day life. However, the court was assured that he was a 'person of high standing' in his community. Over the course of his trial evidence was heard of how the Mansfield empire lay in tatters after the economic crash and how Jim Mansfield Snr had fought a battle with a terminal illness and tried to claw back some wealth for his family as he died. Jim Mansfield Jnr denied he had any role in the kidnapping of Byrne in June 2015, and the court agreed, finding him not guilty. But a damning judgment issued by the court headed by Mr Justice Alexander Owens ruled that he knowingly involved O'Hare and Duffy in his attempts to recover assets lost in the 2008 crash. Justice Alexander Owens, in giving his judgment, also said Mansfield had lied to Gardaí when he said he did not arrange the meeting with O'Hare and Duffy, which ended up with Byrne being kidnapped in June 2015. O'Hare had previously been jailed for seven years in 2019 for falsely imprisoning Byrne, while Duffy got a six-year sentence in 2018 for the same offence.

In jail Mansfield had time to think about the many court proceedings he had issued or threatened against the authorities, including the Garda Commissioner, the Criminal Assets Bureau, and the media who had alluded to his connections with organised crime. When he was informed that the CAB had finally got to the bottom of his links to Daniel Kinahan and Thomas

'Bomber' Kavanagh and was going to seek an order over his mother's former house, he decided it was time to pull back from the denials.

One of the first cases he dropped was a five-year legal battle with the *Sunday World* for exposing his links to criminals. Despite spending years demanding apologies, retractions and compensation for a series of articles written about him, he got his lawyer to drop the case and later agreed to make a donation to the Jack and Jill Children's Foundation charity. In a nine-page legal document, he complained that he and his family had been subjected to an extended 'campaign of vilification' and demanded 'appropriate compensation' for the damage to his reputation. He cited the campaign dating back ten years and first focusing on Mansfield Snr, with suggestions that he was 'very heavily involved in organised crime, working alongside large wholesale drug dealers' which, he stated, 'blithely' portrayed him as a willing accomplice. 'The sheer scale of criminality, its lengthy duration and the fact that much of it was alleged to have been perpetrated from within the family home, would lead any reader to conclude that Jim Mansfield Jnr was a participant in such crimes, or at the very least acquiesced in them, and was and remains content to profit from his father's criminal activities.' In the first letter to the *Sunday World*, Jim Mansfield Jnr also stated that the CAB investigation into him had concluded in 2017 with no findings. 'The articles published by your newspaper amount to a concerted attack on our client's reputation . . . His reputation, both personal and in his professional capacity, has been seriously damaged. He has suffered grave hurt, humiliation and embarrassment,' it stated. Among the demands issued were an unreserved apology, proposals for compensation and admission that the articles were 'sensationalist in style and devoid of evidence'.

The move to drop the proceedings came months after Kinahan and Kavanagh were named as respondents in the CAB case taken against him. During the case, the High Court had heard that Jim Mansfield Jnr was given two suitcases containing €4.5 million as part of a property investment by the Kinahan Cartel, which he was to launder through his empire. The CAB case also heard that in 2014, three years before Mansfield issued the proceedings, Daniel Kinahan had taken control of 10 Coldwater Lakes, which he had been given after his drug money went into the red. The court heard that there had also been attempts to convey legitimate ownership of the property to jailed godfather Thomas 'Bomber' Kavanagh. Evidence was given that the Garda investigation recovered ledgers which tracked payments between the Mansfields and the Kinahan Cartel. The only thing that Mansfield could be grateful for in his foray into prison was the fact that Dessie O'Hare was happy to watch out for him and make sure nothing happened to him.

Following his release in March 2023, he was listed as the sole director of a new property start-up called Swiftbrook Services Limited. The convicted criminal told the Companies Registration Office that he plans to use the company to build new houses, apartments and non-residential properties as the demand for new homes reaches a point not seen since the start of the Celtic Tiger boom. The company, with a share capital of €1 million, was listed out of offices at Keatings Park in Rathcoole, the building where Byrne was brought to meet O'Hare and Duffy before he was kidnapped. Months after his release, the Mansfield family also auctioned off the contents of Finnstown Castle Hotel, which was at that point being used to house refugees at the expense of the Irish government.

Jim Mansfield Jnr's former best pal Lee Cullen hasn't been so lucky. Cullen had managed to escape prison in Ireland despite his links to serious organised crime, cocaine and money laundering, and despite pleading guilty to VAT fraud. After being handed down a suspended sentence and being hit with a hefty CAB bill, he'd decided to start afresh in the UK. The crooked car dealer who'd given Katy French the Range Rover she'd used the night of her cocaine death, moved to a stunning waterside property in posh Stratford-upon-Avon opening a new luxury car dealership. But his clean image was all a front and he landed a massive 18-year sentence after he was nabbed with guns and ammunition. He went on trial but changed his plea to guilty when he heard the weight of evidence against him along with co-accused Paul Frith, 44, and Sean Edwards. Laurence McCarthy, 45, was also convicted when a jury found him guilty after hearing evidence of a conspiracy to recommission firearms to sell to criminals.

Cullen had mixed with criminals for decades, but landing in prison as he approached his 50th year and with a chronic cocaine addiction is a sure sign that crime doesn't pay. Under-cover cops arrested him in June 2021 along with Frith and Edwards in a car in Birmingham city centre, in which two Glock handguns and 25 bullets were found. Later McCarthy was identified as the gang member who had ordered eight Glocks from a supplier in France, which he told a jury was for his son to bring to a Gangsters and Molls party in Limerick. A jury dismissed his claims that he sold the guns to Cullen, who he said collected replica weapons. During the trial, evidence was heard that Cullen had asked his co-accused to bring cocaine with them on the day they were nabbed and that he knew McCarthy as he had borrowed money from him.

Cullen had undoubtedly fallen on hard times and the legacy of his life of crime in Ireland had been hard to shake. Even before he left the country, he'd been ordered to pay back €220,000 in VAT and, at the time, Hugh Hartnett SC, defending, said Cullen had a property in Spain valued at almost €500,000 and that it would be sold to repay the money. The contents of the house had already been sold and a €15,000 cheque had been given to the CAB, he told the court. Mr Hartnett said Cullen's business and his life had been 'destroyed and shattered' as a result of his involvement with crime. He said his business had dwindled to 'almost nothing' and that he was working in Birmingham in England earning £500 a week. The truth was that somebody like Cullen who had enjoyed the high life for decades and who liked to snort lines couldn't ever afford to live on such a paltry salary, and he had secretly re-established himself as a luxury car dealer buying and selling high-end motors and was seen by officers in the company of Thomas 'Bomber' Kavanagh and others connected with the Kinahan Cartel.

Mansfield and Cullen spent years hanging out with Celtic Tiger socialite Marcus Sweeney, who was once the boyfriend of Katy French. He'd been a regular at Citywest but when his name was dragged before the High Court in 2023 and he was described as 'up to his oxters' in organised crime in a case brought by the CAB, any supposition that he was an ordinary businessman was gone. Sweeney's wealth management company, EWM Property Holdings, the High Court heard, was used to launder the cash from one of Ireland's biggest drug gangs. The judge found in favour of the Bureau and its claims that the firm was involved in 'highly dubious' investment schemes, including the land purchase at Waynestown near Dunboyne. Sweeney had also been seen by gardaí in the company of two men at a meeting in Dublin, who were later arrested in possession of nearly €1 million worth of heroin, and he was known to have associated with other Irish criminals suspected of drug dealing and with links to the UK and Turkey. The CAB case centred on land bought by EWM for €102,500 at Waynestown, County Meath, which was paid for with the proceeds of crime. Sweeney had been served a Garda GIM form – given to people who officers believe there is an immediate threat to their life – and this was a direct result of his involvement with criminals and money laundering, and included serious threats, assault and intimidation.

It was a spectacular fall from grace for a man who once peppered the pages of social diaries and whose every new love interest and acquisition was carefully scrutinised and commented upon in sheets and sheets of newspaper commentary. In 2018 the firm was served with an income tax demand in excess of €500,000, and soon afterwards Sweeney met with Kuldip Singh from Birmingham and a Turkish national, both known to be in the drugs trade. When gardaí raided the B&B room where they were staying in Saggart, County Dublin, they found 14 half-kilo blocks of heroin with a street value just shy of €1 million. All three were arrested but Sweeney was later released without charge. Singh would later be jailed for four years and the Turkish national for nine years.

∽

Despite the stories of so many winding up in jail, losing their fortunes or falling foul to their own product, the lure of cocaine, the criminality and the violence around it, continues to be irresistible to many. The business of cocaine, in many ways, seems like a drug itself, with all those who enter the rollercoaster ride of wealth and power believing they can make it out alive and rich to enjoy a luxurious retirement with their spoils. The truth is that very few do, although some like Mickey 'The Pimpernel' Green give it a good go. Having left Ireland, after the fatal car crash which killed the tragic taxi driver, Green settled back on the Costa del Sol and watched on as the CAB sold up his homes in Ireland, which he had been forced to abandon. But losing some assets was the least of his worries as in the UK the secrets of his vast wealth were being touted to police by the same crook who had helped him get off his drunk-driving charge.

Michael Michael had turned a protected witness since he'd provided Green with witnesses for the hit and run, and he was trading all the Pimpernel's financial transactions with cops, including bank accounts he owned and the false passports he used to sneak in and out of England. He'd also implicated him in a number of murders, and when police finally arrested Green in 2000 at the Ritz Hotel Barcelona, both Spanish and UK police announced the end of his career. However, when he eventually got to court a magistrate refused to extradite him, insisting there wasn't enough to prosecute him. Rumours of bribery and corruption surrounded his release back to the Costa del Sol, where he lived out his life in a luxury villa near Estepona. In a twist of fate, it was the sun that got him in the end and in early 2020 he was diagnosed with skin cancer, dying six months later.

His namesake from Cork wasn't quite so blessed and, despite fleeing Irish authorities, Alan 'The Pimpernel' Buckley, the 'co-ordinator' for the southern mafia, was finally arrested with his glamorous girlfriend following a seizure off the Spanish coast of 500kg of cannabis resin. It took nine months and three police forces to finally nab the elusive crook, who vowed he would never get caught with his own contraband, in a sting codenamed Operation Ciana, which nailed his role in the Irish-registered yacht *Colin Hannah* and its €6 million drug cargo. Buckley's girlfriend, Lorna Bowes-Busteed, a wealthy widow and mother of two from Cork, was also caught up in the operation along the Costa del Sol.

The dramatic bust in 2013 came after Buckley had enjoyed a hugely successful career in the drugs business and one that had spanned more than 25 years. After leaving Cork he'd moved to Marbella, where he continued to ship drugs, but when Irish and Spanish police launched a joint offensive against his gang, he was placed under round-the-clock surveillance with his movements and communications monitored. It was a typically sunny day off the coast of Marbella when Guardia Civil speed boats moved in on a little yacht returning from Morocco. The *Colin Hannah* had left Crosshaven in Cork Harbour two years before and when officers in Spain found wrapped bales of cannabis resin inside the boat's hull, land-based Guardia Civil officers moved in and arrested Buckley and his girlfriend. Bowes-Busteed was the daughter of multi-millionaire hotelier Michael Bowes, and the widow of well-known Cork businessman Dick Busteed. She had hooked up with Buckley and moved to Spain after a whirlwind affair, believing he would be her knight in shining armour to help bury the sadness of her past. Instead of a fairytale romance she found herself embroiled in a nightmare underworld of drugs, dirty money and deceit. Buckley was later handed five years for his role in the drug bust, while Bowes-Busteed waited for her jailbird lover, who finally got bail after nine months in prison.

The arrest of the likes of Alan Buckley and the efforts that go into it by police probably show the unfairness of the game between the criminals and those who operate within the law, because the fact is there are far more drug dealers than there are arrests, and most simply get away with it because there isn't enough time or resources to stop them. However, far more successful operations target entire gangs and often cartels. While Mexico and the US have long been playing a game of Whac-A-Mole against the brutal cocaine bosses who spring up all the time, and often the high-profile arrests are politically motivated, in recent years Europe has proved how well it can work together. In particular, the high-profile targeting of the Kinahan

Organised Crime Group has been a blueprint of policing for the future. Together with the DEA and Australian police, Europol has taken on the largest cocaine cartel ever formed in its territory. It has been a complicated and lengthy takedown and one which has required the might of the US, but it is also set to prove that nobody is bigger than the law. The Kinahan mafia had grown rich and confident for years on the Spanish Costa del Sol before migrating to the UAE, but still they couldn't move their business to the Gulf as the majority of it was focused on the countries of Europe, where their cocaine markets are. And despite finding refuge for the top brass of their giant conglomerate in the searing heat of Dubai, they still had to leave behind many of the mechanisms that kept the wheels of the super cartel moving. They also left behind the confidence of years of feeling untouchable as they grew to proportions that could no longer be ignored.

Such was the brazen belief that they were above the law, Johnny and Nicola Morrissey even welcomed a lifestyle magazine into their home to do an interview about their millionaire lifestyle on the Costa del Sol while they laundered Kinahan Cartel cocaine money. The couple posed for photographs and showed off their mansion, sports cars and even their young son as they talked about plans to bring Nero Vodka to the US in 2022. The glamorous photo shoot was a far cry from images of the couple, handcuffed and being led to court by police, less than a year later, in a significant development in the plan to dismantle the billion-dollar Kinahan cocaine empire. In an article entitled 'At Home with Nicola Morrissey' featured in a Marbella lifestyle magazine, the wife of the Kinahan's money launderer and enforcer, Johnny, named during US Treasury sanctions on the group, described how their potato-based vodka had been awarded eight gold industry gongs since it was launched at a glittering extravaganza in Marbella's most exclusive hotel,

Puente Romano Beach Resort, in December 2021. Asked if the Covid-19 pandemic had affected the business, she said that hard work had paid off, and listed some of the Costa's most exclusive eateries, clubs and even the famed Club del Gourmet at El Corte Ingles in Peurto Banús as being keys to its success. Hailed as an iconic businesswoman who juggled family life and her corporate commitments with finesse, she revealed plans for Nero. 'A busy year for sure!' she said of 2022. 'Nero Drinks Company will continue to support and work with local venues, adding more to our client list as well as launching in Mallorca, Tenerife, the UK, and we are finalising plans to launch in America. We are also opening an exclusive, five-star wellness retreat overlooking the sea in La Cala. We have been busy overseeing the luxury building project, gathering an expert team to deliver the latest therapies and treatments. We have a full-time nutritionist, inhouse yoga and meditation specialist, colonic hydrotherapy, cryptotherapy and lots more.'

As she gushed about striking a balance between family life and securing a future for her and Johnny Morrissey's young son, the DEA, Europol and other police forces were watching. What is simply extraordinary and hard to fathom is how the Kinahan organisation believed they could get away with washing €200 million of drugs money through Nero Vodka. Why they considered they could do that in plain sight and with a company linked to a man suspected of involvement in over 30 gangland hits, who had already been targeted by the CAB in Ireland, beggars belief. Johnny Morrissey was a larger-than-life character around Marbella and, along with his Scottish wife, regularly hosted lengthy champagne-fuelled lunches for the C-list celebs who knock around the bars and restaurants of Puerto Banús and Estepona. The pair went out of their way to court celebrity and to be photographed and interviewed in society magazines; at the same time Johnny Morrissey was operating as an enforcer for the Kinahan mob and pushing out its propaganda. He was behind the ill-considered *Blood Feud* book that was the first of a series of marketing ploys by Daniel Kinahan to clean up his image and paint himself as a victim of the Irish media, government and Gardaí as he strove to be an acceptable power broker in world boxing. It was Morrissey who first published the free online book on his social media and later launched a website aimed at identifying 'rats' in the criminal underworld. He was a prolific user of Facebook, Instagram and other social media platforms, where he would regularly treat his followers to videos of his lunches, new cars and lifestyle on the Costa. Nicola mixed with editors, socialites, reality TV stars and businesspeople, and she regularly posed for selfies with glasses of champagne. 'Everything John and I do is to provide a happy and secure life for our son and our family. I love our business but my favourite job is being a mum to Sean ... Like many couples with businesses, John and I sometimes disagree but we respect each other's opinion and understand that we are both working towards the same goal of success,' she told a magazine. When Nero Vodka launched, Michel Euesden, editor of the *EuroWeekly*, a Costa-based news site, gave a speech about female empowerment before welcoming Nicola Morrissey to the stage. Her stepdaughter, Emma, was quoted as saying her dad's wife was: 'A true angel from God, she is honest, hardworking and the most loving person you could ever meet. She is strong and passionate both about Nero Vodka and her family, she is my best friend.'

Dramatic footage released by Spain's Guardia Civil, however, saw the other side of the Morrisseys' world and videos were released of them under arrest in their home while cops from the Netherlands, Spain, Ireland and the US searched for documents, cash and luxury items. Police have said that Nero Vodka was at the centre of the most important money laundering operation in Spain and that €350,000 a day was washed through it. They named the company during the announcement of sanctions on the Kinahan organisation in April 2022 when $5 million was offered for information on the financial dealings of Christy Snr, Christopher Jnr and Daniel. During the course of his arrest, Spanish detectives revealed they believed Morrissey had laundered €200 million for the organisation, but that the cash had not physically moved out of Spain, rather it is spread throughout the world using the ancient money transfer system hawala, discovered by Robert Dawes and later Christy Kinahan Snr after his arrival in Dubai.

A list of 600 cartel associates couldn't believe they could possibly be banned from travelling to the US because of sanctions against the Kinahan Organised Crime Group, and many booked flights in order to check if they would be allowed to board. One who found out in a more public fashion that he was on the banned list was the world champion boxer Tyson Fury and his brother Tommy, whose partner is influencer Molly-Mae. Others are blocked in the other direction and can't come home at all, including Daniel Kinahan's right-hand man Sean McGovern, who couldn't even attend his father's funeral in the wake of the naming by US authorities and the issue of an arrest warrant at home for his role in the feud murder of Noel 'Duck Egg' Kirwan.

Before details of the global crackdown were announced in April 2022, Daniel Kinahan, his father and brother regularly used false passports to travel around the world, but since they were publicly named and rewards were issued for them, they have been grounded in Dubai as international police forces pick away at the financial web they have spun around their riches. Among the revelations that have followed are efforts to buy a fleet of planes, a planned move to Zimbabwe and the use of a tiny island off Iran as a money-laundering hub. Most concerning to the Americans has been the funding of the terrorist group Hezbollah through the laundering of the vast cocaine profits they have accumulated.

But demand for cocaine remains high and many believe it still has not become saturated. In April 2023 police in Spain found the largest cocaine lab ever seen in Europe. Teams of Colombians and Mexicans were discovered to be manning the operation full time in a facility that was producing 440 punds of cocaine every day. The mega lab in the northwest region of Galicia had cooks working in shifts for 24 hours a day to transform the base paste into cocaine ready for consumption. Just two months earlier, a similar but smaller facility was found in Ireland where a cell working for the Kinahan Cartel had set up CCTV cameras to monitor those working for them mixing the drugs. The facility was mixing every one-kilo bale of cocaine with agents to create a three-kilo quantity of the drug, then re-pressing and wrapping it for distribution.

While the Kinahan Cartel had been effectively shut down in Ireland by the dismantling of the Byrne organised crime wing which ran its operations, the cartel has been attempting to keep a presence in the market by employing freelance operators to take their drugs and distribute them; many of these operators had been found to be foreign nationals. They had also attempted to fly cocaine into Ireland, with three aircraft intercepted in one month in 2022 carrying millions of euro worth of the drug. From their base in Dubai and under massive pressure for funds, the cartel leaders had decided to drop the drugs in on a wholesale basis after pre-payment was received from a network of gangs. In a sign of how cocaine is now used all over the country, seizures topping €10 million a go were destined for the midlands. With no insurance and cash paid up front, the seizures actually did hurt the smaller gangs who had to pool their resources to buy the drugs in bulk.

From a business point of view, the Kinahan Cartel cannot be criticised for trying to keep a finger in the pie in Ireland as they struggle to keep money flowing into a network on the brink of collapse. In early 2023 the United Nations Office on Drugs and Crime reported that Irish people are among the highest users of cocaine globally, with one in 40 admitting using the drug during the previous year. Only the Netherlands, Australia and Spain reported higher usage. The cocaine report also warned of the potential of future violence in Ireland due to competition for expanding cocaine markets, the country's use as an entry point to the UK, and the rise in the use of crack cocaine: 'Expanding cocaine use across diverse user groups in Ireland and the UK, as well as Ireland's potential role as a transit country for the UK cocaine market, are likely to further attract Organised Crime Groups, which may lead to violent clashes in the future.'

From a supply point of view, the attraction to cocaine is simple: a kilo of cocaine retailing at around €1,500 at source has a mark-up to €70,000 once it hits the pubs and clubs of Ireland. It's the demand side of things that is probably more curious and where the real problem lies. According to Michael O'Sullivan, former Director of the Maritime Analysis Operation Centre (MAOC) based in Lisbon, Ireland's massive demand for cocaine is being fuelled by cash-rich, educated young people who don't connect a line of white with the violent and powerful cartels who are getting filthy rich from selling it. And he warned that demand will keep growing as long as Ireland and Europe have the money to buy the drugs: 'The South Americans are not going to stop growing it and selling it and getting it in by whatever means is necessary. It will keep growing until there is a decline in the sales of cocaine. What is happening is that more and more young people have more disposable income, and they don't have a problem with it and they don't see why they shouldn't buy it. Back in the 1980s we could tackle it with health education, but cocaine buyers are young and intelligent and while we can do more on the education side, the fact is that they are seeing a lot of "cool" stuff about cocaine. They don't relate it to people getting shot nor the exploitation involved, and they are contributing to that by purchasing it. They are making criminal empires.'

The Victim Impact Statement of a mother to a court often marks the conclusion of an investigation into a drug death but it is merely a glimpse into the devastation left behind in a brutal underworld ruled by the gun. All of these statements are heartbreaking. Sandra Davis said of her son Jordan, killed in 2019, 'We were all robbed of your love', while Elizabeth Woods, the mother of teenager Keane Mulready-Woods, said she hoped no family would go through what hers had. She wished she could see her son one last time and hear him say, 'I love you, Mam.' For the countless victims of gangland murder and the families who mourn their passing there is no end to the grief that is felt for generations to follow when a young life is stolen by a bullet and by the lure of the promise of wealth beyond dreams that cocaine guarantees.

As Europe continues to grapple with its response to the flood of cocaine through its borders and via the large ports of Rotterdam and Antwerp, the wholesalers who ship it in vast quantities to the continent are an ever-moving force who often seem to come full circle in an effort to thwart the authorities.

In the European Union, Ireland now qualifies as having the highest usage rates of the drug with the Health Service Executive expecting the number of new cases of people being treated for addiction to rise a further 55% by 2026. While the largest supply force, the Kinahan Organised Crime Group, remains under pressure from the US and Europol and the vast efforts to dismantle them continue, others are already filling the void as the constant carousel of cocaine and cash continues to fund a growing economy that threatens the very heart and soul of a country hurtling ever forward to the lure of a blinding white storm.

Acknowledgements

Thanks to all those who have shared their wisdom, some from great heights and others from the shadows. Thanks also to publishers Eriu and director Deirdre Nolan.